"十三五"江苏省高等学校重点教材（编号：2019-1-125）

战略管理

主　编·赵　彤　王圣元
副主编·徐　萌　吴小兰

东南大学出版社
SOUTHEAST UNIVERSITY PRESS
·南京·

图书在版编目(CIP)数据

战略管理 / 赵彤，王圣元主编. —南京：东南大学出版社，2021.11

ISBN 978-7-5641-9613-4

Ⅰ.①战… Ⅱ.①赵… ②王… Ⅲ.①企业管理-战略管理 Ⅳ.①F272.1

中国版本图书馆 CIP 数据核字(2021)第 273718 号

战 略 管 理

Zhanlüe Guanli

主　　编	赵彤　王圣元
出版发行	东南大学出版社
社　　址	南京市四牌楼 2 号(邮编:210096　电话:025-83793330)
网　　址	http://www.seupress.com
责任编辑	孙松茜
责任校对	周　菊
封面设计	王　玥
责任印制	周荣虎
经　　销	全国各地新华书店
印　　刷	广东虎彩云印刷有限公司
开　　本	700mm×1000mm　1/16
印　　张	18
字　　数	472 千字
版　　次	2021 年 11 月第 1 版
印　　次	2021 年 11 月第 1 次印刷
书　　号	ISBN 978-7-5641-9613-4
定　　价	68.00 元

(本社图书若有印装质量问题,请直接与营销部联系。电话:025-83791830)

目 录

Chapter 1 Strategic Management

Opening Case①

Lenovo, JD. com Sign CNY12 Billion Strategic Agreement for Mobile Devices

Lenovo's Mobile Business Group announced that they have reached a strategic deal with Chinese B2C e-commerce website JD. com. Under the agreement, Lenovo and JD reached a CNY12 billion strategic pact covering joint product development, marketing, Internet promotion, post-sales logistics, and post-sales services. Meanwhile, Lenovo's first e-commerce platform mobile phone S8 was exclusively launched on JD. com on April 28, 2014. ②

Introduction

You may want to begin this lecture with a general comment that Chapter 1 provides an overview of the strategic management process. In this chapter, the authors introduce a number of terms and models.

1.1 Concept

Strategic competitiveness is achieved when a firm successfully formulates and implements a value-creating strategy. By implementing a value-creating strategy that current and potential competitors are not simultaneously implementing and that competitors are unable to duplicate, or find too costly to imitate, a firm achieves a competitive advantage. ③

Strategy can be defined as an integrated and coordinated set of commitments and actions designed to exploit core competencies and gain a competitive advantage. ④

So long as a firm can sustain (or maintain) a competitive advantage, investors

---

① 课前案例:联想与京东签署移动设备战略协议,价值120亿元人民币。

② 联想和京东达成了价值120亿元人民币的战略协议,涵盖联合产品开发、营销、互联网推广、售后物流和售后服务。与此同时,联想第一款电子商务平台手机S8于2014年4月28日在京东独家发布。

③ 企业成功制定并实施价值创造战略时,就可以实现战略竞争力。如果企业实施的价值创造战略,当前和潜在的竞争对手无法复制,或模仿成本很高,企业便获得竞争优势。

④ 战略是一套整合和协调的承诺和行动集合,旨在开发核心竞争力并获得竞争优势。

will earn above-average returns. Above-average returns represent returns that exceed returns that investors expect to earn from other investments with similar levels of risk (investor uncertainty about the economic gains or losses that will result from a particular investment). In other words, above-average returns exceed investors' expected levels of return for given risk levels.

In smaller new venture firms, performance is sometimes measured in terms of the amount and speed of growth rather than more traditional profitability measures—new ventures require time to earn acceptable returns.

The Strategic Management Process

A framework that can assist firms in their quest for strategic competitiveness is the strategic management process, the full set of commitments, decisions and actions required for a firm to systematically achieve strategic competitiveness and earn above-average returns.

Feedback linkages among the three primary elements indicate the dynamic nature of the strategic management process: strategic inputs, strategic actions and strategic outcomes. ①

(1) Strategic inputs, in the form of information gained by scrutinizing the internal environment and scanning the external environment, are used to develop the firm's vision and mission.

(2) Strategic actions are guided by the firm's vision and mission, and are represented by strategies that are formulated or developed and subsequently implemented or put into action.

(3) Desired strategic outcomes—strategic competitiveness and above-average returns—result when a firm is able to successfully formulate and implement value-creating strategies that others are unable to duplicate.

(4) Feedback links the elements of the strategic management process together and helps firms continuously adjust or revise strategic inputs and strategic actions in order to achieve desired strategic outcomes.

In addition to describing the impact of globalization and technological change on the current business environment, this chapter also will discuss two approaches to the strategic management process.

The first, the industrial organization model, suggests that the external environment

① 三个主要元素之间的反馈联系表明了战略管理过程的动态性质:战略投入、战略行动和战略成果。

should be considered as the primary determinant of a firm's strategic actions.

The second is the resource-based model, which perceives the firm's resources and capabilities (the internal environment) as critical links to strategic competitiveness.

1.2 The Competitive Landscape

This twenty-first century competitive landscape can be described as one in which the fundamental nature of competition is changing in a number of the world's industries. Further, the boundaries of industries are becoming blurred and more difficult to define.

Consider recent changes that have taken place in the telecommunications and TV industries—e. g. , not only cable companies and satellite networks compete for entertainment revenue from television, but telecommunication companies also are stepping into the entertainment business through significant improvements in fiber-optic lines. Partnerships further blur industry boundaries. Many firms are looking into the delivery of video on demand (VOD). Apple iPod has the current lead in offering VOD content, but Netflix is vying hard to compete in this arena since VOD could be the kiss of death to its current online DVD rental service. Blockbuster and Amazon are also seeking a piece of this competitive pie.

The twenty-first century competitive landscape thus implies that traditional sources of competitive advantage—economies of scale and large advertising budgets—may not as important in the future as they were in the past. The rapid and unpredictable technological change that characterizes this new competitive landscape implies that managers must adopt new ways of thinking. The new competitive mind set must value flexibility, speed, innovation, integration, and the challenges that evolve from constantly changing conditions.

A term often used to describe the new realities of competition is hypercompetition, a condition that results from the dynamics of strategic moves and countermoves among innovative, global firms: a condition of rapidly escalating competition that is based on price-quality positioning, efforts to create new know-how and achieve first-mover advantage, and battles to protect or to invade established product or geographic markets.

1.2.1 The Global Economy

A global economy is one in which goods, services, people, skills and ideas move freely across geographic borders. ① The emergence of this global economy results in a number of challenges and opportunities. Today, China is seen as an extremely competitive market in which local market-seeking MNCs (multinational corporations) fiercely compete against other MNCs and local low-cost producers. China has long been viewed as a low-cost producer of goods, but here's an interesting twist. China is now an exporter of local management talent. The expectations of U. S. firms for global business are changing rapidly. GE expects as much as 70 percent of its revenue growth between 2020 and 2030 to be generated by competing in rapidly developing economies (e. g., China and India).

1.2.2 The March of Globalization

Globalization is the increasing economic interdependence among countries as reflected in the flow of goods and services, financial capital, and knowledge across country borders. ② Globalization is the worldwide movement toward economic, financial, trade, and communications integration. Globalization implies the opening of local and nationalistic perspectives to a broader outlook of an interconnected and interdependent world with free transfer of capital, goods, and services across national frontiers. However, it does not include unhindered movement of labor and, as suggested by some economists, may hurt smaller or fragile economies if applied indiscriminately.

This is illustrated by the following:

(1) Financial capital might be obtained in one national market and used to buy raw materials in another one.

(2) Manufacturing equipment bought from another market produces products sold in yet another market.

(3) Globalization enhances the available range of opportunities for firms.

Wal-Mart is trying to achieve boundary-less retailing with global pricing, sourcing, and logistics. Today, Wal-Mart is the world's largest retailer (with over 6,200 total units).

---

① 全球经济是商品、服务、人员、技能和思想可以跨越地理边界、自由流动的经济体。

② 全球化指各国之间的经济相互依赖日益增长，货物、服务、金融资本和知识跨越国界，相互流动。

Because Toyota initially emphasized product reliability and superior customer service, the company's products are in high demand across the globe. Due to the demand for its products, Toyota's competitive actions have forced its global competitors to make reliability and service improvements in their operations.

Global competition has increased performance standards in many dimensions, including quality, cost, productivity, product introduction time, and operational efficiency. Moreover, these standards are not static; they are exacting, requiring continuous improvement from a firm and its employees. Thus, companies must improve their capabilities and individual workers need to sharpen their skills. In the twenty-first century competitive landscape, only firms that meet, and perhaps exceed, global standards are likely to earn strategic competitiveness.

As a result of the new competitive landscape, firms of all sizes must re-think how they can achieve strategic competitiveness by positioning themselves to ask questions from a more global perspective to enable them to (at least) meet or exceed global standards: Where should value-adding activities be performed? Where are the most cost-effective markets for new capital? Can products designed in one market be successfully adapted for sale in others? How can we develop cooperative relationships or joint ventures with other firms that will enable us to capitalize on international growth opportunities?

While globalization seems an attractive strategy for competing in the twenty-first century competitive landscape, there are risks as well. These include such factors as:

(1) the "liability of foreignness" (i. e. , the risk of competing internationally)

(2) over diversification beyond the firm's ability to successfully manage operations in multiple foreign markets

A point to emphasize: entry into international markets requires proper use of the strategic management process.

While global markets are attractive strategic options for some companies, they are not the only source of strategic competitiveness. In fact, for most companies, even for those capable of competing successfully in global markets, it is critical to remain committed to and strategically competitive in the domestic market. And, domestic markets can be testing grounds for possibly entering an international market at some point in the future. ①

---

① 虽然全球市场对一些公司来说是有吸引力的战略选择,但它们并不是战略竞争力的唯一来源。事实上,对于大多数公司来说,即使是那些能够在全球市场上获得成功的公司,保持对国内市场的战略竞争力也是至关重要的。而且,国内市场可能成为未来某个时候进入国际市场的试验场。

1.2.3 Technology and Technological Changes

Three technological trends and conditions are significantly altering the nature of competition:

(1) increasing rate of technological change and diffusion

(2) the information age

(3) increasing knowledge intensity

Technologic Diffusion and Disruptive Technologies

Both the rate of change and the introduction of new technologies have increased greatly over the last 15 to 20 years.

A term that is used to describe rapid and consistent replacement of current technologies by new, information-intensive technologies is perpetual innovation. This implies that innovation must be continuous and carry a high priority for all organizations.

The shorter product life cycles that result from rapid diffusion of innovation often means that products may be replicated within very short time periods, placing a competitive premium on a firm's ability to rapidly introduce new products into the marketplace. In fact, speed-to-market may become the sole source of competitive advantage.①

The rapid diffusion of innovation may have made patents a source of competitive advantage only in the pharmaceutical and chemical industries as many firms do not file patent applications to safeguard (for at least a time) the technical knowledge that would be disclosed explicitly in a patent application.

Disruptive technologies (in line with the Schumpeterian notion of "creative destruction") can destroy the value of existing technologies by replacing them with new ones. Current examples include the success of iPods, PDAs and WiFi.

The Information Age

Changes in information technology have made rapid access to information available to firms all over the world, regardless of size. Consider the rapid growth in the following technologies: personal computers (PCs), cellular phones, computers, personal digital assistants (PDAs), artificial intelligence, virtual reality, and massive

---

① 创新的快速扩散导致产品生命周期缩短,这通常意味着产品可以在很短的时间内得到复制,从而使公司可以快速将新产品引入市场。实践中,新产品上市速度可能成为竞争优势的唯一来源。

data bases. These examples show how information is used differently as a result of new technologies. The ability to access and use information has become an important source of competitive advantage in almost every industry.

(1) Companies are being wired to link to customers, employees, vendors and suppliers around the globe (e-business).

(2) The Internet provides an information-carrying infrastructure available to individuals and firms worldwide.

The ability to access a high level of relatively inexpensive information has created strategic opportunities for many information-intensive businesses. For example, retailers now can use the Internet to provide shopping to customers virtually anywhere.

BusinessWeek and the Boston Consulting Group conduct an annual survey of the top executives of the "1,000 largest global corporations." In May 2020, as a result of this survey, Apple was named by BusinessWeek as the most innovative company for the third consecutive year. Apple was able to rejuvenate itself in 2001 with introduction of its iPod, a portable digital music device, which was followed by its complementary iTunes online music store which offered free downloads of digital music, songs and video clips to iPod users. It not only markets simply designed products, Apple is able to leverage off its aesthetic designs. While Apple focused on differentiation, its competitors were determined to achieve a cost advantage. Dell was very successful as the first computer manufacturer to utilize the internet as a means for customers to buy directly from the manufacturer bypassing the middle-man. In addition to direct selling, Dell did an exemplary job of supply-chain management with firms such as Microsoft and Intel. Apple's success through its stores has outpaced Sony and others and has forced Dell to enter into an alliance with Wal-Mart to bolster sales. The companies that Apple is now outperforming have historically been stronger than Apple. So what is different? Apple seeks to "change the way people behave" versus just competing in the marketplace for traditional products. In doing so, it has been able to establish first mover advantages through radical concepts using elegant design, and relatively perfect market timing recently to establish its advantage. Others seem to compete in commodity businesses with incremental innovations, while Apple creates a new concept in the consumer's mind. For this reason, it is likely that other executives see Apple as a strong innovator in consumer electronics.

Increasing Knowledge Intensity

It is becoming increasingly apparent that knowledge—information, intelligence and expertise—is a critical organizational resource, and increasingly, a source of competitive advantage. As a result,

(1) many companies are working to convert the accumulated knowledge of employees into a corporate asset;

(2) shareholder value is increasingly influenced by the value of a firm's intangible assets, such as knowledge. ①

The implication of this discussion is that, to achieve strategic competitiveness and earn above-average returns, firms must develop the ability to adapt rapidly to change or achieve strategic flexibility.

Strategic flexibility represents the set of capabilities—in all areas of their operations—that firms use to respond to respond to the various demands and opportunities that are found in dynamic, uncertain environments. This implies that firms must develop certain capabilities, including the capacity to learn continuously, which will provide the firm with new skill sets. However, those working within firms to develop strategic flexibility should understand that the task is not an easy one, largely because of inertia that can build up over time. A firm's focus and past core competencies may actually slow change and strategic flexibility.

Two models describing key strategic inputs to a firm's strategic actions are discussed next: the Industrial Organization (or externally-focused) model and the Resource-Based (or internally-focused) model.

1.3 The I/O Model of Above-Average Returns

The I/O or Industrial Organization model adopts an external perspective to explain that forces outside of the organization represent the dominant influences on a firm's strategic actions. ② In other words, this model presumes that the characteristics of and conditions present in the external environment determine the appropriateness of strategies that are formulated and implemented in order for a firm to earn above-average returns. In short, the I/O model specifies that the choice of industries in which to compete has more influence on firm performance than the decisions made by managers inside their firm.

---

① 知识——信息、情报和专业知识是一种关键的组织资源,并日益成为竞争优势的来源。因此(1)许多公司正在努力将员工积累的知识转化为企业资产;(2)股东价值越来越受到公司无形资产(如知识)价值的影响。

② 产业组织模型采用外部视角来解释组织外部的力量对企业战略行动起主导影响作用。

Four Assumptions

The I/O model is based on the following four assumptions:

(1) The external environment-the general, industry and competitive environments impose pressures and constraints on firms and determines strategies that will result in superior returns. In other words, the external environment pressures the firm to adopt strategies to meet that pressure while simultaneously constraining or limiting the scope of strategies that might be appropriate and eventually successful.

(2) Most firms competing in an industry or in an industry segment control similar sets of strategically relevant resources and thus pursue similar strategies. This assumption presumes that, given a similar availability of resources, most firms competing in a specific industry (or industry segment) have similar capabilities and thus follow strategies that are similar. In other words, there are few significant differences among firms in an industry.

(3) Resources used to implement strategies are highly mobile across firms. Significant differences in strategically relevant resources among firms in an industry tend to disappear because of resource mobility. Thus, any resource differences soon disappear as they are observed and acquired or learned by other firms in the industry.

(4) Organizational decision-makers are assumed to be rational and committed to acting only in the best interests of the firm. The implication of this assumption is that organizational decision-makers will consistently exhibit profit-maximizing behaviors.

According to the I/O model, firms must pay careful attention to the structured characteristics of the industry in which they choose to compete, searching for one that is the most attractive to the firm, given the firm's strategically relevant resources. Then, the firm must be able to successfully implement strategies required by the industry's characteristics to be able to increase their level of competitiveness. The five forces model is an analytical tool used to address and describe these industry characteristics.①

The I/O Model of Above-Average Returns

Based on its four underlying assumptions, the I/O model prescribes a five-step process for firms to achieve above-average returns:②

---

① 根据I/O模型,企业必须关注其选择竞争的行业的结构性特征,根据企业的相关战略资源,寻找对企业最具吸引力的行业。然后,企业必须能够成功实施行业特征所要求的战略,以提高其竞争力水平。五力模型是一种用于解决和描述这些行业特征的分析工具。

② 产业组织模型有四个基本假设,根据这些假设,界定企业实现高于平均回报的五步流程。

(1) Study the external environment—general, industry and competitive—to determine the characteristics of the external environment that will both determine and constrain the firm's strategic alternatives. ①

(2) Select an industry (or industries) with a high potential for returns based on the structural characteristics of the industry. A model for assessing these characteristics, the Five Forces Model of Competition. ②

(3) Based on the characteristics of the industry in which the firm chooses to compete, strategies that are linked with above-average returns should be selected. A model or framework that can be used to assess the requirements and risks of these strategies (the Generic Strategies called cost leadership & differentiation). ③

(4) Acquire or develop the critical resources—skills and assets—needed to successfully implement the strategy that has been selected. ④

(5) The I/O model indicates that above-average returns will accrue to firms that successfully implement relevant strategic actions that enable the firm to leverage its strengths (skills and resources) to meet the demands or pressures and constraints of the industry in which they have elected to compete. ⑤

The I/O model has been supported by research indicating:

(1) 20% of firm profitability can be explained by industry characteristics.

(2) 30% of firm profitability can be attributed to firm characteristics and the actions taken by the firm.

(3) Overall, this indicates a reciprocal relationship—or even an interrelationship—between industry characteristics (attractiveness) and firm strategies that result in firm performance.

1.4 The Resource-Based Model of Above-Average Returns

The resource-based model adopts an internal perspective to explain how a firm's

---

① 研究外部环境,包括一般环境、行业环境和竞争环境,以确定外部环境的特征,研究将决定和约束公司的战略选择。

② 根据行业的结构特点,选择具有高回报潜力的行业,这些行业的竞争特点可以用竞争的五力模型来评估。

③ 根据公司选择参与竞争的行业的特点,选择回报高于平均水平的战略。可用模型或框架(通用策略包括成本领先和差异化)来评估这些策略的需求和风险。

④ 获得或开发成功实施战略所需的关键资源——技能和资产。

⑤ 产业组织模型表明,企业如果成功实施相关战略行动,将获得高于平均水平的回报,有了这些战略行动,企业能够利用其优势(技能和资源)来满足他们所选择行业的需求,解决行业的压力和约束。

unique bundle or collection of internal resources and capabilities represent the foundation upon which value-creating strategies should be built. ①

Resources are inputs into a firm's production process, such as capital equipment, individual employee's skills, patents, brand names, finance and talented managers. These resources can be tangible or intangible. ②

Capabilities are the capacity for a set of resources to perform a task or activity. ③ Thus, according to the resource-based model, a firm's resources and capabilities—found in its internal environment—are more critical to determining the appropriateness of strategic actions than are the conditions and characteristics of the external environment. So, strategies should be selected that enable the firm to best exploit its core competencies, relative to opportunities in the external environment. Core competencies are resources and capabilities that serve as a source of competitive advantage for a firm. Often related to functional skills, core competencies—when developed, nurtured, and applied throughout a firm—may result in strategic competitiveness. ④

The Resource-Based Model of Above-Average Returns

The resource-based model of above-average returns is grounded in the uniqueness of a firm's internal resources and capabilities. The five-step model describes the linkages between resource identification and strategy selection that will lead to above-average returns. ⑤

(1) Firms should identify their internal resources and assess their strengths and weaknesses. The strengths and weaknesses of firm resources should be assessed relative to competitors. ⑥

(2) Firms should identify the set of resources that provide the firm with capabilities that are unique to the firm, relative to its competitors. The firm should identify those capabilities that enable the firm to perform a task or activity better than

---

① 资源模型采用内部视角来阐释,企业独特的资源和能力的组合是建立价值创造战略的基础。

② 资源是企业生产过程的输入,如资本设备、员工个人技能、专利、品牌、财务和人才管理。这些资源可以是有形的或无形的。

③ 能力是指综合执行一组资源的任务或活动。

④ 核心竞争力是产生企业竞争优势的资源和能力,通常与职能技能相关,一旦在公司内发展、培养和应用,核心能力会形成战略竞争力。

⑤ 基于资源的超额收益模型建立在企业内部资源和能力的独特性的基础上。五步流程模型描述了资源识别和战略选择之间的关联,这种关联可能带来高于平均水平的回报。

⑥ 企业应确定其内部资源并评估其优缺点。企业资源的优势和劣势应相对于竞争对手进行评估。

its competitors. ①

(3) Firms should determine the potential for their unique sets of resources and capabilities to outperform rivals in terms of returns. Determine how a firm's resources and capabilities can be used to gain competitive advantage. ②

(4) Locate and compete in an attractive industry. Determine the industry that provides the best fit between the characteristics of the industry and the firm's resources and capabilities. ③

(5) To attain a sustainable competitive advantage and earn above-average returns, firms should formulate and implement strategies that enable them to exploit their resources and capabilities to take advantage of opportunities in the external environment better than their competitors. ④

Resources and capabilities can lead to a competitive advantage when they are valuable, rare, costly to imitate, and non-substitutable.

(1) Resources are valuable when they support taking advantage of opportunities or neutralizing external threats.

(2) Resources are rare when possessed by few, if any, competitors.

(3) Resources are costly to imitate when other firms cannot obtain them inexpensively (relative to other firms).

(4) Resources are non-substitutable when they have no structural equivalents.

1.5 Vision and Mission

1.5.1 Vision

Vision is a picture of what the firm wants to be and, in broad terms, what it wants to ultimately achieve. Vision is "big picture" thinking with passion that helps people feel what they are supposed to be doing. ⑤

---

① 企业应确定其资源,能让企业获得竞争对手没有的独特能力。企业应确定有能力能够使企业比竞争对手更好地完成任务或活动。

② 企业应该确定其独特的资源和能力,有潜力在回报方面有胜过竞争对手;并确定如何利用公司的资源和能力获得竞争优势。

③ 在有吸引力的行业中定位和竞争。确定在行业特征和企业资源、能力之间提供最佳匹配的行业。

④ 企业为了获得可持续的竞争优势并获得高于平均水平的回报,应制定和实施战略,利用自身的资源和能力,更好地利用外部环境中的机遇。

⑤ 愿景是指企业想要成为什么样的企业,从广义上讲,指企业最终想要达到什么样的目标。愿景是充满激情的"大局"思维,帮助人们感受到他们应该做的事情。

Vision statements:

(1) reflect a firm's values and aspirations.

(2) are intended to capture the heart and mind of each employee (and, hopefully, many of its other stakeholders).

(3) tend to be enduring while it is missions that can change in light of changing environmental conditions.

(4) tend to be relatively short and concise, easily remembered. ①

Examples of vision statements:

(1) Our vision is to be the world's best quick service restaurant. (McDonald's)

(2) Our mission is to be recognized by our customers as the leader in applications engineering. We always focus on the activities customers' desire; we are highly motivated and strive to advance our technical knowledge in the areas of material, part design and fabrication technology. (LNP, a GE Plastics Company)

(3) We must be a great company with great people. (LG Electronics)

The CEO is responsible for working with others to form the firm's vision. However, experience shows that the most effective vision statement results when the CEO involves a host of people to develop it.

A vision statement should be clearly tied to the conditions in the firm's external and internal environments and it must be achievable. Moreover, the decisions and actions of those involved with developing the vision must be consistent with that vision.

A strongly-worded vision statement emphasizes "winning" (in some fashion), and this can create a mental struggle for some students. The problem is that a focus on winning ultimately will mean that some companies will be put out of business and employees will end up losing their jobs. It is important to point out that many who experience dislocation as a result of a business failure will soon be employed at the "winning" firm (which is in expansion mode), at another firm in the same industry, or in an entirely different industry. Those who are not quickly reabsorbed often are those who have the skills that least fit the demands of the industry. In the end, though, there is no getting around the fact that a competitive marketplace can produce significant hardship for some, and there is no need to argue otherwise; however, the number of customers who are better served by firms that are continuously improving dwarfs the number of individuals who are dislocated. Thus, in the "big picture," we

① 愿景陈述:(1) 反映企业的价值观和抱负。(2) 旨在捕捉每位员工(希望还有其他利益相关者)的内心和思想。(3) 在任务执行过程中,往往是持久的,可以根据环境条件的变化而改变。(4) 相对简短,易于记忆。

are all better off as a result. If the notion of winning is difficult to accept, then it is good to think of the alternative—a non-responsive economy with few new products, a tendency toward inefficiency, and poorly served customers.

1.5.2 Mission

A firm's mission is an externally focused application of its vision that states the firm's unique purpose and the scope of its operations in product and market terms.

As with the vision, the final responsibility for forming the firm's mission rests with the CEO, though the CEO and other top-level managers tend to involve a larger number of people in forming the mission. This is because middle- and first-level managers and other employees have more direct contact with customers and their markets.

A firm's vision and mission must provide the guidance that enables the firm to achieve the desired strategic outcomes—strategic competitiveness and above-average returns—that enable the firm to satisfy the demands of those parties having an interest in the firm's success: organizational stakeholders.

Earning above-average returns often is not mentioned in mission statements. The reasons for this are that all firms want to earn above-average returns and that desired financial outcomes result from properly serving certain customers while trying to achieve the firm's intended future. In fact, research has shown that having an effectively formed vision and mission has a positive effect on performance (growth in sales, profits, employment and net worth).

1.6 Stakeholders

Stakeholders are the individuals and groups who can affect and are affected by the strategic outcomes achieved and who have enforceable claims on a firm's performance.

Classification of Stakeholders

The stakeholder concept reflects that individuals and groups have a "stake" in the strategic outcomes of the firm because they can be either positively or negatively affected by those outcomes and because achieving the strategic outcomes may be dependent upon the support or active participation of certain stakeholder groups.

The following table was developed to organize a discussion of each stakeholder group's expectations or demands, potential conflicts and stakeholder management strategies.

Table 1 - 1 Examples of a Company's Stakeholders①

Stakeholders	Stakeholder's concerns
Government	taxation, VAT, legislation, employment, truthful reporting, diversity, legalities, externalities.
Employees	rates of pay, job security, compensation, respect, truthful communication.
Customers	value, quality, customer care, ethical products.
Suppliers	providers of products and services used in the end product for the customer, equitable business opportunities.
Creditors	credit score, new contracts, liquidity.
Community	jobs, involvement, environmental protection, shares, truthful communication.
Trade Unions	quality, worker protection, jobs.
Owner(s)	profitability, longevity, market share, market standing, succession planning, raising capital, growth, social goals.
Investors	return on investment, income.

From reviewing the primary expectations or demands of each stakeholder group, it becomes obvious that a potential for conflict exists. For instance, shareholders generally invest for wealth-maximization purposes and are therefore interested in a firm's maximizing its return on investment or ROI. However, if a firm increases its ROI by making short-term decisions, the firm can negatively affect employee or customer stakeholders.

If the firm is strategically competitive and earns above average returns, it can afford to simultaneously satisfy all stakeholders. When earning average or below-average returns, tradeoffs must be made. At the level of average returns, firms must at least minimally satisfy all stakeholders. When returns are below average, some stakeholders can be minimally satisfied, while others may be dissatisfied.

For example, reducing the level of research and development expenditures (to

① 利益相关者关注的事项:(1)政府:税收,增值税,立法,就业,真实报告,多样性,合法性,外部性。(2)员工:薪资,工作保障,薪酬,尊重,如实沟通。(3)客户:价值,质量,客户关怀,道德产品。(4)供应商:为最终产品中的客户提供产品和服务,为客户提供公平的商机。(5)债权人:信用评分,新合同,流动性。(6)社区:工作,参与,环境保护,分享,如实沟通。(7)工会:质量,工人保护,工作。(8)所有者:盈利能力,寿命,市场份额,市场地位,继任计划,筹集资金,增长,社会目标。(9)投资者:投资回报,收益。

increase short-term profits) enables the firm to pay out the additional short-term profits to shareholders as dividends. However, if reducing R&D expenditures results in a decline in the long-term strategic competitiveness of the firm's products or services, it is possible that employees will not enjoy a secure or rewarding career environment (which violates a primary union expectation or demand for job security for its membership). At the same time, customers may be offered products that are less reliable at unattractive prices, relative to those offered by firms that did not reduce R&D expenditures.

Thus, the stakeholder management process may involve a series of trade-offs that is dependent on the extent to which the firm is dependent on the support of each affected stakeholder and the firm's ability to earn above-average returns.

Stakeholder management has introduced some interesting notions into business practice. For example, business schools typically teach that there are three main stakeholder groups (owners, customers, and employees) and that they should be tended to in that order. That is, it is important to begin with the idea that the primary purpose of the firm is to maximize shareholder wealth (i. e., tend to the interests of the owners first). Then, it is common to introduce notions such as, "The customer is always right." This suggests that customer interests are to be tended to next. Finally, we get around to looking to the needs of employees, if resources make that possible. This is the standard approach, but some firms have turned this formulation on its head. For example, Southwest Airlines has been extremely successful by taking great efforts to select the right employees and treat them well, which then spills over into appropriate treatment of the customer. As you might guess, the company assumes that these emphases will naturally lead to positive outcomes for the stockholders as well (as has been the case). This issue can lead to interesting discussions with students about their thoughts on the topic.

本章课程思政学习专题

中美经贸摩擦

1. 时代背景

当前,以美国为首的贸易保护主义、单边主义持续蔓延,贸易与投资争端不断加剧,全球产业格局和金融稳定受到强烈冲击,世界经济运行风险和不确定性显著上升。中国秉持"共商、共建、共享"原则,通过"一带一路"建设向世界提供"中国智慧与中国方案”,为发展中国家构筑完善的基础设施,为其经济腾飞创造良好的条件,致力于逐步解决全球经济发展与分配过程中的严重失衡问题,积极推动新一阶段的全球化和缩小区域发展差距,愿同世界各国和平共处、合作共赢,共建人类命运共同体,为创造世界经济更加美好的明天不懈努力。

中美建交40多年来,两国经贸关系既有合作又有摩擦。特朗普执政后,以“美国优先”为宗旨,奉行贸易单边主义和保护主义,采取加征关税、限制投资等经贸限制措施,单方面挑起中美经贸摩擦。从表面来看,中美经贸摩擦的起因是中美贸易逆差,美国经贸谈判的诉求是减少对华贸易逆差;但本质上,中美经贸摩擦不是简单的经贸之争,而是美国以冷战思维判断中国,视中国为强劲的战略竞争对手,打着贸易保护主义名头阻碍中国发展,是在位霸权国家对新兴大国崛起的遏制,是由于发展模式、意识形态、文化文明、价值观等差异所引发的世界领导权更迭之争。中美经贸摩擦在短期内可能是边打边谈,其逻辑演化的过程应是“磋商谈判—对抗升级—再磋商谈判—和平妥协或全面对抗”。因此,要客观、理性地认清美国的真实意图,进一步弘扬“人类命运共同体”理念,深入推进“一带一路”建设;坚持开放引领,加强机制对接,推动贸易畅通高质量发展;坚持自主研发、科技创新,助推实体经济发展;加快推进人民币国际化进程,逐步建立高效监管协调机制;全面提升自身经济活力,以不变应万变,应对中美贸易摩擦引起的外部冲击。

中美经贸摩擦是当前世界经济中备受关注的焦点之一,因为在全球价值链分工体系下,分别作为目前世界上最大的发展中国家和最大的发达国家,两国经贸关系的发展所具有的关键意义,已经完全超出了中美两国自身,在某种程度上已然成为影响世界经济增长和繁荣发展的重要变量。

自2018年7月美国对价值340亿美元的中国商品加征25%进口关税措施正式落地开始,美国不断升级对华经贸摩擦,突出表现为加征关税商品范围不断扩大、关税水平不断提高以及摩擦领域不断蔓延等。可以说,美方发起并且不断升级的对华经贸摩擦,不仅严重威胁中美双边经贸关系,致使中美双方同时遭受损失,而且极大地危害了全球经贸秩序,对世界经济也产生了严重的负面影响,尤其是给已经构建起来的合理有序的全球价值链分工体系带来了严重的冲击效应、破坏效应和割裂效应。令人欣慰的是,2019年10月11日,中美第十三轮高级别经贸磋商初步达成了“第一阶段”协议,并于12月13日就贸易协议文本达成一致。其中,美方承诺将取消部分对华拟加征和已加征的关税,并且会加大对中国输美产品关税豁免的力度。这一阶段性的成果似乎表明,中美经贸摩擦出现了暂时缓和迹象,中美经贸摩擦第一阶段象征性地结束了。那么,究竟该如何看待中美经贸摩擦的这一阶段性变化?第一阶段中美经贸协议的达成,是否意味着中美经贸摩擦可以鸣金收兵?应对中美经贸摩擦,究竟应该采取怎样的短期应对措施?长期的有效应对机制又该如何建设？这些问题需要理论和实践部门深入思考。

2. 美国对华经贸摩擦的真实战略意图

美国对华发起经贸摩擦，所凭借的主要口实就是所谓中美之间的巨额贸易逆差以及所谓中国盗窃美国的知识产权、强制美国在华企业转让技术等。这几项莫须有的“罪名”其实都是不成立的，而是有着其他更为深刻的战略意图。

长期贸易顺差并非是中国主动刻意追求的结果，而是全球价值链分工演进、产业和产品增值环节国际梯度转移、美国消费行为和习惯以及美元霸权地位等多种因素促成的结果，是市场经济在全球化条件下的一种规律使然。贸易保护主义只会通过贸易转移效应而转移贸易失衡的主体对象，却无法改变美国贸易逆差的局面。特朗普政府还简单地将贸易失衡等同于利益失衡。美国作为全球价值链分工体系中的高端控制者和主导者，由于掌控和收获着全球价值增值中最高端的部分，因此实际上是经济全球化的最大受益者。

美国发起对华经贸摩擦的依据，从根本上看是不存在和站不住脚的，也不是美国真正想要的。比如，从产业互补和比较优势的分工原理角度看，如果美国真正是因为贸易失衡并追求中美贸易更加平衡的发展，那么其打击和制裁中国的出口产品和产业，选择的应该是中国出口产品和产业中最具比较优势的；而不应在一开始拟定征税清单时，就选择了中国并不具备显著比较优势的、技术含量相对较高的产品，更不应该对中国从美进口量最大的芯片等采取断供举措。美国政府发动对华经贸摩擦在口实和行动上的矛盾和不统一，恰恰更加有利于我们透过现象（甚至可以说假象）看到本质。那么，美国发起对华经贸摩擦的本质和战略意图究竟是什么？

美国当前发起并不断升级对华贸易摩擦，根本的战略意图是遏制中国的和平崛起，继续维护美国的全球霸权地位以及对经济全球化发展的绝对主导权。

3. 美国发起对华经贸摩擦的本质原因

（1）全球要素分工兴起为发展中国家带来了战略机遇

由于全球价值链旨在说明产品生产的不同环节和阶段，或者说不同增值环节，被配置到不同国家和地区的新型生产和组织模式，但却并没有很好地反映当前生产要素流动及其在国际分工和贸易中的重要作用，因而还未能从本质上刻画当前国际分工的真实模式。基于产品生产环节的全球分解以及要素跨境流动的双重特征事实，当前国际分工的本质可以概括为全球要素分工。以要素分工为主要特征的新一轮经济全球化，的确为发展中国家带来了重要的发展机遇。中国改革开放的伟大事业也正是在此背景下开展的。正是由于实施了正确的开放发展战略，中国劳动人民通过勤劳实干，抓住了经济全球化带来的战略机遇，获得了开放型经济发展的巨大成功。全球要素分工至少从两种作用机制上，为发展中国家通过融入经济全球化实现经济发展，带来了重要的战略机遇：一种是产品价值增值环节的全球分解;一种是生产要素的跨境流动。

(2) 全球要素分工下利益格局的改变触动了美国传统霸权

从本质上看,全球要素分工这种新型分工模式并非零和博弈,而是更加具有互利共赢的特质,在有助于推动经济全球化繁荣发展的同时,实现发达国家和发展国家在发展水平上更加协调、均衡。只不过,长期处于霸权地位的美国是不愿意看到这种"均势"化发展的。此外,在全球要素分工推动下产业和产品生产环节的国际梯度转移,在有助于实现跨国公司利益最大化的同时,也进一步深化了劳资矛盾,使得资本主义社会的劳资矛盾在新型国际分工条件下有了新的表现,即技术进步加上产业空心化,不仅使得普通劳动者收入下降,甚至带来了失业等更为严重的影响。也就是说,经济全球化虽然使得美国在整体层面上仍然是最大的获益者,但是其内部的利益分配失衡却愈发严重,即导致内部不同利益集团的"非均势"化发展。

4. 思考问题

(1) 应对中美经贸摩擦的短期战略举措有哪些?

(2) 如何建设应对中美经贸摩擦的长期机制?

Chapter 2 The External Environment Analysis

Opening Case

Strategic CRM for Chinese Auto OEMs

CRM strategy is the overall guidance to the development of the entire customer relationship management. Without an appropriate CRM strategy hardly will investment in other aspects such as Process, IT Infrastructure, Culture and Organization be fruitful①. Shanghai VW introduced Touran into the Chinese market trying to develop its MPV customer segment in China. It is a model with high technology content and quality to be proud of—Touran gained a "five stars" Euro NCAP rating②. However, Touran didn't make a big splash as it did in the foreign markets. It was not favored by Chinese consumers. There could be a number of causes leading to this unsuccess. But, it is for sure that a successful introduction of new model is required to have a right target segment and selection of core product based on a full understanding on customer needs③.

Introduction

This chapter can be introduced with a general statement regarding the importance of understanding what is happening outside of the firm itself and how what is happening can affect the firm's ability to achieve strategic competitiveness and earn above-average returns. This importance is illustrated by the Opening Case, which discusses the impact events in the external environment can have on a firm's performance, despite efforts to adjust to industry dynamics.

The Importance of Analyzing the Firm's External Environment.

Environmental conditions in the current global economy differ from those

① 客户关系管理战略是整个客户关系管理发展的总体指导。没有正确的客户关系管理战略,流程、IT 基础设施、文化和组织等方面的投资便难有产出。

② 上海大众为了发展 MPV 客户细分市场,将途安引入中国市场。途安车型技术含量高、质量好,在欧洲 NCAP 评级中高达"五星级"。

③ 然而,途安并没有像在国外市场那样引起轰动,没有受到中国消费者的青睐。导致这一失败的原因可能有很多。但是,要想引进新车型,必然要求在充分了解客户需求的基础上,形成正确的目标细分,选择核心的产品。

previously faced by firms:

(1) Technological advances require more timely and effective competitive actions and responses.

(2) Rapid sociological changes abroad affect labor practices and product demand of diverse consumers.

(3) Governmental policies and laws affect where and how firms may choose to compete.

Understanding the external environment helps to build the firm's base of knowledge and information which can (1) help to build new capabilities, (2) buffer the firm from environmental impacts, and (3) build bridges to influential stakeholders.

2.1 The General, Industry, and Competitor Environments

2.1.1 The External Environment

(1) The General Environment

Demographic

Political/Legal

Social/ Cultural

Economic

Technological

Global

(2) The Industry Environment

Threat of New Entrants

Power of Buyers

Power of Suppliers

Intensity of Rivalry

Product Substitutes

(3) The Competitor Environment

The general environment is composed of elements in the broader society that can indirectly influence an industry and the firms within the industry. But firms cannot directly control the general environment's segments and elements①.

2.1.2 The General Environment: Segments and Elements

The industry environment is the constellation of factors—threat of new entrants, suppliers, buyers, product substitutes, and the intensity of rivalry among competitors—that directly influence a firm and its competitive decisions and responses.

(1) Competitor analysis represents the firm's understanding of its current competitors. This understanding will complement information and insights derived from investigating the general and industry environments.

The following are important distinctions to make regarding different external analyses:

① Analysis of the general environment focuses on the future.

② Industry analysis focuses on factors and conditions influencing firm profitability within its industry.

③ Competitor analysis focuses on predicting the dynamics of rivals' actions, responses, and intentions.

Performance improves when the firm integrates the insights provided by analyses of the general environment, the industry environment, and the competitor environment.

(2) The strategic challenge is to develop an understanding of the implications of these elements and factors for a firm's competitive position. Processes and frameworks for the analysis of the external environment are provided in this chapter.

2.2 External Environmental Analysis

(1) In addition to increasing a firm's awareness and understanding of an increasingly turbulent, complex, and global general environment, external environmental analysis also is necessary to enable the firm's managers to interpret information to identify opportunities and threats②.

(2) Opportunities represent conditions in the general environment that may help a company achieve strategic competitiveness by presenting it with possibilities, while

---

① 一般环境是由广泛的社会因素组成的,这些因素可以间接影响一个行业和行业内的企业。但企业不能直接控制一般环境的各个环节和要素。

② 外部环境分析能使企业更好地认识和理解日益动荡复杂和全球化的一般环境,也能使企业的管理者能够解读信息,识别机遇和威胁。

threats are conditions that may hinder or constrain a company's efforts to achieve strategic competitiveness①.

(3) Information used to analyze the general environment can come from multiple sources: publications, observation, attendance at trade shows, or conversations with customers, suppliers, and employees of public-sector organizations. And this information can be formally gathered by individuals occupying traditional "boundary spanning" roles (such as a position in sales, purchasing, or public relations) or by assigning information-gathering responsibility to a special group or team.

(4) One strategy that firms can use to enhance their awareness of conditions in the external environment is to establish an analysis process involving scanning, monitoring, forecasting, and assessing.

2.2.1 Scanning

Scanning entails the study of all segments in the general environment. Firms use the scanning process to either detect early warning signals regarding potential changes or to detect changes that are already underway. In most cases, information and data being collected or observed are ambiguous, incomplete, and appear to be unconnected. Scanning is most important in highly volatile environments, and the scanning system should fit the organizational context (e. g. , scanning systems designed for volatile environments are not suitable for firms competing in a stable environment)②.

Scanning may signal a future change in the needs and lifestyles of baby boomers as they approach retirement age. This may not only provide opportunities for financial institutions as they prepare for an increase in the number of retirees, but also may provide opportunities for packagers and marketers of retirement communities and other products specifically targeted to this segment③.

The Internet provides significant opportunities to obtain information. For example,

---

① 机会代表一般环境中可以帮助公司展示可能性以获得战略竞争力的条件,而威胁则是可能阻碍或限制公司获得战略竞争力的条件。

② 扫描指对一般环境中的所有要素进行研究。通过扫描,公司可以侦测到潜在变化的预警信号,或者发现已有的变化。多数情况下,收集或观察中的信息和数据既不明确,也不完整,并且看起来互不相关。易变环境中,扫描最重要,同时,扫描系统应与公司的组织框架一致(例如,为易变环境公司设计的扫描系统不适用于稳定环境中的公司)。

③ 通过扫描分析会发现,当婴儿潮一代接近退休年龄时,未来的需求和生活方式会发生变化。这不仅为金融机构提供了机会,因为金融机构为退休人数的增加做出了准备;也为退休社区的包装商和营销商以及专门针对这一细分市场的产品提供了机会。

Amazon. com records significant information about individuals visiting its website, particularly if a purchase is made. Amazon then welcomes the individual by name when s/he visits the website again. It even sends messages to the individual about specials and new products similar to that purchased in previous visits. Additionally, many websites and advertisers on the Internet obtain information surreptitiously from those who visit their sites via the use of "cookies".

2.2.2 Monitoring

Monitoring represents a process whereby analysts observe environmental changes (over time) to see if, in fact, an important trend begins to emerge①.

The critical issue in monitoring is that analysts be able to detect meaning from the data and information collected during the scanning process. (Remind students that this data is generally ambiguous, incomplete and unconnected.) For example, in the United States, middle class African Americans are growing in number and wealth and are pursuing investment options, an opportunity in the economic segment that companies in the financial planning sector could monitor②.

Effective monitoring requires the firm to identify important stakeholders. Because the importance of different stakeholders can vary over a firm's life cycle, careful attention must be given to the firm's needs and its stakeholder groups over time. Scanning and monitoring can also provide information about successfully commercializing new technologies③.

2.2.3 Forecasting

The next step is for analysts to take the information and data gathered during the scanning and monitoring phases and attempt to project forward. Forecasting represents the process where analysts develop feasible projections of what might happen—and how quickly—as a result of the changes and trends detected through scanning and monitoring. Because of uncertainty, forecasting events and outcomes accurately is a

---

① 分析人员观察环境变化,判断是否有新趋势出现的长期过程叫作监测。

② 监测中的关键问题是,分析人员能否从扫描过程中收集的数据和信息中发现意义(提醒:这些数据通常不明确、不完整,不相关)。例如,在美国,中产的非洲裔美国人数量和财富在增长,并且正在寻求投资选择,这就为金融规划部门的公司监控经济成分提供了机会。

③ 有效的监测要求公司识别重要的利益相关者。由于不同利益相关者在公司的生命周期中可能起到不同作用,因此必须长期关注公司的需求及其利益相关者群体。通过扫描和监测,还可以获得信息,将新技术成功商业化。

challenging task①.

2.2.4 Assessing

Assessing represents the step in the external analysis process where all of the other steps come together. The objective of assessing is to determine the timing and significance of the effects of changes and trends in the environment on the strategic management of a firm. Getting the strategy right will depend on the accuracy of the assessment②.

It is good to alert students to the fact that a major challenge for managers and firms engaging in the process of external analysis is to recognize biases and assumptions that may affect the analysis process. This is important, because these may limit the accuracy of forecasts and assessments. For example, managers may choose to disregard certain information, thus missing critical indicators of future environmental changes. Or, past experiences may prejudice the ways that opportunities or threats are perceived—if they are perceived at all. One solution might be to solicit multiple inputs so a single source is not able to manipulate the information and to seek frequent feedback regarding the accuracy or usefulness of forecasts and assessments.

2.3 Segments of the General Environment

The general environment consists of six segments: demographic, economic, political/legal, social/cultural, global, and technological. The challenge is to scan, monitor, forecast, and assess all six segments of the general environment, focusing the primary effort on those elements in each segment of the general environment that have the greatest potential impact on the firm.

In the twenty-first century competitive landscape, analysts are cautioned against confining their analysis to domestic markets alone. Any analysis of the general environment and its segments should recognize global elements that may have an impact on the firm.

External analysis efforts should focus on segments most important to the firm's

---

① 下一步是分析员利用在扫描和监视阶段收集的信息和数据，并尝试向前推进。通过扫描和监测阶段侦测到变化趋势后，分析人员对于变化可能导致的后果开发出可行的项目计划。由于具有不确定性，预测事件和结果是一项具有挑战性的任务。

② 评估是将外部分析中所有的步骤结合起来。环境的变化趋势影响公司的战略管理，评估的目的正是为了确定这种影响的时机和意义。正确的战略取决于评估的准确性。

strategic competitiveness to identify environmental changes, trends, opportunities, and threats that can be matched with the firm's core competencies so that it can achieve strategic competitiveness and earn above-average returns.

2.3.1 The Demographic Segment

(1) The demographic segment is concerned with a population's size, age structure, geographic distribution, ethnic mix, and distribution of income①.

(2) While each of the elements of this segment are discussed below, you might note that the challenge for analysts (and managers) is to determine what the changes that have been identified in the demographic characteristics or elements of a population imply for the future strategic competitiveness of the firm②.

Population Size

While population size itself may be important to firms that require a "critical mass" of potential customers, changes in the specific make-up of a population's size may have even more critical implications. One of the most important changes in a population's size is changes in a nation's birth rate and/or family size, as well as demographic changes in the population of developed versus developing countries.

Age Structure

Changes in a nation's birth rate or life expectancy can have important implications for firms. Are people living longer? What is the life expectancy of infants? These will impact the health care system (and firms serving that segment) and the development of products and services targeted to an older (or younger) population.

Geographic Distribution

Population shifts from one region of a nation to another or from metropolitan to non-metropolitan areas may have an impact on a firm's strategic competitiveness. Issues that should be considered include:

(1) The attractiveness of a firm's location may be influenced by governmental support, and a shrinking population may imply a shrinking tax base and a lesser availability of official financial support.

---

① 人口因素涉及人口的规模、年龄结构、地理分布、民族结构和收入分配。

② 下文将讨论人口因素中所有的因素,分析师(或经理)面临的挑战是能否确定人口因素中的变化对公司未来战略竞争力的影响。

(2) Firms may have to consider relocation if tax demands require it.

(3) Advances in communications technology will have a profound effect on geographic distribution and the workforce.

Ethnic Mix

This reflects the changes in the ethnic make-up of a population and has implications both for a firm's potential customers and for the workforce. Issues that should be addressed include:

(1) Will new products and services be demanded or can existing ones be modified?

(2) How will changes in the ethnicity of a population affect the composition of the workforce?

(3) Are managers prepared to manage a more culturally diverse workforce?

(4) How can the firm position itself to take advantage of increased workforce heterogeneity?

Income Distribution

Changes in income distribution are important because changes in the levels of individual and group purchasing power and discretionary income often result in changes in spending (consumption) and savings patterns. Tracking, forecasting, and assessing changes in income patterns may identify new opportunities for firms.

Income and its distribution have always been a central concern of economic theory and economic policy. Classical economists such as Adam Smith, Thomas Malthus and David Ricardo were mainly concerned with factor income distribution, that is, the distribution of income between the main factors of production, land, labour and capital.

Modern economists have also addressed this issue, but have been more concerned with the distribution of income across individuals and households. Important theoretical and policy concerns include the relationship between income inequality and economic growth.

The distribution of income within a society may be represented by the Lorenz curve. The Lorenz curve is closely associated with measures of income inequality, such as the Gini coefficient.

2.3.2 The Economic Segment

The economic segment of the general environment refers to the nature and direction of the economy in which a firm competes or may compete. Analysts must scan, monitor, forecast, and assess a number of key economic indicators or elements, including levels and trends of: ①

Inflation Rates and Interest Rates

In economics, inflation is a sustained increase in the general price level of goods and services in an economy over a period of time. When the price level rises, each unit of currency buys fewer goods and services. Consequently, inflation reflects a reduction in the purchasing power per unit of money—a loss of real value in the medium of exchange and unit of account within the economy. A chief measure of price inflation is the inflation rate, the annualized percentage change in a general price index (normally the consumer price index) over time. The opposite of inflation is deflation. ②

Inflation affects an economy in various ways, both positive and negative. Negative effects of inflation include an increase in the opportunity cost of holding money, uncertainty over future inflation which may discourage investment and savings, and if inflation were rapid enough, shortages of goods as consumers begin hoarding out of concern that prices will increase in the future.

Inflation also has positive effects: Fundamentally, inflation gives everyone an incentive to spend and invest, because if they don't, their money will be worth less in the future. This spending and investment can benefit the economy. Inflation reduces the real burden of debt, both public and private. If you have a fixed-rate mortgage on your house, your salary is likely to increase over time due to inflation, but your mortgage payment will stay the same. Over time, your mortgage payment will become a smaller percentage of your earnings, which means that you will have more money to spend. Inflation keeps nominal interest rates above zero, so that central banks can reduce interest rates, when necessary, to stimulate the economy. Inflation reduces unemployment to the extent that unemployment is caused by nominal wage rigidity. When demand for labor falls but nominal wages do not, as typically occurs during a recession, the supply and demand for labor cannot reach equilibrium, and

---

① 一般环境的经济因素是指公司所在经济的性质或方向。分析师需要对一系列经济指标或因素进行扫描、监控、预测及评估。

② 通货膨胀是一个经济体中商品和服务的总体价格水平在一段时间内的持续上涨。当价格水平上升时,每单位货币购买的商品和服务就会减少。因此,通货膨胀反映了单位货币购买力的下降——经济中交换媒介和记账单位的实际价值损失。物价通胀的主要衡量指标是通货膨胀率,即一个总物价指数(通常是消费物价指数)随时间年化百分比的变化。通货膨胀的反面是通货紧缩。

unemployment results. By reducing the real value of a given nominal wage, inflation increases the demand for labor, and therefore reduces unemployment.

Economists generally believe that high rates of inflation and hyperinflation are caused by an excessive growth of the money supply. However, money supply growth does not necessarily cause inflation. Some economists maintain that under the conditions of a liquidity trap, large monetary injections are like "pushing on a string". Views on which factors determine low to moderate rates of inflation are more varied. Low or moderate inflation may be attributed to fluctuations in real demand for goods and services, or changes in available supplies such as during scarcities. However, the consensus view is that a long sustained period of inflation is caused by money supply growing faster than the rate of economic growth.

Today, most economists favor a low and steady rate of inflation. Low (as opposed to zero or negative) inflation reduces the severity of economic recessions by enabling the labor market to adjust more quickly in a downturn, and reduces the risk that a liquidity trap prevents monetary policy from stabilizing the economy. The task of keeping the rate of inflation low and stable is usually given to monetary authorities. Generally, these monetary authorities are the central banks that control monetary policy through the setting of interest rates, through open market operations, and through the setting of banking reserve requirements.

Increases in quantity of the money or in the overall money supply (or debasement of the means of exchange) have occurred in many different societies throughout history, changing with different forms of money used. For instance, when gold was used as currency, the government could collect gold coins, melt them down, mix them with other metals such as silver, copper or lead, and reissue them at the same nominal value. By diluting the gold with other metals, the government could issue more coins without also needing to increase the amount of gold used to make them. When the cost of each coin is lowered in this way, the government profits from an increase in seigniorage. This practice would increase the money supply but at the same time the relative value of each coin would be lowered. As the relative value of the coins becomes lower, consumers would need to give more coins in exchange for the same goods and services as before. These goods and services would experience a price increase as the value of each coin is reduced.

During the Song Dynasty, China introduced the practice of printing paper money in order to create fiat currency. During the Yuan Dynasty, the government spent a great deal of money fighting costly wars, and reacted by printing more, leading to inflation. The problem of inflation became so severe that the people stopped using paper money, which they saw as "worthless paper". Fearing the inflation that plagued the Yuan Dynasty, the Ming Dynasty initially rejected the use of paper money, using only copper coins. The dynasty did not issue paper currency until 1375.

By the nineteenth century, economists categorized three separate factors that cause a rise or fall in the price of goods: a change in the value or production costs of the good, a change in the price of money which then was usually a fluctuation in the commodity price of the metallic content in the currency, and currency depreciation resulting from an increased supply of currency relative to the quantity of redeemable metal backing the currency. Following the proliferation of private banknote currency printed during the American Civil War, the term "inflation" started to appear as a direct reference to the currency depreciation that occurred as the quantity of redeemable banknotes outstripped the quantity of metal available for their redemption. At that time, the term inflation referred to the devaluation of the currency, and not to a rise in the price of goods.

This relationship between the over-supply of banknotes and a resulting depreciation in their value was noted by earlier classical economists such as David Hume and David Ricardo, who would go on to examine and debate what effect a currency devaluation (later termed monetary inflation) has on the price of goods (later termed price inflation, and eventually just inflation).

The adoption of fiat currency by many countries, from the 18th century onwards, made much larger variations in the supply of money possible. Since then, huge increases in the supply of paper money have taken place in a number of countries, producing hyperinflation—episodes of extreme inflation rates much higher than those observed in earlier periods of commodity money. The hyperinflation in the Weimar Republic of Germany is a notable example.

Trade Deficits and Surpluses

The commercial balance or net exports (sometimes symbolized as NX), is the difference between the monetary value of exports and imports of output in an economy over a certain period, measured in the currency of that economy. It is the relationship between a nation's imports and exports. A positive balance is known as a trade surplus if it consists of exporting more than is imported; a negative balance is referred to as a trade deficit or, informally, a trade gap. The balance of trade is sometimes divided into a goods and a services balance. [①]

Trade, in general connotation, means the purchase and sales of commodities. In International Trade, purchase and sale are replaced by imports and exports. Balance of Trade is simply the difference between the value of exports and value of imports. Thus, the Balance of Trade denotes the differences of imports and exports of a merchandise of a country during the course of year. It indicates the value of exports and imports of the country in question. If the value of its exports over a period exceeds its value of imports, it is called favorable balance of trade and, conversely, if the value of total imports exceeds the total value of exports over a period, it is unfavorable balance of trade. The favorable balance of trade indicates good economic condition of the country.

The balance of trade forms part of the current account, which includes other transactions such as income from the net international investment position as well as international aid. If the current account is in surplus, the country's net international asset position increases correspondingly. Equally, a deficit decreases the net international asset position. The trade balance is identical to the difference between a country's output and its domestic demand.

Measuring the balance of trade can be problematic because of problems with recording and collecting data. As an illustration of this problem, when official data for all the world's countries are added up, exports exceed imports by almost 1%; it appears the world is running a positive balance of trade with itself. This cannot be true, because all transactions involve an equal credit or debit in the account of each nation. The discrepancy is widely believed to be explained by transactions intended to launder money or evade taxes, smuggling and other visibility problems. However, especially for developed countries, accuracy is likely.

In addition, the trade balance is likely to differ across the business cycle. In export-led growth (such as oil and early industrial goods), the balance of trade will improve during an economic expansion. However, with domestic demand led growth (as in the United States and Australia) the trade balance will worsen at the same stage in the business cycle.

Monetary balance of trade is different from physical balance of trade (which is expressed in amount of raw materials, known also as Total Material Consumption). Developed countries usually import a lot of raw materials from developing countries.

---

① 商业余额或净出口(有时用 NX 表示)是一个经济体在一定时期内出口和进口的货币价值之间的差额,以该经济体的货币计量。它是一个国家的进口和出口之间的关系。如果出口大于进口,则称为贸易顺差;负差额被称为贸易逆差或非正式的贸易差额。贸易差额有时分为商品差额和服务差额。

Typically, these imported materials are transformed into finished products, and might be exported after adding value. Financial trade balance statistics conceal material flow. Most developed countries have a large physical trade deficit, because they have a large ecological footprint. Civil society organizations point out the predatory nature of this imbalance, and campaign for ecological debt repayment.

Annual trade surpluses are immediate and direct additions to their nations' GDPs. To some extent exports induce additional increases to GDP that are not reflected within the export products' prices; thus contributions to GDP from trade surpluses are generally understated.

Products' prices generally reflect their producers' production supporting expenditures. Producers often benefit from some production supporting goods and services at lesser or no cost to the producers.

For example, governments may deliberately locate or increase the capacity of their infrastructure, or provide other additional considerations to retain or attract producers within their own jurisdictions. The curriculum of a nation's schools and colleges may provide job applicants specifically suited to the producer's needs, or provide specialized research and development. All national factors of production, including education, contribute to GDP, and unless globally traded products fully reflect those goods and services, these other export supporting contributions are not entirely identified and attributed to their nations' global trade.

Annual trade deficits are immediate and indirect reducers of their nations' GDPs. Trade deficits make no net contribution to their nations' GDPs but the importing nations indirectly deny themselves of the benefits earned by producing nations. Among what's being denied is familiarity with methods, practices, the manipulation of tools, materials and fabrication processes.

The economic differences between domestic and imported goods occur prior to the goods entry within the final purchasers' nations. After domestic goods have reached their producers shipping dock or imported goods have been unloaded on to the importing nation's cargo vessel or entry port's dock, similar goods have similar economic attributes.

Although supporting products not reflected within the prices of specific items are all captured within the producing nation's GDP, those supporting but not reflected within prices of globally traded goods are not attributed to nations' global trade. Trade surpluses' contributions and trade deficits' detriments to their nation's GDPs are understated. The entire benefits of production are earned by the exporting nations and denied to the importing nation.

Budget Deficits and Surpluses

A government budget is a government document presenting the government's proposed revenues and spending for a financial year. The budget is also known as the Annual Financial Statement of the country. This document estimates the anticipated government revenues and government expenditures for the ensuing (current) financial year. For example, only certain types of revenue may be imposed and collected. Property tax is frequently the basis for municipal and county revenues, while sales tax and/or income tax are the basis for state revenues, and income tax and corporate tax are the basis for national revenues.

Personal Savings Rates & Business Savings Rates

A savings and loan or "thrift" is a financial institution that accepts savings deposits and makes mortgage, car and other personal loans to individual members (a cooperative venture known in the United Kingdom as a building society).

Gross Domestic Product

Gross domestic product (GDP) is defined by the Organization for Economic Co-operation and Development (OECD) as "an aggregate measure of production equal to the sum of the gross values added of all resident, institutional units engaged in production (plus any taxes, and minus any subsidies, on products not included in the value of their outputs)".

GDP estimates are commonly used to measure the economic performance of a whole country or region, but can also measure the relative contribution of an industry sector. This is possible because GDP is a measure of "value added" rather than sales; it adds each firm's value added (the value of its output minus the value of goods that are used up in producing it). For example, a firm buys steel and adds value to it by producing a car; double counting would occur if GDP added together the value of the steel and the value of the car. Because it is based on value added, GDP also increases when an enterprise reduces its use of materials or other resources ("intermediate consumption") to produce the same output.

The more familiar use of GDP estimates is to calculate the growth of the economy from year to year (and recently from quarter to quarter). The pattern of GDP growth is held to indicate the success or failure of economic policy and to determine whether an economy is "in recession".

The history of the concept of GDP should be distinguished from the history of changes in ways of estimating it. The value added by firms is relatively easy to calculate from their accounts, but the value added by the public sector, by financial industries, and by intangible asset creation is more complex. These activities are increasingly important in developed economies, and the international conventions governing their estimation and their inclusion or exclusion in GDP regularly change in an attempt to keep up with industrial advances. In the words of one academic economist, "The actual number for GDP is therefore the product of a vast patchwork of statistics and a complicated set of processes carried out on the raw data to fit them to the conceptual framework."

GDP can be determined in three ways, all of which should, in principle, give the same result. They are the production (or output or value added) approach, the income approach, or the expenditure approach.

The most direct of the three is the production approach, which sums the outputs of every class of enterprise to arrive at the total. The expenditure approach works on the principle that all of the product must be bought by somebody, therefore the value of the total product must be equal to people's total expenditures in buying things. The income approach works on the principle that the incomes of the productive factors ("producers", colloquially) must be equal to the value of their product, and determines GDP by finding the sum of all producers' incomes. For both domestic and key international markets. In addition, the implications of changes and trends in the economic segment may affect the political/legal segment both domestically and in other global markets. This may be of critical importance as nations eliminate or reduce trade barriers and integrate their economies.

2.3.3 The Political/Legal Segment

The political/legal segment is the arena in which organizations and interest groups compete for attention, resources, and a voice in overseeing the body of laws and regulations guiding the interactions among nations. In other words, this segment is concerned with how interest groups and organizations attempt to influence representatives of governments (and governmental agencies) and how they, in turn, are influenced by them①.

Because of the influence that this segment can have on the nature of competition as well as on the overall profitability of industries and individual firms, analysts must assess changes and trends in administration philosophies regarding:

Anti-Trust Regulations and Enforcement

Competition law is a law that promotes or seeks to maintain market competition by regulating anti-competitive conduct by companies. Competition law is implemented through public and private enforcement.

In Japan, the competition law prevents certain forms of conglomerates. Competition law is considered as a tool to stimulate economic growth in many of Asia's developing countries, including India. There has also been speculation that competition law has solved some problems like monetary problems in Israel and the lack of effective institutions and regulations in Indonesia. In addition, competition law has promoted fairness in China and Indonesia as well as international integration in Vietnam.

Competition law is known as antitrust law in the United States and European Union, and as anti-monopoly law in China and Russia. In previous years it has been known as trade practices law in the United Kingdom and Australia.

The history of competition law reaches back to the Roman Empire. The business practices of market traders, guilds and governments have always been subject to scrutiny, and sometimes severe sanctions. Since the 20th century, competition law has become global. The two largest and most influential systems of competition regulation are United States antitrust law and European Union competition law. National and regional competition authorities across the world have formed international support and enforcement networks.

Tax Laws

Tax laws are enacted by the National People's Congress, e. g. , the Individual Income Tax Law of the People's Republic of China; or enacted by the Standing Committee of the National People's Congress, e. g. , the Tax Collection and Administration Law of the People's Republic of China.

---

① 政治/法律因素指组织及利益集团竞争的战场，争夺注意力、资源，争取监督国际活动所遵循的法律法规体系的话语权。换言之，政治/法律因素涉及组织和利益集团如何影响政府代表（及部门），又如何被后者影响。

The administrative regulations and rules concerning taxation are formulated by the State Council, e. g. , the Detailed Rules for the Implementation of the Tax Collection and Administration Law of the People's Republic of China, the Detailed Regulations for the Implementation of the Individual Income Tax Law of the People's Republic of China, the Provisional Regulations of the People's Republic of China on Value Added Tax.

The departmental rules concerning taxation are formulated by the Ministry of Finance, the State Administration of Taxation, the Tariff and Classification Committee of the State Council, and the General Administration of Customs, e. g. , the Detailed Rules for the Implementation of the Provisional Regulations of the People's Republic of China on Value Added Tax, the Provisional Measures for Voluntary Reporting of the Individual Income Tax.

The formulation of tax laws follows four steps: drafting, examination, voting and promulgation. The four steps for the formulation of tax administrative regulations and rules are: planning, drafting, verification and promulgation. The four steps mentioned above take place in accordance with laws, regulations and rules.

Industry Deregulation

A regulation is a legal norm intended to shape conduct that is a byproduct of imperfection. A regulation may be used to prescribe or proscribe conduct ("command-and-control" regulation), to calibrate incentives ("incentive" regulation), or to change preferences ("preferences shaping regulation"). In statist mechanisms it can also be extended to monitoring and enforcement of rules as established by primary and/or delegated legislation. In this form, it is generally a written instrument containing rules having the force of statist law (as opposed to natural law). Other forms of regulation are self regulation. In general, regulations are written by executive agencies as a way to enforce laws passed by the legislature. Because of the actual or potential interference in choices, the idea of regulation and most issues related to regulation tend to be in controversy.

Regulation creates limits, constrains a right, creates or limits a duty, or allocates a responsibility. Regulation can take many forms: legal restrictions promulgated by a government authority, contractual obligations that bind many parties (for example, "insurance regulations" that arise out of contracts between insurers or reinsures and their insured), self-regulation by an industry such as through a trade association, social regulation (e. g. norms), co-regulation, third-party regulation, certification, accreditation or market regulation. In its legal sense regulation can and should be distinguished from primary legislation (by Parliament of elected legislative body) on the one hand and judge-made law on the other.

Regulation mandated by a state attempts to produce outcomes which might not otherwise occur, produce or prevent outcomes in different places to what might otherwise occur, produce or prevent outcomes in different timescales than would otherwise occur. In this way, regulations can be seen as implementation artifacts of policy statements. Common examples of regulation include controls on market entries, prices, wages, development approvals, pollution effects, employment for certain people in certain industries, standards of production for certain goods, the military forces and services. The economics of imposing or removing regulations relating to markets is analyzed in regulatory economics.

Regulation of businesses existed in the ancient early Egyptian, Indian, Greek, and Roman civilizations. Standardized weights and measures existed to an extent in the ancient world, and gold may have operated to some degree as an international currency. In China, a national currency system existed and paper currency was invented. Sophisticated law existed in Ancient Rome. In the European Early Middle Ages, law and standardization declined with the Roman Empire, but regulation existed in the form of norms, customs, and privileges; this regulation was aided by the unified Christian identity and a sense of honor in regard to contracts.

Labor Laws

Labor law mediates the relationship between workers (employees), employers, trade unions and the government. Collective labor law relates to the tripartite relationship between employee, employer and union. Individual labor law concerns employees' rights at work and through the contract for work. Employment standards are social norms (in some cases also technical standards) for the minimum socially acceptable conditions under which employees or contractors are allowed to work.

Labor law arose in parallel with the Industrial Revolution as the relationship between worker and employer changed from small-scale production studios to large-scale factories. Workers sought better conditions and the right to join (or avoid joining) a labor union, while employers sought a more predictable, flexible and less costly workforce. The state of labor law at any one time is therefore both the product of, and a component of struggles between various social forces.

As England was the first country to industrialize, it was also the first to face the often appalling consequences of industrial revolution in a less regulated economic framework. Over the course of the late 18th and early to mid-19th century the foundation for modern labor law was slowly laid, as some of the more egregious aspects of working conditions were steadily ameliorated through legislation.

Free Trade Versus Protectionism

Free trade is a policy in international markets in which governments do not restrict imports or exports. Free trade is exemplified by the European Union/European Economic Area and the North American Free Trade Agreement, which have established open markets. Most nations are today members of the World Trade Organization (WTO) multilateral trade agreements. However, most governments still impose some protectionist policies that are intended to support local employment, such as applying tariffs to imports or subsidies to exports. Governments may also restrict free trade to limit exports of natural resources. Other barriers that may hinder trade include import quotas, taxes, and non-tariff barriers, such as regulatory legislation.

Protectionism is the economic policy of restraining trade between states (countries) through methods such as tariffs on imported goods, restrictive quotas, and a variety of other governmentregulations designed to allow (according to proponents) fair competition between imports and goods and services produced domestically.

This policy contrasts with free trade, where government barriers to trade are kept to a minimum. In recent years, protectionism has become closely aligned with anti-globalization and anti-immigration. The term is mostly used in the context of economics, where protectionism refers to policies or doctrines which protect businesses and workers within a country by restricting or regulating trade with foreign nations.

A variety of policies have been used to achieve protectionist goals. These include:

Tariffs: Typically, tariffs (or taxes) are imposed on imported goods. Tariff rates usually vary according to the type of goods imported. Import tariffs will increase the cost to importers, and increase the price of imported goods in the local markets, thus lowering the quantity of goods imported, to favor local producers. Tariffs may also be imposed on exports, and in an economy with floating exchange rates, export tariffs have similar effects as import tariffs. However, since export tariffs are often perceived as "hurting" local industries, while import tariffs are perceived as "helping" local industries, export tariffs are seldom implemented.

Import quotas: To reduce the quantity and therefore increase the market price of imported goods. The economic effects of an import quota are similar to that of a tariff, except that the tax revenue gain from a tariff will instead be distributed to those who receive import licenses. Economists often suggest that import licenses be auctioned to the highest bidder, or that import quotas be replaced by an equivalent tariff.

Administrative barriers: Countries are sometimes accused of using their various administrative rules (e. g. regarding food safety, environmental standards, electrical safety, etc.) as a way to introduce barriers to imports.

Anti-dumping legislation: Supporters of anti-dumping laws argue that they prevent "dumping" of cheaper foreign goods that would cause local firms to close down. However, in practice, anti-dumping laws are usually used to impose trade tariffs on foreign exporters.

Direct subsidies: Government subsidies (in the form of lump-sum payments or cheap loans) are sometimes given to local firms that cannot compete well against imports. These subsidies are purported to "protect" local jobs, and to help local firms adjust to the world markets.

Export subsidies: Export subsidies are often used by governments to increase exports. Export subsidies have the opposite effect of export tariffs because exporters get payment, which is a percentage or proportion of the value of exported. Export subsidies increase the amount of trade, and in a country with floating exchange rates, have effects similar to import subsidies.

Exchange rate manipulation: A government may intervene in the foreign exchange market to lower the value of its currency by selling its currency in the foreign exchange market. Doing so will raise the cost of imports and lower the cost of exports, leading to an improvement in its trade balance. However, such a policy is only effective in the short run, as it will most likely lead to inflation in the country, which will in turn raise the cost of exports, and reduce the relative price of imports.

International patent systems: There is an argument for viewing national patent systems as a cloak for protectionist trade policies at a national level. Two strands of this argument exist: one when patents held by one country form part of a system of exploitable relative advantage in trade negotiations against another and a second where adhering to a worldwide system of patents confers "good citizenship" status despite "de facto protectionism". There were also reputation advantages for states to be seen to be sticking to intellectual property systems.

2.3.4 The Sociocultural Segment

The sociocultural segment is concerned with different societies' social attitudes and cultural values. This segment is important because the attitudes and values of society influence and thus are reflected in changes in a society's economic, demographic, political/legal, and technological segments①.

Analysts are especially cautioned to pay attention to sociocultural changes and effects that they may have on②:

(1) Workforce composition—and the implications for managing—resulting from an increase in the number of women, and increased ethnic and cultural diversity③.

(2) Changes in attitudes about the growing number of contingency workers④.

(3) Shifts in population toward suburban life, and resulting transportation issues⑤.

(4) Shifts in work and career preferences, including a trend to work from home made possible by technology advances⑥.

2.3.5 The Technological Segment

As noted in many of the other segments of the general environment—and as discussed in Chapter 1 as a key driver of the new competitive landscape—technological changes can have broad effects on society. The technological segment includes institutions and activities involved with creating new knowledge and translating that knowledge into new outputs, products, processes, and materials⑦.

Firms should pay careful attention to the technological segment, since early adopters can gain market share and above average returns⑧.

Important technology-related issues that might affect a broad variety of firms include⑨:

(1) Increasing plant automation.

(2) Internet technologies and their application to commerce and data gathering.

---

① 社会文化因素指不同国家的社会态度及文化价值观。这一因素很重要,社会态度及价值观不但影响社会的经济、人口、政治/法律及技术因素,也体现于这些因素之中。

② 分析师尤其应该注意社会文化变化及其对以下方面的影响。

③ 劳动力构成及其对管理的意义:由女性劳工数量增加、种族及文化多样性增加导致。

④ 对人数日益增加的临时工的态度变化。

⑤ 郊区人口变化及因此带来的交通问题。

⑥ 职业偏好变化,如:科技发展使得居家办公成为趋势。

⑦ 技术因素包含从事创造新知识并将其转化为新产出、新产品、新程序及新材料的机构和行为。

⑧ 公司需特别注意技术因素,更早获得新技术的公司更容易抢占市场份额,获得高于平均的收益。

⑨ 与技术相关、并能影响大量公司的重要因素有:装置自动化程度提高,网络技术及其在商务及信息收集中的应用,无线技术的使用。

(3) Uses of wireless technology.

2.3.6 The Global Segment

The 21st-century competitive landscape requires that firms also must analyze global factors. Among the global factors that should be assessed are:

(1) The potential impact of significant international events such as peace in the Middle East or the recent entry of China into the WTO①.

(2) The identification of both important emerging global markets and global markets that are changing②.

(3) The trend toward increasing global outsourcing③.

(4) The differences between cultural and institutional attributes of individual global markets④.

(5) Global market expansion opportunities⑤.

(6) The opportunities to learn from doing business in other countries⑥.

(7) Expanding access to the resources firms need for success⑦.

2.4 Industry Environment Analysis

An industry is a group of firms producing products that are close substitutes for each other. As they compete for market share, the strategies implemented by these companies influence each other and include a broad mix of competitive strategies as each company pursues strategic competitiveness and above-average returns⑧.

It should be noted that, unlike the general environment which has an indirect effect on strategic competitiveness and firm profitability, the effect of the industry environment is more direct. Industry—and individual firm—profitability and the

---

① 国际重大事件的潜在影响,如中东和平,中国加入世界贸易组织。

② 区分正在兴起的国际市场和发生变化的国际市场,二者同等重要。

③ 国际外包的兴起。

④ 全球市场中文化特征与制度特征的区别。

⑤ 全球市场扩张的机遇。

⑥ 向他国学习经营的机遇。

⑦ 增加企业获得成功必需资源(如资本)的途径。

⑧ 行业指生产可以互相替代产品的多家企业。这些企业相互竞争,追求竞争优势和高于平均的回报,因此采用了一系列竞争性战略,不同企业的策略相互产生影响。

intensity of competition in an industry are a function of five competitive forces①.

The Five Forces Model of Competition

(1) The Five Forces Model of Competition indicates that these forces interact to determine the intensity or strength of competition, which ultimately determines the profitability of the industry②.

① Threat of New Entrants.

② Threat of Substitute Products.

③ Bargaining Power of Buyers (Customers).

④ Bargaining Power of Suppliers.

⑤ Rivalry Among Competing Firms in an Industry.

(2) Assessing the relative strength of the five competitive forces is important to a firm's ability to achieve strategic competitiveness and earn above-average returns.

Viewed differently, competition should be seen as groupings of alternative ways that customers can obtain desired results. Thus, any analysis of an industry must expand beyond the traditional practice of concentrating on direct competitors to include potential competitors. For example:

① Suppliers can become competitors by integrating forward.

② Buyers or customers can become competitors by integrating backward.

③ Firms that are not competitors today could produce products that serve as substitutes for existing products offered by firms in an industry, transforming themselves into competitors.

2.4.1 Threat of New Entrants

New entrants to an industry are important because, with new competitors, the intensity of competitive rivalry in an industry generally increases. This is because new competitors may bring substantial resources into the industry and may be interested in capturing a significant market share. If a new competitor brings additional capacity to the industry when product demand is not increasing, prices that can be charged to consumers generally will fall. One result may be a decline in sales and lower returns for many firms in the industry.

---

① 需要注意的是,一般环境对战略竞争力及公司盈利的影响是间接的,而行业环境的影响更为直接。行业收益、个体的企业收益及竞争强度是竞争五力的功能之一。

② 竞争的五力模型中,五种力量相互作用,决定竞争的强度,最终决定行业的收益。新进入者的威胁,替代品的威胁,购买者的议价能力,供应商的议价能力,同业竞争者的竞争程度。

The seriousness or extent of the threat of new entrants is affected by two factors: barriers to entry and expected reactions from—or the potential for retaliation by—incumbent firms in the industry.

Barriers to Entry: Barriers to entering an industry are present when entry is difficult or when it is too costly and places potential entrants at a competitive disadvantage (relative to firms already competing in the industry). There are seven factors that represent potentially significant entry barriers that can emerge as an industry evolves or might be explicitly "erected" by current participants in the industry to protect profitability by deterring new competitors from entry.

Economies of scale refers to the relationship between quantity produced and unit cost: As the quantity of a product produced during a given time period increases, the cost of manufacturing each unit declines.

Economies of scale can serve as an entry barrier when existing firms in the industry have achieved these scale economies and a potential new entrant is only able to enter the industry on a small scale (and produce at a higher cost per unit).

Economies of scale can be overcome as a potential entry barrier by firms that produce multiple customized products or that enter an industry on a large-enough scale. New manufacturing technology facilitated by advanced information systems has allowed the development of "mass customization" in an increasing number of industries, and online ordering has enhanced the ability of customers to obtain customized products (often referred to as "markets of one").

Product Differentiation: Customers may perceive that products offered by existing firms in the industry are unique as a result of service offered, effective advertising campaigns, or being first to offer a product of service to the market. If customers perceive a product or service as unique, they generally are loyal to that brand. Thus, new entrants may be required to spend a great deal of money over a long period of time to overcome customer loyalty to existing products.

While new entrants may be able to overcome perceived uniqueness and brand loyalty, the cost of such strategies generally will be high: offering lower prices, adding additional features, or allocating significant funds to a major advertising and promotion campaign. In the short run, new entrants that try to overcome uniqueness and brand loyalty may suffer lower profits or may be forced to operate at a loss.

Capital Requirements: Firms choosing to enter any industry must commit resources for facilities, to purchase inventory, to pay salaries and benefits, etc. While entry may seem attractive (because there are no apparent barriers to entry), a potential new entrant may not have sufficient capital to enter the industry.

Switching Costs: These are the one-time costs customers will incur when buying from a different supplier. These can include such explicit costs as retraining of employees or retooling of equipment as well as the psychological cost of changing relationships. Incumbent firms in the industry generally try to establish switching costs to offset new entrants that try to win customers with substantially lower prices or an improved (or, to some extent, different) product.

Access to Distribution Channels: As existing firms in an industry generally have developed effective channels for distributing products, these same channels may not be available to new firms entering an industry. Thus, access (or lack thereof) may serve as an effective barrier to entry.

This may be particularly true for consumer nondurable goods (e. g., because of the limited amount of shelf space available in retail stores) and in international markets. In the case of some durable goods or industrial products, to overcome the barrier, new entrants must again incur costs in excess of those paid by existing firms, either through lower prices or price breaks, costly promotion campaigns, or advertising allowances. New entrants may have to incur significant costs to establish a proprietary distribution channel. As in the case of product differentiation or uniqueness barriers, new entrants may suffer lower profits or operate at a loss as they battle to gain access to distribution channels.

Cost Disadvantages Independent of Scale: Existing firms in an industry often are able to achieve cost advantages that cannot be costlessly duplicated by new entrants (i. e., other than those related to economies of scale and access to distribution channels). These can include proprietary process (or product) technology, more favorable access to or control of raw materials, the best locations, or favorable government subsidies.

Potential entrants must find ways to overcome these disadvantages to be able to effectively compete in the industry. This may mean successfully adapting technologies from other industries and/or non-competing products for use in the target industry, developing new sources of raw materials, making product (or service) enhancements to overcome location-related disadvantages, or selling at a lower price to attract customers.

Government Policy: Governments (at all levels) are able to control entry into an industry through licensing and permit requirements. For example, at the firm level, entry into the banking industry is regulated at both the federal and state levels, while liquor sales are regulated at the state and local levels. In some cases, state and/or federal licensing requirements limit entry into the personal services industry (securities sales and law), while in others only state requirements may limit entry (barbers and beauticians).

Expected Retaliation: Even if a firm concludes that it can successfully overcome all of the entry barriers, it still must take into account or anticipate reactions that might be expected from existing firms.

Strong retaliation is likely when existing firms have a heavy investment in fixed assets (especially when there are few alternative uses for those assets) or when industry growth is slow or declining. Retaliation could take the form of announcements of anticipated future investments to increase capacity, new product plans, price-cutting or a study to assess the impact of lower prices (this might imply price-cutting as a "promised" entry barrier-creation strategy by existing firms).

Small entrepreneurial firms can avoid retaliation by identifying and serving neglected market segments. For example, Honda first entered the U.S. market by concentrating on small-engine motorcycles, a market that firms such as Harley-Davidson ignored. After consolidating its position, Honda went on the offensive by introducing larger motorcycles and competing in the broader market.

2.4.2 Bargaining Power of Suppliers

The bargaining power of suppliers depends on suppliers' economic bargaining power relative to firms competing in the industry. Suppliers are powerful when firm profitability is reduced by suppliers' actions. Suppliers can exert their power by raising prices or by restricting the quantity and/or quality of goods available for sale.

Suppliers are powerful relative to firms competing in the industry when:

(1) the supplier segment of the industry is dominated by a few large companies and is more concentrated than the industry to which it sells.

(2) satisfactory substitute products are not available to industry firms.

(3) industry firms are not a significant customer group for the supplier group.

(4) suppliers' goods are critical to buyers' marketplace success.

(5) effectiveness of suppliers' products has created high switching costs for buyers.

(6) suppliers represent a credible threat to integrate forward into the buyers' industry, especially when suppliers have substantial resources and provide highly differentiated products.

In the airline industry, suppliers' bargaining power is changing. There are few suppliers, but demand for the major aircraft is also low. Boeing and Airbus compete strongly for most orders of major aircraft. However, China recently announced plans to enter the market by building large commercial aircraft, significant in a country which is projected to purchase thousands.

2.4.3 Bargaining Power of Buyers

While firms seek to maximize their return on invested capital, buyers are interested in purchasing products at the lowest possible price (the price at which sellers will earn the lowest acceptable return). To reduce cost or maximize value, customers bargain for higher quality or greater levels of service at the lowest possible price by encouraging competition among firms in the industry.

Buyer groups are powerful relative to firms competing in the industry when:

(1) buyers are important to sellers because they purchase a large portion of the supply industry's total sales.

(2) products purchased from a supply industry represent a significant portion of the seller's annual revenues.

(3) buyers are able to switch to another supplier's product at little, if any, cost.

(4) suppliers' products are undifferentiated and standardized, and the buyers represent a real threat to integrate backwards into the suppliers' industry using resources or expertise.

Armed with greater amounts of information about the manufacturer's costs and the power of the Internet as a shopping and distribution alternative, consumers appear to be increasing their bargaining power in many industries. One reason for this shift is that individual buyers incur virtually zero switching costs when they decide to purchase from one manufacturer rather than another or from one dealer as opposed to a second or third one.

2.4.4 Threat of Substitute Products

All firms must recognize that they compete against firms producing substitute products, those products that are capable of satisfying similar customer needs but come from outside the industry and thus have different characteristics. In effect, prices charged for substitute products represent the upper limit on the prices that suppliers can charge for their products.

The threat of substitute products is greatest when:

(1) buyers or customers face few, if any switching costs.

(2) prices of the substitute products are lower.

(3) quality and performance capabilities of substitutes are equal to/greater than those of the industry's products.

Firms can offset the attractiveness of substitute products by differentiating their products in ways that are perceived by customers as relevant. Viable strategies might include price, product quality, product features, location, or service level.

2.4.5 Intensity of Rivalry among Competitors

The intensity of rivalry in an industry depends upon the extent to which firms in an industry compete with one another to achieve strategic competitiveness and earn above-average returns because success is measured relative to other firms in the industry. Competition can be based on price, quality, or innovation.

Because of the interrelated nature of firms' actions, action taken by one firm generally will result in retaliation by competitors (also known as competitive response). In addition to actions and reactions that result as firms attempt to offset the other competitive forces in the industry—threat of new entry, power of suppliers and buyers, and threat of substitute products—the intensity of competitive rivalry is also a function of a number of other factors.

Numerous or Equally Balanced Competitors

Industries with a high number of firms can be characterized by intense rivalry when firms feel that they can make competitive moves that will go unnoticed by other firms in the industry. However, other firms will generally notice these moves and offer countermoves of their own in response. Patterns of frequent actions and reactions often result in intense rivalry, such as in local restaurant, retailing, or dry-cleaning industries.

Rivalry also will be intense in an industry that has only a few firms of equivalent resources and power. The firms' resource bases enable each to take frequent action to improve their competitive positions which, in turn, produces a reaction or countermove by competitors. Battles for market share in the fast food industry between McDonald's and Burger King; in the automobile industry between such firms as General Motors, Ford, and Toyota; and in athletic shoes between Nike and Reebok are examples of intense rivalry between relatively equivalent competitors. Of course, Boeing versus

Airbus is an especially useful example.

Slow Industry Growth

(1) When a market is growing at a level where there seem to be "enough customers for everyone", competition generally centers around effective use of resources so that a firm can effectively serve a larger, growing customer base. Because of sufficient growth in the market, firms do not concentrate on taking customers away from other firms.

(2) The intensity of competition often results in a reduction in industry profitability as observed in the fast food industry with the battle for a slower growing traditional, U. S. customer base between McDonald's, Burger King, and Wendy's. The intensity of competition can be illustrated by the various competitive strategies followed by firms in the fast food industry:

① rapid and continuous introduction of new products and new packaging schemes.

② the introduction of innovative-pricing strategies.

③ product and/or service differentiation.

High Fixed Costs or High Storage Costs

When an industry is characterized by high fixed costs relative to total costs, firms produce in quantities that are sufficient to use a large percentage, if not all of their production capacity so that fixed costs can be spread over the maximum volume of output. While this may lower per unit costs, it also can result in excess supply if market growth is not sufficient to absorb the excess inventory. The intensity of competitive rivalry increases as firms use price reductions, rebates, and other discounts or special terms to reduce inventory as observed in the automobile industry from the 1980s to the present.

High storage costs, especially those related to perishable or time-sensitive products (such as fruits and vegetables) also can result in high levels of competitive intensity as such products rapidly lose their value if not sold within a given time period. Pricing strategies often are used to sell such products.

Lack of Differentiation or Low Switching Costs

Products that are not characterized by brand loyalty or perceived uniqueness are generally viewed by buyers as commodities. For such products, industry rivalry is more intense and competition is based primarily on price, service, and other features of interest to consumers.

Switching costs can be used to decrease the likelihood that customers will switch to competitors' products. Products for which customers incur no or few switching costs are subject to intense price- and service-based competition, similar to undifferentiated products.

High Strategic Stakes

The intensity of competitive rivalry increases when success in an industry is important to a large number of firms (such as the domestic airline industry following deregulation). For example, the success of a diversified firm may be important to its effectiveness in other industries, especially when the firm is in interdependent or related industries.

Geographic stakes may also be high. The importance of geographic stakes can be illustrated by the intense rivalry in the U.S. automobile industry as Japanese manufacturers recognized the strategic importance of a U.S. marketplace presence and U.S. manufacturers responded.

High Exit Barriers

Exit barriers—created by economic, strategic, and emotional factors that cause companies to remain in an industry, even though the profitability of doing so is in question—also can increase the intensity of competition in an industry. The higher the barriers to exit, the greater the probability that competitive actions and reactions will include price cuts and extensive promotions.

Some sources of exit barriers include:

(1) investments in specialized assets, or assets whose value is linked to use in a particular industry or location, with little or no value as salvage or in other uses.

(2) fixed costs of exit, such as labor agreements or a requirement to repay federal, state or local aid packages.

(3) strategic relationships, interdependencies within the organization (e.g., shared facilities, market access).

(4) emotional barriers, such as loyalty to employees or fear for one's own career.

(5) government and/or social restrictions based on concern for job losses or the economic impact of exit.

2.5 Interpreting Industry Analyses

(1) Effective industry analyses are products of careful study and interpretation of data from multiple sources. Because of globalization, international markets and rivalry must be included in the firm's analyses; in fact, research shows international variables may have more impact on strategic competitiveness than domestic ones, in some cases①.

(2) Following study of the five industry forces, the firm has the insights required to determine an industry's attractiveness in terms of the potential to earn adequate or superior returns on its invested capital. In general, the stronger the competitive forces, the lower the profit potential for an industry's firms. An unattractive industry has low entry barriers, suppliers and buyers with strong bargaining positions, strong competitive threats from product substitutes, and intense rivalry among competitors, which make it difficult for firms to achieve strategic competitiveness and earn above-average returns. An attractive industry has the mirror image of these features and offers little potential for favorable performance②.

2.6 Strategic Groups

As implied by the previous discussion, not all firms in an industry may adopt the same strategies in their quest for strategic competitiveness and above-average returns. However, many firms in an industry may follow similar strategies. These firms are generally classified as strategic groups, or groups of firms in an industry following the same or similar strategies along the same strategic dimensions③.

(1) Membership in a particular strategic group is determined by the essential characteristics of a firm's strategy.

---

① 有效的行业分析需对不同来源的数据进行仔细地分析与解读。由于市场全球化，企业分析时需考虑国际市场与国际竞争对手。实际上，有调查显示，在某些案例中，国际变量对战略竞争力的影响大过国内变量。

② 企业研究五力模式后，能洞悉行业的吸引力，了解行业是否具有凭借投资的资本，获得足量甚至超量回报的潜力。总的来说，竞争力越强，企业的回报潜力越低。吸引力不高的行业准入门槛低，购买者供应商议价能力强，替代品威胁大，同业者竞争力强，因此企业很难获得战略竞争力，也很难获得超过平均的收益。吸引力高的行业则正好相反，良好表现的潜力不大。

③ 同一行业中，许多企业采用相似的策略，这些企业被归为战略集团，战略集团也指采用同一战略维度中相同或相似策略的企业。

(2) extent of technological leadership.

① degree of product quality.

② pricing policies.

③ choice of distribution channels.

④ degree and type of customer service.

(3) The strategic group concept can be useful in analyzing the competitive structure of an industry and can serve as a framework for assessing competition, positioning alternatives, and potential profitability of firms in an industry.

High mobility barriers, high rivalry, and low resources among the firms within an industry will limit the formation of strategic groups. However, research suggests that once formed, strategic group membership remains relatively stable over time, making analysis easier and more useful.

Use of the strategic group concept requires that analysts be aware of several implications:

① A firm's major or primary competitors are those in its strategic group, thus competitive rivalry within the strategic group is expected to be more intense than rivalry with other firms in the industry.

② The relative strengths of the five competitive forces will differ among groups, thus firms in different groups may adopt different competitive strategies.

③ The closer the strategic groups on the relevant dimensions, the greater the likelihood of their rivalry.

本章课程思政学习专题

海外市场风险对中国企业国际化的影响①

1. 中国企业国际化面临的环境风险

改革开放以后,中国开始活跃在世界舞台,大量企业纷纷投身于国外市场的开拓,国际贸易得到了前所未有的发展,成为拉动经济增长的三驾马车之一。尤其是加入 WTO 之后,出口贸易更是上了一个新台阶。根据国家统计局数据显示,2005—2016 年间出口额的平均增速达到 10.08%,2017 年出口额达到 1.8 万亿元人民币。而出口并不是企业参与国际竞争的唯一方式,为了获取能源、地理、劳动

① 陈阵,李亚茹.海外市场风险如何影响中国企业的国际化进程?[J].世界经济研究,2019(5):92－106＋136.

力等要素的优势,企业开始在国外市场建立分销网络,设立工厂和子公司。于是,在出口快速增长的同时,中国对外直接投资在2004年后迅速增长,2007—2016年间中国对外直接投资的平均增速高达64%。

值得关注的是,在中国企业出口与对外直接投资迅速增长的同时,我们发现海外市场风险的不确定性程度在不断提升。2018年以来,中美之间的贸易摩擦愈演愈烈,两国间的关税不断提高,这对于中国企业在美国市场的出口产生了严重的负面影响。在中国企业"走出去"进程中,"一带一路"沿线国家无疑是投资的重要市场,然而东道国政权更迭、经济波动、政府债务居高不下等因素极大地遏制了中国企业进入这些新兴市场的热情。

2. 思考问题①

(1)海外市场风险对于中国企业的国际化路径影响几何?

(2)这种风险不确定性对于中国企业的出口和对外直接投资的动态行为产生了哪些方面的影响?

① 相关研究发现:企业在国外市场的出口经验对于初始投资该市场的概率有正向影响。更重要的是,出口经验的作用在很大程度上取决于国外市场的不确定性。当企业投资于市场条件更为不确定的目的地时,获得出口经验就显得更为重要。我们的分析表明,将企业国际化进程决策纳入企业的动态战略具有重要意义,可以防范和抵御由于国外市场风险不确定性所带来的经营风险。从动态角度看,出口与对外直接投资之间不是简单的替代关系,企业可以通过支付相对低的成本通过出口进入国外市场,以获取相应的供求信息,从而引导企业进行对外直接投资。在国外市场建立分销网络或者子公司能够在一定程度上扩大市场份额,增加出口同类产品的数量以及新产品的进入。同时,企业成功在海外市场建立子公司,又可以鼓励企业对其他类似海外市场尝试出口。

Chapter 3 The Internal Organization

Opening Case

R&D Center of AVIC Aircraft Corporation LTD. Officially Launched

On January 22nd 2014, R&D center of AVIC Aircraft Corporation LTD. was officially launched in Yanliang, Xi'an. The center has absorbed all the assets and staff related to aviation research and development originally owned by the Xi'an and Hanzhong divisions of AVIC Aircraft Corporation. Meanwhile, AVIC Aircraft will enter into cooperation on aircraft research and development and sign related agreements with AVIC The First Aircraft Institute, which will help improve the corporation's research and development ability. The center will be managed as a business division of research and development. According to information, the center will undertake all the work related to development planning, advanced research, model approval, engineering development, large system integration and technology and service assurance of model projects and product development. Also, it will be responsible for all the development work of medium and large transport aircraft, bombardment aircraft, fighter bomber, medium and large special aircraft, civil aircraft and large UAVs.

Introduction

Firms follow two competing models to generate the inputs needed to formulate and implement strategies. Chapter 2 focused on the external environment, which is the foundation of the I/O model. The emphasis in Chapter 3 is on internal resources and their potential to create competitive advantage for the firm, which falls in line with the resource-based model.

3.1 Analyzing the Internal Organization

3.1.1 The Context of Internal Analysis①

In the global economy, traditional factors such as labor costs, access to financial

① 内部分析的背景。

resources and raw materials, and protected or regulated markets continue to be sources of competitive advantage, but to a lesser degree (mostly because the advantages created by these more traditional sources can be overcome by competitors through an international strategy and by the flow of resources throughout the global economy)①.

Increasingly, those analyzing their firm's internal environment should use a global mind-set (i. e., the ability to study an internal environment in ways that are not dependent on the assumptions of a single country, culture, or context).

Analysis of the firm's internal environment requires that evaluators examine the firm's portfolio of resources and the bundles of heterogeneous resources and capabilities managers have created. Understanding how to leverage the firm's unique bundle of resources and capabilities is a key outcome decision makers seek when analyzing the internal environment.

It might be appropriate at this point in the discussion to remind students of the primary differences between the I/O and resource-based models. The I/O model presumes that resources and capabilities are distributed homogeneously among firms and freely move between them; the primary determining factor is how firms react to changes in the external environment. The resource-based model presumes a heterogeneous distribution of resources and capabilities and assumes that they do not move freely between firms.

By using or exploiting their core competencies, firms are in a position to develop and perform value-creating strategies better than their competitors or to create and perform value-creating strategies that competitors either are unable or unwilling to imitate.

3.1.2 Components of Internal Analysis②

(1) A firm's tangible and intangible resources (for example, its facilities and corporate culture, respectively) represent sources of capabilities③.

(2) These capabilities (teams or bundles of resources) represent sources of core competencies④.

---

① 经济全球化背景下,传统元素仍然是竞争优势的来源,如劳工成本、金融资源及原材料来源、受保护或受管制市场,但影响力已降低,主要原因是竞争者采用国际战略,享有全球经济带来的资源,因此抵消了传统因素的影响力。

② 内部分析的要素。

③ 企业的有形资源和无形资源(前者如设备,后者如企业文化)代表能力资源。

④ 能力(各种资源)意味着核心竞争力的来源。

(3) When exploited and nurtured (and valuable, costly to imitate, rare, and non-substitutable), core competencies are potential sources of competitive advantage[①].

(4) If a firm is able to use its core competencies to achieve a competitive advantage, it will achieve strategic competitiveness and earn above-average returns so long as competitors are unable or unwilling to imitate them successfully[②].

The importance of a firm's internal characteristics—represented by its resources and capabilities—highlights a shift in the priorities and prescriptions of strategic management research. The field has evolved or developed from a position that understanding industry characteristics and then positioning the firm to take advantage of industry characteristics relative to competitors was of primary importance to recognizing that it is a firm's resources and capabilities (which represent sources of core competencies) that should serve as the foundation for firm strategy. This shift recognizes that industry attractiveness is not dependent only on industry characteristics. Industry attractiveness is ultimately determined by both industry characteristics (which can be translated into opportunities and threats) or what a firm might do and its internal strengths (its resources, capabilities, and core competencies) which determine what a firm is capable of doing to take advantage of (or exploit) external opportunities.

3.1.3 Creating Value[③]

Some thoughts on "value":

(1) Firms create value by exploiting core competencies and meeting the standards of global competition.

(2) Value is measured by the product's performance and by its attributes for which customers are willing to pay.

---

① 核心竞争力,一旦得以开发和培育(有价值,模仿成本高,稀缺,不可替代),就会成为竞争优势的源泉。

② 如果企业能够利用核心竞争力获得竞争优势,只要竞争对手不能或不愿模仿,就能获得战略竞争力及超过平均的收益。

③ 创造价值。(1) 企业通过开发核心竞争力,满足国际竞争的标准来创造价值。(2) 价值通过产品的性能及顾客愿意为其买单的特性来衡量。(3) 企业要为顾客提供价值,这种价值应高于竞争对手创造的价值,这样,才能产生竞争优势。(4) 顾客认为国际品牌比国内品牌价值更高。(5) 企业创新使用和整合资源以创造价值。(6) 最终,价值成为获得超出平均收益的根本。(7) 优势的最重要来源是核心能力以及产品与市场定位。(8)除了对一般环境、行业环境、竞争环境的分析,企业的核心能力决定其对策略的选择。

(3) Firms must provide value to customers which is superior to the value provided by competitors in order to create a competitive advantage.

(4) Customers perceive higher value in global rather than domestic-only brands.

(5) Firms create value by innovatively bundling and leveraging their resources and capabilities.

(6) Ultimately, value is the foundation for earning above-average profits.

(7) Core competencies, combined with product-market positions, are the most important sources of advantage.

(8) The core competencies of a firm, in addition to analysis of its general, industry, and competitor environments, should drive its selection of strategies.

3.1.4 The Challenge of Analyzing the Internal Organization①

Correctly identifying, developing, deploying, and protecting firm resources, capabilities, and core competencies requires managers to make difficult decisions. In part, these challenges are a result of characteristics of both the internal and external environments of the firm. This challenge is multiplied because of three conditions that characterize important strategic decisions-uncertainty, complexity, and intraorganizational conflict②.

Conditions Affecting Managerial Decisions about Resources, Capabilities, and Core Competencies

The conditions or decision characteristics are:

(1) Uncertainty regarding the assessment of the general and industry environments, assessments, and predictability of competitive actions, and customer preferences.

(2) Complexity regarding the nature of any interrelatedness of the causes of change in the environment and how the environments are perceived, especially regarding decisions as to which of the firm's resources and capabilities might serve as the foundation for competitive advantage.

(3) Intraorganizational conflicts among managers making decisions about which core competencies are to be nurtured and about how the nurturing should take place.

---

① 内部组织分析的挑战。

② 管理者要想辨别、开发、部署及保护企业的资源、能力及核心竞争力,需要作出艰难的决策。这些挑战部分是内外部环境共同作用的结果。重大的战略决策具有三个特征:不确定性、复杂性及组织内冲突,三点使得上述挑战难度翻倍。

Uncertainty is present because of the inherent difficulty in identifying, assessing, and predicting changes and trends in characteristics of the external environment. Among these characteristics are correctly predicting the extent, direction, and timing of changes in the general environment, such as those resulting from societal values, political and economic conditions, customer preferences, and emerging technologies from other industries (and how they might ultimately affect the firm).

Complexity is increased because of the uncertain nature of interrelationships among the characteristics of the external environment and the related challenge regarding how to assess the effects of changes in one set of characteristics on other characteristics. The issue becomes more complex when managers must relate the complex external environment to their assessment of the firm's internal environment and thus affects decisions regarding the firm's resources, capabilities, and core competencies, and their relationship to opportunities in the external environment that can be exploited successfully to achieve a competitive advantage.

Intraorganizational conflicts often develop as a result of uncertainty and complexity. When managers make decisions regarding the identification of the firm's capabilities and choose to nurture them (with resources) to develop core competencies that can be exploited to achieve a competitive advantage, they must make these important decisions without absolute certainty that the decision is correct. And, such decisions may result in changes or shifts in power and interrelationships among individuals and groups within the firm. When this occurs, there may be conflict as those who are affected adversely—or perceive that they will be so affected—may resist these changes. In some cases, managers faced with decisions that may have unpleasant consequences or are uncomfortable often experience denial, an unconscious coping mechanism used to block out and not initiate major changes that may have some pain associated with them.

Thus, managers that must make decisions under conditions of uncertainty, complexity, and intraorganizational conflicts must exercise judgment, a capacity for making a successful decision in a timely manner when no correct model is available or when relevant data are unreliable or incomplete.

When exercising judgment, decision makers often take intelligent risks. In the current competitive landscape, executive judgment can be a particularly important source of competitive advantage. One reason is that, over time, effective judgment allows a firm to build a strong reputation and retain the loyalty of stakeholders whose support is linked to above-average returns.

Significant changes in the value-creating potential of a firm's resources and capabilities can occur in a rapidly changing global economy. Because these changes affect a company's power and social structure, inertia or resistance to change may surface. Even though these reactions may happen, decision makers should not deny the changes needed to assure the firm's strategic competitiveness. By denying the need for change, difficult experiences can be avoided in the short run.

Strategic Focus

Geely Cars: The Quality Is There, So Why Aren't the Cars Selling?[①]

Once defined as "cheap, tin-pot vehicles", Geely automobiles suffered from multiple manufacturing defects. But in a move to reposition itself in a very competitive business, Geely Motor Company became intent on establishing a new image of producing high-quality vehicles. In a study done by a well-known market research and auto-industry consulting firm, Geely held leadership positions in five different categories (including large car, minivan, and SUV). These evaluations supported Geely's goal of establishing a brand that stood for quality. Geely's quality ratings get a higher level.

With quality endorsements by highly respected third parties, Geely felt that its quality efforts had been validated and that it was in a position to become a new player in a market dominated by Japanese and European quality automakers. Unfortunately for Geely, the market has yet to recognize it as a manufacturer of high-quality vehicles. Is this an example of having one chance to make a first impression? What suggestions do students have for Geely to recreate itself and establish an image of quality?

3.2 Resources, Capabilities, and Core Competencies[②]

This section develops the background and relationships between resources, capabilities, and core competencies that represent potential sources upon which a firm can build the foundation for a competitive advantage.

3.2.1 Resources

Resources represent inputs into a firm's production process, such as capital

---

① 吉利汽车：汽车有质量，却为何无销量？

② 资源、能力及核心竞争力。

equipment, the skills of individual employees, brand names, financial resources, and talented managers[①].

By themselves—or individually—resources generally will not enable a firm to achieve a competitive advantage. They must be combined or integrated with other firm resources to establish a capability. When these capabilities are identified and nurtured, they can result in core competencies, which may lead to a competitive advantage. A firm's resources can be classified either as tangible or intangible.

Tangible Resources

Tangible resources are assets that can be seen or quantified, such as a firm's physical assets (e. g., its plant and equipment). Tangible resources are classified in one of four ways.

A firm's tangible resources generally can be placed into one of four categories:[②]

(1) Financial resources, such as borrowing capacity.

(2) Organizational resources, such as its formal reporting structure and systems.

(3) Physical resources, such as location.

(4) Technological resources, such as patents and trademarks.

One statement made in the chapter deserves special attention. Paraphrased slightly, the authors declare that the value of tangible resources is constrained because they are difficult to leverage: it is hard to derive more business or additional value from a tangible resource. For example, an airplane is a tangible resource or asset, but it can only be used on one route at a time, and it is equally impossible to put the same crew on five different routes at the same time. This is also true for the financial investment made in the airplane, but intangible assets such as a new innovation in manufacturing processes can be applied to many assembly lines. These dynamics are considered next.

Intangible Resources

A firm's intangible resources may be less visible, but they are no less important. In fact, they may be more important as a source of core competencies. Intangible resources range from innovation resources, such as knowledge, trust, and organizational routines, to the firm's people-dependent or subjective resources of know-

① 资源指企业生产过程中的输入,如固定设备、员工技能、品牌名称、财政资源以及优秀管理者。

② 公司的有形资源通常可分为四类:(1) 金融资源,如借贷能力。(2) 组织资源,如其正式结构和系统。(3) 物质资源,如位置。(4) 技术资源,如专利和商标。

how, networks, organizational culture, to the firm's reputation for its goods and services and the way it interacts with others (such as employees, suppliers, or customers).

A firm's intangible resources can be classified as: ①

(1) Human resources, such as knowledge, trust, and managerial capabilities.

(2) Innovation resources, such as scientific capabilities and capacity to innovate.

(3) Reputational resources, such as the firm's reputation with customers or suppliers.

Because tangible resources are those that can be seen (such as plants), touched (such as equipment), documented (such as contracts with suppliers of raw materials), or quantified (such as the value of a specific asset), they generally will not, by themselves, represent capabilities that will serve as sources of core competencies. However, they still have value and will contribute to the development of capabilities and core competencies.

Because they cannot be quantified, touched, or seen, and are more difficult to explain, intangible resources are more likely to be sources of sustainable competitive advantage. And, if they also are difficult for competitors to identify and/or understand, they also may represent the most likely source(s) of a firm's capabilities, core competencies, and sustained competitive advantage.

One can report to the class that two surveys asked managers to identify the source of their firms' competitive advantage or overall success. In both instances, one intangible asset was identified as the most important: Company Reputation/Reputation for Quality. As time permits, you may want to have the class discuss what makes a company's reputation. This also can be assigned as a "thought-provoking" question for an outside assignment or for future class discussion.

3.2.2 Capabilities

As implied in the definition, a firm's capabilities represent its capacity to integrate individual firm resources to achieve a desired objective, though this ability does not emerge overnight②.

Capabilities develop over time as a result of complex interactions that take

① 公司的无形资源可分为:(1) 人力资源,如知识、信任和管理能力。(2) 创新资源,如科学能力和创新能力。(3) 声誉资源,如公司在客户或供应商中的声誉。

② 顾名思义,企业能力是指企业整合各种资源以达到既定目标的能力,这种能力无法一蹴而就。

advantage of the interrelationships between a firm's tangible and intangible resources that are based on the development, transmission, and exchange or sharing of information and knowledge as carried out by the firm's employees (its human capital)[①].

A firm's ability to achieve a competitive advantage is thus reflected in its knowledge base and the ability of its human capital to successfully exploit firm capabilities. Thus, human capital is of significant value in the firm's ability to develop capabilities and core competencies to achieve strategic competitiveness.

As discussed in the chapter, the strategic value of resources is increased when they are integrated or combined. Unique combinations of the firm's tangible and intangible resources can be molded into capabilities—what the firm can do when it deploys teams of resources working together. You can use a firm like Microsoft to illustrate this point.

The knowledge possessed by the firm's human capital may be one of the most significant sources of a firm's competitive advantage because it represents everything that the firm has learned, and thus everything that it knows about successfully linking or bundling sets of individual resources to develop capabilities as a foundation for developing core competencies and, ultimately, to achieve a competitive advantage.

A number of firms have gone so far as to hire Chief Learning Officers (CLO) to find ways for the organization to acquire, internalize, and share knowledge in competitively relevant ways. Managing knowledge is critical since enterprises view this as their primary source of competitive advantage and believe it should be used in ways that will create value for customers.

Establishing and nurturing the skills and abilities of the workforce is of critical importance to a firm's ability not only to establish, but to sustain a competitive advantage by acquiring new knowledge and developing new skills that will enhance existing capabilities and core competencies, as well as aid in the development of new ones.

Firms use a variety of methods to nurture the value of their human capital. For example, Microsoft contends its best asset is the intellectual potential of its employees. To support the trend, the firm strives to hire people who are more talented than the current set of employees in hopes of defending and extending the domain of its

---

① 企业员工(即企业的人力资本)开发、传播、交换或分享信息,因此形成了有形与无形资源,能力的长期发展便是源于这些资源之间复杂的相互交换。

intellectual property. It is not uncommon for prospective employees to be asked questions like, "Why are manhole covers round?" (The answer: A round cover cannot fall into the hole no matter which way it is turned.) Such questions may seem silly, but the goal is to identify people with powerful reasoning skills, and thus (conceivably) the capacity to generate outstanding software solutions.

Firms also have functional area capabilities they have nurtured and are now considered as core competencies. As a result, these core competencies provide the foundation for the firm's competitive advantage.

3.2.3 Core Competencies

Once a firm has identified its resources and capabilities, it is ready to identify its core competencies, the resources and capabilities that are a source of competitive advantage for the firm over its competitors. Core competencies emerge over time through an organizational process of accumulating and learning how to deploy different resources and capabilities①. As the capacity to take action, core competencies are the "crown jewels of a company," the activities the company performs especially well compared with competitors and through which the firm adds unique value to its goods or services over a long period.

Resources and capabilities serve as the foundation upon which firms formulate and implement value-creating strategies so that the firm can achieve strategic competitiveness and earn above-average returns. However, if a firm has a deficiency in some of its resources, it may not be able to achieve strategic competitiveness. For example, insufficient financial resources may prevent a firm from implementing the processes or integrating the activities required to add superior value by limiting its ability to hire workers with the necessary skills or to invest in the capital assets (facilities and equipment) that are needed.

Thus, firms not only are challenged to scan the external environment to identify opportunities that can be exploited, but also to have an in-depth understanding of their resources and capabilities. This enables the firm to develop strategies to exploit external opportunities while it also avoids competing in areas where the firm's resources and capabilities are inadequate.

Not all of a firm's resources and capabilities are strategic assets—that is, assets

---

① 一旦企业确认了自身的资源及能力，就能够确认核心能力了，即生成竞争优势的资源与能力。在企业积累并学习如何部署不同资源与能力的长期过程中，核心竞争力便产生了。

that have competitive value and the potential to serve as a source of competitive advantage. Some resources and capabilities may result in incompetence, because they represent competitive areas in which the firm is weak compared to competitors. Thus, some resources or capabilities may stifle or prevent the development of a core competence.

When the firm's resources and capabilities result in a core competence, the firm will be able to produce goods or services with features and characteristics that are valued by customers. This implies that firms can implement value-creating strategies only when its capabilities and resources can be combined to form core competencies.

The question is asked: "How many core competencies are required for a competitive advantage?" McKinsey & Company recommends that firms identify 3 or 4 competencies around which to frame their strategic actions.

In support of the "McKinsey Rule", it is interesting to note that McDonald's has four main competencies (in real estate, restaurant operations, marketing, and its global infrastructure). Also, with the actual manufacturing of automobiles and trucks expected to become a declining part of its operations, Ford Motor Company is framing its twenty-first century competitive success around competencies in the areas of design, branding, sales, and service operations.

3.3 Identification of Core Competencies

This section discusses two conceptual tools/frameworks firms can use to identify competitive advantages:

(1) Four criteria determine which of the firm's resources and capabilities are core competencies.

(2) Value chain analysis, a tool for determining which value-creating competencies should be maintained, upgraded, and developed and which should be outsourced.

3.3.1 Four Criteria for Sustainable Competitive Advantage[①]

Four criteria should be used to determine whether or not a firm's capabilities are core competencies and can be a source of competitive advantage.

It is important to understand that a firm's capabilities must meet all four of the

① 可持续性竞争优势的四个标准。

criteria noted earlier before they can be core competencies and enable the firm to achieve a sustainable competitive advantage.

However, a short-term competitive advantage is available when firm capabilities are valuable, rare, and non-substitutable. The length of time that a firm possessing such capabilities can expect to sustain a competitive advantage depends on how long it takes for competitors to successfully imitate the value-creating activity or process, or reproduce valued features or characteristics of the product or service.

Thus, the ability to sustain a competitive advantage is dependent on firm capabilities being valuable, rare, non-substitutable, and costly to imitate.

Valuable

Capabilities that are valuable help a firm exploit opportunities and/or neutralize threats in the external environment. Valuable capabilities allow a firm to develop and implement strategies that create customer value.

Rare

Capabilities are rare when they are possessed by few, if any, current or potential competitors. If many firms have the same capabilities, the same value-creating strategies will be selected. As a result, none of the firms will be able to achieve a sustainable competitive advantage. A competitive advantage will be achieved by firms that develop and exploit capabilities that are different from those held by other firms.

Costly-to-Imitate

Capabilities are costly to imitate when other firms are unable to develop them except at a cost disadvantage relative to firms that already have them. This usually is a result of one or a combination of three conditions:

(1) Unique historical conditions can make duplication of capabilities costly. For example, establishing facilities in a key location that can preempt competition when no other locations have similar value-related characteristics or developing a unique organizational culture in the early stages of the organization's life may not be cheap to duplicate by firms that are developing theirs at a different time.

A unique culture may not only serve as a source of competitive advantage, but also can be a source of competitive disadvantage. The latter may be the case when a firm's culture prevents it from recognizing or successfully adapting to changes in a turbulent environment.

This may explain why such companies as IBM and General Motors, whose cultures developed early in each company's history—and during relatively calm or stable environments—were able to rely on formal controls and multiple approvals of strategies and be successful. However, their respective cultures, grounded in rigidity and bureaucracy, may have prevented them from successfully adapting to rapid environmental change in a fast-paced global environment.

(2) Causal ambiguity also may prevent competitors from perfectly imitating a competency if the link between a firm's capabilities and core competencies is not identified or understood. Competitors may not be able to identify or determine how a firm uses its competencies to achieve a sustainable competitive advantage.

(3) Social complexity means that a firm's capabilities are the product of complex social phenomena such as interpersonal relationships within the firm (e. g., how managers and subordinates at Hewlett-Packard work with each other) or a firm's reputation with its customers and suppliers.

Nonsubstitutable

A firm's capabilities are nonsubstitutable when they do not have strategic equivalents. Firm resources are strategically equivalent when they each can be separately exploited to implement the same strategies. If capabilities are invisible, it is even more difficult for competitors to identify viable substitutes. Examples of capabilities that can be difficult to identify or to find suitable substitutes for include firm-specific knowledge and trust-based working relationships.

Outcomes from Combinations of the Criteria for Sustainable Competitive Advantage

(1) Resources and capabilities that are neither valuable, rare, costly-to-imitate, nor nonsubstitutable mean that the firm will be at a competitive disadvantage and will earn below-average returns.

(2) Resources and capabilities that are valuable, but are neither rare nor costly to imitate and may or may not be nonsubstitutable mean that the firm can achieve competitive parity and earn average returns.

(3) Resources and capabilities that are both valuable and rare, but are not costly to imitate and may or may not be nonsubstitutable, may enable the firm to achieve a temporary competitive advantage and will earn above-average to average returns.

(4) Resources and capabilities that are valuable, rare, costly-to-imitate, and nonsubstitutable will enable the firm to achieve a sustainable competitive disadvantage and earn above-average returns.

3.3.2 Value Chain Analysis[①]

A framework that firms can use to identify and evaluate the ways in which their resources and capabilities can add value is value chain analysis.

The Basic Value Chain[②]

Primary activities represent traditional line activities such as inbound logistics, operations, outbound logistics, marketing and sales, and service[③].

Support activities are represented by a firm's staff activities and include its financial infrastructure, human resource management practices, technological development, and procurement activities[④].

Examining the Value-Creating Potential of Primary Activities

(1) Inbound logistics: Examine all activities related to the receipt, control, warehousing, inventory, and distribution of raw materials or component parts into the production process.

(2) Operations: Activities to be examined are all of those necessary to convert the inputs (raw materials or components) available as a result of inbound logistics into finished products. Examples include machining, assembly, equipment maintenance, and packaging.

(3) Outbound logistics: This category represents the firm's activities involved with the collection, storage, and physical distribution of products to customers. Examples include warehousing or storage of finished products, material handling, and order processing.

(4) Marketing and sales: Several marketing and sales activities must be completed to both induce customers to purchase products and ensure that products are available. Activities include developing advertising and promotion campaigns; selecting and developing distribution channels; and selecting, training, developing, and supporting a sales force.

(5) Service: These are the activities that a firm offers to enhance or maintain a

---

① 价值链分析法。

② 基本价值链。

③ 基本活动是指传统的线性活动,如进货物流、业务操作、出货物流、营销、销售及服务。

④ 支持活动指企业的员工活动,包括企业的金融基础设施、人力资源管理活动、技术开发及采购活动。

product's value, including installation, product use training, adjustment, repair, and warranty services.

Examining the Value-Creating Potential of Support Activities

(1) Procurement: These are activities that are completed to purchase the inputs needed to produce a firm's products, including items consumed or used in the manufacturing process (such as raw materials or component parts), supplies, and fixed assets (machinery, equipment and facilities).

(2) Technological development: All activities that are completed to either improve a firm's products or its production processes. This includes basic research, process and equipment design, product design, and servicing procedures.

(3) Human resource management: These activities are related to the recruiting, hiring, training, developing, and compensating (including performance assessment and reward systems) of a firm's employees.

(4) Firm infrastructure: These activities support the activities performed in the firm's value chain, including general management practices, planning, finance, accounting, legal, and government relations. By performing its infrastructure-related activities, a firm identifies external opportunities and threats, and internal strengths and weaknesses related to firm resources and capabilities, and supports or nurtures its core competencies.

Using the value chain framework enables managers to study the firm's resources and capabilities in relationship to the primary and support activities performed to design, manufacture, and distribute products, and to assess them relative to competitors' capabilities. For these activities to be sources of competitive advantage, a firm must be able to:

(1) perform primary or support activities in a manner superior to the ways that competitors perform them.

(2) perform a primary or support activity that no competitor is able to perform to create superior value for customers and achieve a competitive advantage.

This implies that, given that individual firms are comprised of unique or heterogeneous bundles of activities, reconfiguring the value chain may enable a firm to develop unique value-creating activities.

Prominent Application of the Internet in the Value Chain

This is a very involved figure, but it helps to illustrate the vast potential of the Internet to change the way managers think about the value chain. Explaining the ins-

and-outs of the figure will take a good bit of time, but it is worth the investment.

The managerial challenge is that the value-creation process is difficult and there is no one best way to assess a firm's primary and support activities or to evaluate the value-creating potential of those activities either within the firm or relative to competitors, because of incomplete or ambiguous data.

By being objective, managers may be able to use the value chain framework to identify new, unique ways to combine resources and capabilities to create value that are difficult for competitors to recognize, understand, or imitate. The longer a firm is able to keep competitors "in the dark" as to how resources and capabilities have been combined to create value, the longer a firm will be able to sustain a competitive advantage.

Firms can use outsourcing as an alternative to identify primary or support activities for which its resources and capabilities are not core competencies and do not enable the firm to add superior value and achieve competitive advantage.

3.4 Outsourcing①

Outsourcing describes a firm's decision to purchase a value-creating activity from an external supplier. Outsourcing has become important—and may become more important in the future—for two reasons②:

(1) There are limits to the abilities of firms to possess all of the bundles of resources and capabilities that are required to achieve superior performance (relative to competitors) in all its primary and support activities③.

(2) With limited resources and capabilities, firms can increase their ability to develop resources and capabilities to form core competencies and achieve competitive advantage by nurturing a few core competencies④.

Firms engaging in outsourcing can increase their flexibility, mitigate risks, and reduce their capital investment. In business, outsourcing involves the contracting out of a business process to another party (compare business process outsourcing). The

---

① 外包。

② 外包是指企业决定从外部供货商处购买价值创造活动。外包很重要,未来将更加重要,两个原因如下。

③ 企业能力有限,在基本活动及支持活动中,(与竞争者相比)不具有获得优秀表现的所有能力与资源。

④ 在资源与能力有限的前提下,企业可以开发资源,提高能力,通过建立少数核心能力来提高竞争优势。

concept "outsourcing" came from American Glossary "outside resorting" and it dates back to at least 1981. Which means to use outside resources and experts for to develop, expanded and···An organization. Outsourcing sometimes involves transferring employees and assets from one firm to another, but not always. Outsourcing is also the practice of handing over control of public services to for-profit corporations. Outsourcing can also be viewed as any assistance from an intermediary that is more capable of or familiar with certain practices than us. It is just a way of seeking for help.

Outsourcing includes both foreign and domestic contracting, and sometimes includes off shoring (relocating a business function to another country). Financial savings from lower international labor rates can provide a major motivation for outsourcing or off shoring. The opposite of outsourcing, insourcing, entails bringing processes handled by third-party firms in-house, and is sometimes accomplished via vertical integration. However, a business can provide a contract service to another business without necessarily in sourcing that business process. Outsourcing is a very important tool for reducing cost and improving quality, if an organization does one or all its work by itself, its work may affect its production quality. So, an organization must realize some important areas, from which its cost is reduced and its products stay in high quality.

A company wants to outsource only to firms possessing a core competence in terms of performing the primary or support activity that is being outsourced. This was the case between Nissan and IBM. In fact, the firm's services division, the group to which Nissan outsourced some of its computer operations, was the fastest-growing part of IBM. A few years back, IBM sold its Global Network division to AT&T at a price of $5 billion. As part of this transaction, IBM agreed to pay AT&T Solutions $5 billion to run its global telecom network through 2004, a deal that allows AT&T and IBM to concentrate their efforts on different operations (those in which the companies have core competencies).

Other research suggests that outsourcing does not work effectively without extensive internal capabilities to coordinate external sourcing as well as core competencies.

To ensure that the appropriate primary and support activities are outsourced, four skills are essential for managers involved in outsourcing programs:

(1) strategic thinking-understanding whether/how outsourcing creates competitive advantage within the company.

(2) deal making-able to secure rights from external providers that can be fully used by internal managers.

(3) partnership governance-able to oversee and govern appropriately the relationship with the company to which the services were outsourced.

(4) change management-because outsourcing can significantly change how an organization operates, managers administering these programs must also be able to manage that change, including resolving employee resistance that accompanies any significant change effort.

Outsourcing can take several forms, depending on a firm's strategic objectives. Examples of outsourcing strategies that, while different, enable outsourcing firms to achieve their strategic objectives while changing the face of college campuses include:

(1) Universities and colleges outsourcing the management of college bookstores to Follett College Stores and Barnes & Noble.

(2) Food Service management companies such as ARA and Marriott licensing with Burger King to establish national chain restaurants on college campuses.

(3) Colleges in the U. S. contracting with private firms to manage or build on-campus housing.

3.5 Strategic Decisions

Tools such as outsourcing help the firm focus on its core competencies as the source of its competitive advantages. However, evidence shows that the value-creating ability of core competencies should never be taken for granted. Moreover, the ability of a core competence to be a permanent competitive advantage can't be assumed. ①

All core competencies have the potential to become core rigidities. As Leslie Wexner, CEO of The Limited, Inc., says: "Success doesn't beget success. Success begets failure because the more that you know a thing works, the less likely you are to think that it won't work. When you've had a long string of victories, it's harder to foresee your own vulnerabilities." Thus, each competence is a strength and a weakness—a strength because it is the source of competitive advantage and, hence, strategic competitiveness, and a weakness because, if emphasized when it is no longer competitively relevant, it can sow the seeds of organizational inertia.

① 外包等工具有助于企业将核心竞争力作为竞争优势的来源。然而,证据表明,核心竞争力的价值创造能力决不能被视为理所当然。此外,不能假设核心竞争力具有成为永久竞争优势的能力。

Events occurring in the firm's external environment create conditions through which core competencies can become core rigidities, generate inertia, and stifle innovation. According to one observer, "Often the flip side, the dark side, of core capabilities is revealed due to external events when new competitors figure out a better way to serve the firm's customers, when new technologies emerge, or when political or social events shift the ground underneath."

In the final analysis, changes in the external environment do not cause core competencies to become core rigidities; rather, strategic myopia and inflexibility on the part of managers are the cause. Thus, nurturing existing competencies must be balanced by efforts to encourage the development of new competencies.

本章课程思政学习专题

传统企业的内部创业①

1. 传统企业的内部创业

为应对移动互联时代的挑战,不少传统企业试图借助内部创业的方式实现转型升级。随着数字技术应用的普及,众多创业公司顺势崛起,并试图重构传统行业。例如,借助智能手机的定位功能,网约车平台能够根据乘客的用车需求和物理位置实时匹配周边的空车,这给巡游出租车行业带来了极大的挑战。为了抓住机会并应对挑战,越来越多的传统企业开始借助内部创业的方式寻找业务方向,实现转型升级。内部创业指在现有的组织内由个人或者团队创造一个新的组织或者发起创业的过程。

内部创业对于传统企业而言具有战略意义,包括给母公司带来新的产品和服务改变内部的结构、流程和能力;从根本上改变竞争方式,重新定义公司与行业竞争对手的关系;甚至重构商业模式,与竞争对手形成差别优势。现有的研究都围绕在传统企业如何支持内部创业上,例如有研究指出现有组织的管理支持、资源供给以及风险承担等都会影响到内部创业。

然而,传统企业在对内部创业提供支持的同时,无形中也会施加限制,例如有研究指出文化冲突会阻碍内部创业的发展,而现有研究忽略了这一点。对于内部创业来讲,传统企业带来的支持和制约同时存在,因此必须将这两种情况都考虑进来,讨论其对内部创业的影响。

尽管内部创业背靠母公司,有丰富的资源可以利用,但大多数的内部创业仍

① 王冰,毛基业. 传统企业的内部创业组织如何获取正当性[J]. 管理评论,2020,32(4):104-116.

然没能“背靠大树乘上凉”,最终以失败告终。

2. 中国情境下的研究发现

尽管内部创业能够背靠企业借力生长,但这实际上是把双刃剑,内部创业在获取母公司赋能的同时,还会受到母公司的约束,这种约束会带来正当性不足的问题。内部创业既需要考虑内部正当性,也需要考虑外部正当性。为了更快地获取正当性,内部创业组织可以采用渐进式的策略,即先在内部获取正当性,然后再逐渐增强内部和外部的正当性。三种正当性之间也存在促进关系,即先在局部打造道义正当性和实用正当性,之后进一步获取认知正当性。正当性的获取是组织成员积极参与、利用外部资源和内部资源共同努力的结果。在这个过程中,组织需要根据不同的阶段获取不同的关键资源,并对获取的资源进行恰当的捆绑和利用,以发挥资源的价值。影响内部创业获取正当性的关键资源包括高管支持、社交网络、企业背书、制度支持和资金支持等。高管支持,尤其是高管的创业认知有助于发现新的机会,能够帮助组织获取局部的实用正当性;网络资源和背书资源能够促进组织获取局部的道义正当性。

3. 思考问题

传统企业内部创业将会对企业的内部能力产生怎样的影响?

Chapter 4 Business-Level Strategy

Opening Case

The Business-Level Strategy of CAC Showed by FC-1 Project

The PAC JF-17 Thunder or CAC FC-1Xiaolong is a lightweight, single-engine, multi-role combat aircraft developed jointly by the Pakistan Aeronautical Complex (PAC) and the Chengdu Aircraft Corporation (CAC) of China. The JF-17 can be used for aerial reconnaissance, ground attack and aircraft interception. Its designation "JF-17" by Pakistan is short for "Joint Fighter-17", while the designation and name "FC-1 Xiaolong" by China means "Fighter China-1 Fierce Dragon". The JF-17 can deploy diverse ordnance, including air-to-air and air-to-surface missiles, and a 23 mm GSh-23-2 twin-barrel autocannon. Powered by a RD-93 afterburning turbofan it has a top speed of Mach 1.6. The JF-17 is to become the backbone of the Pakistan Air Force (PAF), complementing the General Dynamics F-16 Fighting Falcon. The PAF inducted its first JF-17 squadron in February 2010 and four years later 49 units were in service (one lost in a crash), and 110 units were on order.

Introduction

Firms that perform well, even in very competitive industries, will follow some pattern of decision-making and execution that is internally consistent. That is, the firm will line up its resource commitments in a way that reinforces the direction of the enterprise. If these decisions are inconsistent, the outcome will be resource commitments that work against one another and hinder the progress of the business. This chapter will lay out the basic strategy patterns that can lead to competitive advantage. Knowing these will help students understand how to make the most of the firm's potentials.

4.1 Business-Level Strategy

As stated in Chapter 1, strategies represent integrated and coordinated sets of actions that are taken to exploit core competencies and gain a competitive advantage.

To be more specific, strategies are purposeful, precede the taking of actions to which they apply, and demonstrate a shared understanding of the firm's vision and mission. An effectively formulated strategy marshals, integrates, and allocates the firm's resources, capabilities, and competencies so that it will be properly aligned with its external environment. A properly developed strategy also rationalizes the firm's vision and mission along with the actions taken to achieve them.

Determining the businesses in which the firm will compete is a question of corporate-level strategy and is discussed later. Competition in individual product markets is a question of business-level strategy.

The firm's core competencies should be focused on satisfying customer needs or preferences through business-level strategies, which detail actions taken to provide value to customers and gain a competitive advantage by exploiting core competencies in specific, individual product or service markets. In other words, business-level strategies are developed based on a firm's core competencies and indicate how an organization chooses to compete in a particular market to gain a competitive advantage over competitors.

Indicate that, following a discussion of the customer, two broad categories of business-level strategies will be discussed in this chapter:

Cost leadership, a strategy that provides products—goods or services—with features acceptable to customers at the lowest competitive price. For example, many of Chinese Taiwan's PC manufacturers target the low-priced segment of the PC market through extreme forms of the cost leadership strategy. To drive their costs lower and to exploit the competitive advantage their low-cost structures provide, these companies rely on suppliers from Chinese mainland to supply low-priced components that will allow the PC manufacturers to drive production costs still lower①.

Differentiation, a strategy that provides products that customers perceive as being unique in ways that are important to them and, because this uniqueness offers value, customers are willing to pay a premium price for them. Jaguar is a manufacturer of high-prestige cars for which customers are willing pay high prices②.

---

① 有了成本领先策略,产品(商品或服务)能以最低的竞争价格为客户所接受。例如,中国台湾的电脑生产商将低价的细分市场作为目标,将成本领先策略用到极致。为了压低成本,并开发这种策略的竞争优势,这些台湾企业依赖于中国大陆供货商提供低价配件,能将电脑成本降至更低。

② 采用差异化策略,客户认为产品很重要,不可取代,这种不可取代性便是价值,客户愿意为此支付高昂的价格。例如捷豹出品的汽车广受好评,客户愿意为其支付溢价。

A customer focus requires that firms simultaneously evaluate or consider[①]

(1) who to serve,

(2) what customer needs will be satisfied, and

(3) how those needs will be satisfied through the strategy selected.

4.2 Customers: Their Relationship with Business-Level Strategies[②]

To survive and achieve strategic competitiveness in the twenty-first century competitive landscape, firms must[③]:

(1) identify who their customers are.

(2) determine customer needs or preferences.

(3) focus on satisfying the needs of some group of customers.

(4) determine how to compete (select a strategy) that enables them to satisfy customer needs.

4.2.1 Effectively Managing Relationships with Customers[④]

Key connections in managing customer relationships are as follows[⑤]:

(1) The firm's relationships with its customers are strengthened when it delivers superior value to them.

(2) Delivering superior value often results in increased loyalty from customers.

(3) Customer loyalty is positively related to profitability.

A number of companies have become skilled at managing all aspects of their relationship with their customers.

(4) Amazon. com is known for the quality of information it maintains about its customers, the service it renders, and its ability to anticipate customers' needs.

(5) Cemex uses the Internet to link its customers, cement plants, and main

---

① 顾客导向要求企业同时评估并思考以下问题:服务谁?需要满足什么样的客户需求?如何运用策略满足这些需求?

② 客户:与业务层战略的关系。

③ 企业为了获得战略竞争力,并在21世纪的竞争环境中生存下来,需要:明确客户群;确认客户需求或偏好;专注满足某类客户的需求;决策如何竞争(选择策略),满足客户需求。

④ 客户关系的有效管理。

⑤ 管理与客户的关系的关键点如下:企业向客户传递卓越价值时,便巩固了与客户的关系;传递卓越价值通常会带来客户忠诚度的提高;客户忠诚与利润正相关。

control room, allowing the firm to automate orders and optimize truck deliveries in highly congested Mexico City.

4.2.2 Reach, Richness, and Affiliation[①]

In the Internet age, firms can maintain competitive advantage by[②]:

(1) thinking continuously about accessing and connecting with customers (reach).

(2) maintaining information with depth and detail for (and from) customers (richness).

(3) facilitating useful interactions (affiliation).

4.2.3 Who: Determining the Customers to Serve

The first step is to identify customers based on differences in needs or preferences (often called market segmentation). This enables the firm to have a better grasp on what might be important to customers because of the lack of any in-depth insights relevant for decision making that are provided by central tendencies (averages) of the market in general.

Basis for Customer Segmentation

Dimensions that can be used to identify potential customers include the following factors:

For Consumer Markets: For Industrial Markets:

Demographic Factors End-use Segments

Socioeconomic Factors Product Segments

Geographic Factors Geographic Segments

Psychological Factors Common Buying Factor Segments

Consumption Patterns Customer Size Segments

Perceptual Factors

Once customers have been segmented into groups, firms must determine whether or not differences in needs or preferences among customer groups are significant. If they are not, firms might decide to offer a standard product to all customers (a standard product being one that appeals to or satisfies the needs of an average or typical

---

① 延伸性、丰富性、关联性。

② 互联网时代,企业可以通过以下方式获得竞争优势:不断思考如何与客户缔结联系(延伸性);为客户提供(或从客户处获得)的信息的深度及广度(丰富性);促进有效互动(关联性)。

customer). They also may do this because they believe that the product cannot easily be customized or differentiated, or the firm's competencies may be best suited to manufacturing standard products. Firms that offer standard, undifferentiated products typically offer them at the lowest competitive price as they follow a cost leadership strategy. However, firms that choose to ignore significant differences in customer needs may find that they no longer are strategically competitive.

It is imperative that firms pay careful attention to differences in customer needs among customer groups and not arbitrarily "lump" them together because:

(1) Almost any identifiable human or organizational characteristic can be used to sub-divide a market into segments that differ from one another on a given characteristic.

(2) Customer characteristics are often combined to segment markets into specific groups that have unique needs.

(3) Demographic factors can also be used to segment markets into generations with unique interests and needs.

4.2.4 What: Determining Which Customer Needs to Satisfy①

One challenge for firms is to identify ways in which they can bundle their resources and capabilities to create value for customers, because, given the choice, customers are most interested in purchasing products that both satisfy their needs and provide value②.

After the firm decides who it will serve, it must identify the targeted customer group's needs that its goods or services can satisfy. This is important in that successful firms learn how to deliver to customers what they want and when they want it.

In a general sense, needs (wants) are related to a product's benefits and features. Having close and frequent interactions with both current and potential customers helps the firm identify those individuals' and groups' current and future needs. From a strategic perspective, a basic need of all customers is to buy products that create value for them.

The most effective firms continuously strive to anticipate changes in customers' needs. Failure to do this results in the loss of customers to competitors who are offering

---

① 满足客户的什么需求?

② 企业面临的挑战之一是能否整合资源与能力,为客户创造价值。有选择的前提下,客户最感兴趣的产品既能满足需求,又能提供价值。

greater value in terms of product features and functionalities.

In any given industry, there is great variety among consumers in terms of their needs, e.g., high-quality, lower-cost with acceptable quality, quick delivery.

Diversified food and soft-drink producer PepsiCo believes that "any one consumer has different needs at different times of the day".

4.2.5 How: Determining Core Competencies Necessary to Satisfy Customers' Needs[①]

Core competencies are resources and capabilities that serve as a source of competitive advantage for the firm over its rivals. Firms use core competencies (how) to implement value-creating strategies and thereby satisfy customers' needs. Only those firms with the capacity to continuously improve, innovate, and upgrade their competencies can expect to meet and hopefully exceed customers' expectations across time[②].

4.3 The Purpose of a Business-Level Strategy[③]

Choosing to perform activities differently or to perform different activities than rivals is the essence of business-level strategy[④]. Thus, the firm's business-level strategy is a deliberate choice about how it will perform the value chain's primary and support activities in ways that create unique value. Indeed, in the complex twenty-first century competitive landscape, successful use of a business-level strategy results only when the firm learns how to integrate the activities it performs in ways that create competitive advantages that can be used to create value for customers.

Fit among activities is a key to the sustainability of competitive advantage for all firms. As Michael Porter observes, "Strategic fit among many activities is fundamental not only to competitive advantage, but also to the sustainability of that advantage. It is harder for a rival to match an array of interlocked activities than it is merely to imitate a particular sales-force approach, match a process technology, or replicate a set of

---

① 确定满足客户需求所需的核心能力。

② 核心能力指能力及资源,是企业竞争优势的来源。企业利用核心能力(即"怎样")实施创造价值的策略,并因此满足客户需求。企业只有不断改进、革新、升级自身能力,才能满足客户期待,甚至未来超越客户期待。

③ 业务层战略的目的。

④ 业务层战略的核心是选择实施与对手不同的行为,或选择与对手不同的实施方法。

product features. Positions built on systems of activities are far more sustainable than those built on individual activities."

4.4 Types of Business-Level Strategies[①]

Business-level strategy is concerned with a firm's position in an industry, relative to competitors. Firms are challenged to select business-level strategies to position themselves favorably by performing activities differently or performing different activities as compared to its rivals. Thus, the firm's business-level strategy is a deliberate choice about how it will perform the value chain's primary and support activities in ways that create unique value.

4.4.1 Cost Leadership Strategy

The cost leadership strategy is an integrated set of actions taken to produce goods or services with features that are acceptable to customers at the lowest cost, relative to that of competitors[②].

Firms that choose a cost-leadership strategy offer relatively standardized products with characteristics or features that typical customers accept (but with competitive levels of differentiation) at the lowest competitive price[③].

Firms that wish to be successful by following a cost-leadership strategy must maintain constant efforts aimed at lowering costs (relative to rivals' costs) and creating value for customers. Cost-reduction strategies can include:

(1) Building efficient-scale facilities.

(2) Establishing tight control of production and overhead costs.

(3) Minimizing the costs of sales, product research and development, and service.

(4) Investing in state-of-the-art manufacturing technologies.

Implementing and maintaining a cost leadership strategy means that a firm must consider its value chain of primary and secondary activities and effectively link those activities, if it is to be successful.

---

① 业务层战略的种类。

② 成本领先策略指采取一系列行为,以最低的成本生产出为客户所接受的产品或服务。

③ 选择成本领先策略的企业以最低竞争价格提供相对标准的产品,为一般客户所接受(具有一定程度差异性)。

As primary activities, inbound logistics and outbound logistics often account for much of the total cost to produce some goods and services. Research suggests that a competitive advantage in logistics creates more value with cost leadership strategies than with differentiation strategies, prompting cost leaders to focus on these primary activities.

Cost leaders also carefully examine all support activities to find additional sources of potential cost reductions.

Examples of Value-Creating Activities Associated with the Cost Leadership Strategy

The firm's focus throughout each of its primary and secondary value-creating activities is on the following:

(1) simplification of processes and procedures.

(2) achieving efficiency and effectiveness.

(3) reducing costs.

(4) monitoring costs of activities provided by others that interface with the firm's inbound or outbound logistics.

A firm that successfully implements a cost leadership strategy can earn above-average returns even when the five competitive forces are strong①.

Rivalry with Existing Competitors

Achieving the lowest cost position means that a firm's rivals will hesitate to compete based on price because, in a price war, the low cost firm will still earn profits even after its competitors compete away all profits. Having the low-cost position is a valuable defense against rivals.

Bargaining Power of Buyers (Customers)

Achieving the low cost position provides some protection against powerful customers who attempt to drive down prices. If customers attempt to drive prices below the cost of the next most efficient firm, that firm might choose to exit the market (rather than remain and earn below average profits), leaving the low cost firm with a monopoly position. If that happens, customers would lose any bargaining power as the monopoly firm would be in a position to raise prices.

① 即使企业面临强劲的五种竞争力,成功实施成本领先策略即能获得高于平均的收益。竞争五力包括:与现有竞争者的竞争;买方议价能力;供货商议价能力;潜在入市者;产品替代者。

Bargaining Power of Suppliers

Because they have achieved the lowest cost position in the industry, the cost leadership strategy enables a firm to absorb a greater amount of cost increases from powerful suppliers before it must raise prices charged to customers. This may enable the firm to be alone among its competitors in earning above-average returns. In addition, a low-cost leader that also has a dominant market share may be in a position to force suppliers to reduce prices or to hold down the level of price increases, and thus reduce the power of suppliers. Again, Wal-Mart is a good example of a firm that follows this pattern.

Potential Entrants

Firms successfully following cost leadership strategies generally must produce and sell in large volumes to earn above-average returns. And, with a continuous focus on efficiency and reducing costs, cost leadership firms create barriers to entry. New entrants must either enter the industry at a large scale (large enough to achieve the same economies of scale as the next lowest cost firm) or be satisfied with average profits until they move sufficiently far down the experience curve to match the efficiencies of the low-cost leader.

Product Substitutes

The cost leader is in a more attractive position relative to substitute products than are other firms in the industry. To retain customers, the cost leader can more easily reduce prices to maintain the price-value relationship and retain customers.

Competitive Risks of the Cost Leadership Strategy①

Despite the attractiveness of the cost leadership strategy, it is accompanied by risks such as the following②:

(1) Technological innovations by competitors could eliminate the cost leader's cost advantage.

(2) Overly focusing on process efficiency may cause the cost leader to overlook needed differentiation features.

(3) Competitors may successfully imitate the low-cost leader's value chain

---

① 成本领先策略的竞争风险。

② 成本领先策略虽然具有吸引力,但仍有如下风险:(1) 竞争对手的技术革新会抵消成本领先优势。(2) 过分关注过程效率可能导致成本领先者忽视必要的差别特性。(3) 竞争者可以模仿低成本领先者的价值链配置并获得成功。

configuration.

In the event of any of the above, the low-cost leader is challenged to increase value to customers. This may mean reducing prices or adding product features without raising prices. However, if prices are reduced too low, it may be difficult for the firm to earn satisfactory margins and customers may resist any price increases.

4.4.2 Differentiation Strategy

In contrast to the cost leadership strategy, implementation of a differentiation strategy means that value is provided to customers through the unique features and characteristics of a firm's products rather than by the lowest price①.

Because differentiated products satisfy customers' unique needs or preferences, firms can charge a premium price for differentiated products. But the premium cannot exceed what customers are willing to pay.

For the firm to be able to outperform its competitors and earn above-average returns, the price charged for the differentiated product must exceed the cost of differentiation. In other words, the price charged must exceed total product cost. Because of this, the differentiated product's premium prices generally exceed the low price of the standard product.

Firms that follow a differentiation strategy concentrate or focus on product innovation and developing product features that customers value rather than on maintaining the lowest competitive price (the case for cost leadership strategy). Often this strategy seeks to differentiate the product/service on as many dimensions as possible.

Products can be differentiated in a number of ways so that they stand apart from standardized products②:

(1) superior quality,

(2) unusual or unique features,

(3) more responsive customer service,

(4) rapid product innovation,

(5) advanced technological features,

(6) engineering design and performance

---

① 与成本领先策略不同,差异性策略指企业向客户提供的价值源自企业产品的独特性,而非低价。

② 与标准化产品不同,产品差别化体现在以下方面:质量上乘;具有不常见或独有的特征;客户服务反应更积极;产品创新迅速;采用先进的技术;工程设计及实施;附加特征;代表声望或地位的形象。

(7) additional features,

(8) an image of prestige or status.

Some examples of differentiation strategies would include the following:

(1) Ralph Lauren differentiates its clothing lines through image.

(2) Lexus cars are differentiated by prestige and image.

(3) Apple (iPod and iPhone) are differentiated by innovative design.

(4) McKinsey and Company offers differentiated consulting services.

Successfully implementing (and maintaining) a differentiation strategy requires a firm to consider its value chain of primary and secondary activities and effectively link.

Examples of Value-Creating Activities Associated with the Differentiation Strategy

The firm's focus in its primary and secondary value-creating activities is on

(1) establishing the importance of quality,

(2) accuracy, speed, and responsiveness,

(3) understanding and meeting customers' unique preferences,

(4) monitoring the speed, reliability, and quality of activities provided by others that interface with the firm's inbound and outbound logistics.

A firm that successfully implements a differentiation strategy can earn above-average returns even when the five competitive forces are strong.

Rivalry with Existing Competitors

Achieving customer loyalty means differentiating products in ways that are meaningful to customers. Brand loyalty means that customers will be less sensitive to price increases. As long as the firm satisfies the differentiated needs of loyal customers, it may be insulated from price-based competition.

Bargaining Power of Buyers (Customers)

Through meaningful differentiation, firms develop products that are considered unique. This uniqueness may insulate the firm from competitive rivalry and reduce customer sensitivity to price increases. By satisfying customer preferences in ways that no competitor can, firms also are able to charge higher prices.

Bargaining Power of Suppliers

Because of the differentiator's focus on product quality and responsiveness to customer preferences, suppliers also may be forced to provide differentiators with higher quality materials, components, or services, which can drive up the firm's per-unit costs.

Since the differentiator charges premium prices, they are somewhat insulated from suppliers' price increases (as the differentiator can absorb a greater level of cost increases from powerful suppliers through its higher margins). Alternatively, because of lower price sensitivity by customers, differentiators may be able to raise prices to cover increased supplier-related costs.

Potential Entrants

The principal barrier to entry is customers' loyalty to the uniquely differentiated brand. This means that a potential entrant must either overcome (or surpass) the uniqueness of existing products or provide similarly differentiated products at a lower price to increase customer value.

Product Substitutes

Brand loyalty may insulate differentiated products from substitutes. Without brand loyalty, customers may switch to substitutes that offer similar features at a lower price or to products with more attractive features at the same price.

Competitive Risks of the Differentiation Strategy

Like the cost leadership strategy, the differentiation strategy also carries risks such as the following:

(1) Customers may decide that the cost of uniqueness is too high. In other words, the price differential between the standardized and differentiated product is too high. Perhaps the firm provides a greater level of uniqueness than customers are willing to pay for.

(2) The firm's means of differentiation no longer provides value to customers. For instance, what is the value of prestige or exclusivity? And, how long will they last as customers become more sophisticated?

(3) Customer learning may reduce the customer's perception of the value of the firm's differentiation. Through experience, customers may learn that the extra price for a differentiated good is no longer a value.

(4) A fourth risk is concerned with counterfeiting. Increasingly, counterfeit goods (products that attempt to convey differentiated features to customers at significantly reduced prices) are a concern for many firms using the differentiated strategy.

In the event of any of the above, differentiators are challenged to increase value to customers. This may mean reducing prices, adding product features without raising prices, or developing new efficiencies in its value chain of primary and secondary activities.

By implementing a cost leadership or differentiation strategy, firms choose to compete by exploiting their core competencies on an industry-wide basis and adopt a broad competitive reach.

Alternatively, firms can choose to follow a focus strategy by seeking to use their core competencies to serve the needs of a particular customer group in an industry. In other words, firms focus on specific, smaller segments of customers rather than across the entire market.

Markets can be segmented by:

(1) particular buyer group,

(2) different segments of a product line,

(3) different geographic market.

Firms may choose to follow a focus strategy because:

(1) they can serve a narrow segment more effectively than competitors that choose to compete industry wide.

(2) the narrow segment's needs are so special that industry-wide competitors choose not to meet them.

(3) certain narrow segments are being poorly served by industry-wide competitors.

Focused Cost Leadership Strategy

Firms that compete by following cost leadership strategies to serve narrow market niches generally target the smallest buyers in an industry (those who purchase in such small quantities that industry-wide competitors cannot serve them at the same low cost)[①].

Global furniture retailer Ikea provides customers with "good design and function at low prices" through use of the focused cost leadership strategy. Ikea does this by offering low-cost, modular furniture (assembled by customers), using self-service as an alternative to having sales associates follow and pressure customers to buy. Ikea displays its products in room-like settings so that customer can view different combinations of furniture, eliminating the need for assistance from sales associates or decorators to visualize the setting and reducing employee costs. Customers also pick up

---

① 企业采取成本领先策略,市场定位较窄,通常将目标客户定位为行业中的最小买家(这些买家购买数量少,行业内的竞争者无法提供如此低价)。

their own purchases to reduce the firm's costs. However, the company also differentiates somewhat. For example, stores address the needs of shoppers (e. g., extended hours and in-store childcare) while they shop.

Focused Differentiation Strategy

Firms following focused differentiation strategies produce customized products for small market segments[①].

They can be successful when either the quantities involved are too small for industry-wide competitors to handle economically, or when the extent of customization (or differentiation) requested is beyond the capabilities of the industry-wide differentiator[②].

Examples of focused differentiators follow:

(1) Upscale apartment buildings in various locations are being designed to serve the needs of technologically savvy city dwellers, offering differentiated features such as high-speed digital Internet access and other sophisticated telecommunications services.

(2) Manufacturers such as Ferrari, Aston Martin, and Lamborghini compete in the tiny supercar category with prices starting at $150,000 and running as high as $600,000. These cars are more than just transportation.

Just as was noted for industry-wide differentiators and low-cost producers, firms choosing to focus must be particularly adept at completing primary and secondary value chain activities in a superior way. Issues related to the five competitive forces are similar to those discussed for the differentiation and cost leadership strategies; however, the competitive scope of the focus is on a narrow segment rather than the industry.

Competitive Risks of Focus Strategies

The competitive risks of focus firms are similar to those previously noted for the cost leadership and differentiation strategies with the following additions:

(1) Competitors may successfully focus on an even smaller segment of the market, "outfocusing" the focuser, or focus only on the most profitable slice of the focuser's chosen segment.

For example, Confederate Motor Co. is producing a highly differentiated

---

① 采用集中化差别策略的企业为小的市场细分提供定制产品。

② 如果这些企业的业务量很小,小到行业内竞争者无法因此获得盈利,或者定制程度超出了竞争者的差别化能力,这些企业采用集中化差别策略便会成功。

motorcycle that might appeal to some of Harley Davidson's customers. Obsessed with making a "fiercely American motorcycle" (one that is even more American than are Harley's products), Confederate's motorcycles are produced entirely by hand labor. In fact, a full week is required to make a single bike. Digital technology is used to design Confederate's products, which have a radical appearance. At a price of $62,000 or above, the firm's products will appeal only to customers wanting to buy a truly differentiated product such as the F113 Hellcat (which is receiving "rave reviews in the motorcycling press").

(2) An industry-wide competitor may recognize the attractiveness of the segment served by the focuser and mobilize its superior resources to better serve the segment's needs.

(3) Preferences and needs of the narrow segment may become more similar to the broader market, reducing or eliminating the advantages of focusing.

4.4.3 Integrated Cost Leadership/Differentiation Strategy

This new hybrid strategy may become even more important—and more popular—as global competition rises①.

Compared to firms relying on a single generic strategy, firms that integrate the generic strategies may position themselves to improve their ability to adapt quickly to environmental changes②.

Successfully pursuing the cost leadership and differentiation strategies simultaneously yields additive benefits③:

(1) Differentiation enables the firm to charge premium prices.

(2) Cost leadership enables the firm to charge the lowest competitive price.

Flexible Manufacturing Systems

A flexible manufacturing system is a computer-controlled process used to produce a variety of products in moderate, flexible quantities. It enables firms to achieve the flexibility necessary to simultaneously respond to changes in customer needs and preferences while maintaining the low-cost advantages of large-scale manufacturing.

---

① 随着全球竞争越来越多,这种混合型的新策略将会越来越重要,也越来越普遍。

② 不同于一些企业依赖于单一种类的策略,许多企业整合策略,敦促自身提高能力,更快适应环境变化。

③ 同时采用成本领先策略及差别策略有如下好处:采用差别策略,企业赚取溢价;采用成本领先策略,企业收取最低竞争价格。

This increases a firm's ability to engage in an integrated low-cost/differentiation strategy①.

Information Networks

Information networks enable a firm to coordinate interdependencies between internally-and externally-performed value-creating activities to increase flexibility and responsiveness. Examples include real-time linkages between manufacturers and suppliers or subcontractors, or between retailers and suppliers. These linkages can improve time-to-market of new products by coordinating design and production activities and reduce out-of-stock occurrences by shortening the order-restock cycle②.

Customer relationship management (CRM) is one form of an information-based network process that firms use to better understand customers and their needs. An effective CRM system provides a 360-degree view of the company's relationship with customers, encompassing all contact points, involving all business processes, and incorporating all communication media and sales channels. The firm can then use this information to determine the trade-offs its customers are willing to make between differentiated features and low cost, which is vital for companies using the integrated cost leadership/differentiation strategy.

Enterprise Resource Planning is an information system used to identify and plan the resources required across the firm to receive, record, produce, and ship customer orders. For example, salespeople for aircraft parts distributor Aviall use handheld equipment to scan bar-code labels on bins in customers' facilities to determine when parts need to be restocked. Data gathered through this procedure are uploaded via the Web to the Aviall back-end replenishment and ERP system, allowing the order fulfillment process to begin within minutes of scanning. Growth in ERP applications such as the one used at Aviall has been significant. Full installations of an ERP system are expensive, running into the tens of millions of dollars for large-scale applications.

Improving efficiency on a company-wide basis is a primary objective of using an ERP system. Efficiency improvements result from the use of systems through which financial and operational data are moved rapidly from one department to another. The

---

① 柔性制造系统用计算机控制,用来生产弹性数量产品的过程。有了这个系统,企业既可以灵活应对客户的需求及偏好变化,又能保留大规模生产的低价优势。企业因此可以更好地实行整合性成本领先/差异化策略。

② 企业使用信息网络后,可以调整内外部价值创造活动的相互依赖,提高灵活性和响应能力。比如,生产商与供货商、承包商之间的实时联系。有了这种实时联系,企业可以通过缩短订货—补货周期来调整设计与生产活动,减少缺货情况,并因此缩短新产品的上市时间。

transfer of sales data from Aviall salespeople to the order entry point at the firm's manufacturing facility demonstrates the rapid movement of information from one function to another. Integrating data across parties that are involved with detailing product specifications and then manufacturing those products and distributing them in ways that are consistent with customers' unique needs enable the firm to respond with flexibility to customer preferences relative to cost and differentiation.

TQM(Total Quality Management) Systems

These systems have been established to improve product quality (from a customer perspective) and to improve productivity in the performance of the internal value-creating activities①.

Firms develop and use TQM systems in order to (1) increase customer satisfaction, (2) cut costs, and (3) reduce the amount of time required to introduce innovative products to the marketplace.

Improving product quality focuses on product reliability, performance and utility, and enables the firm to differentiate its products and charge higher prices, while lowering the costs of manufacturing and service. Total quality management consists of organization-wide efforts to install and make permanent a climate in which an organization continuously improves its ability to deliver high-quality products and services to customers. While there is no widely agreed-upon approach, TQM efforts typically draw heavily on the previously developed tools and techniques of quality control. TQM enjoyed widespread attention during the late 1980s and early 1990s before being overshadowed by ISO 9000, Lean manufacturing, and Six Sigma. Following are the key assumptions upon which total quality management (TQM) systems are based:

(1) The costs of poor quality exceed the costs of developing processes that produce high quality products and services (in other words, it is less costly to do things right the first time).

(2) Employees care about their work and will take the initiative to improve it (but, only if the firm provides the resources, tools, and training necessary and management listens to their ideas).

(3) Since organizations are systems of highly interdependent parts, decision processes must be integrated and include participation from all affected functional areas.

---

① 建立这一系统是为了(站在客户角度)改善产品质量,在内部价值创造活动中提高生产力。

(4) Responsibility for effective TQM rests with top-level managers who must support TQM processes and appropriately design the firm so that employees can function effectively.

Competitive Risks of the Integrated Cost Leadership/Differentiation Strategy

This is a risky strategy, as it is difficult for firms to perform primary and support activities in ways that allow them to produce relatively inexpensive products with levels of differentiation that create value for the target customers. Moreover, to properly use this strategy across time, firms must be able to simultaneously reduce costs incurred to produce products (as required by the cost leadership strategy) while increasing products' differentiation (as required by the differentiation strategy)①.

Being "stuck-in-the-middle" implies that the firm will not be able to manage successfully the five competitive forces and will not achieve strategic competitiveness. In fact, these firms can only earn average profits when industry structure is favorable or when other firms in the industry also are "stuck-in-the-middle".

本章课程思政学习专题

绿色产品垂直差异化②

1. 绿色产品垂直差异化

世界环境问题变得越来越严重,可持续生产与消费作为解决资源紧缺与环境恶化问题的关键措施备受关注。随着绿色经济的不断发展及消费者环保意识的不断提高,消费者在生活过程中会更加关注产品对环境的影响,绿色产品作为创新技术和环保设计相融合的环保型产品也因此备受青睐,尤其是对环保意识和社会责任感更加强烈的绿色消费者而言,绿色消费者会越来越倾向于购买绿色产品。相关研究发现,超过60%的受访者愿意为绿色产品支付高溢价,平均而言,消费者愿意支付的溢价是正常定价的16.8%。2016年,中国循环经济协会可再生能源专委会(CREIA)委托益普索市场咨询有限公司(IPSOS)对中国十座主要城市的3000名消费者进行调研,发现消费者购买绿色电力的意愿强烈,超过97%

---

① 这一策略具有风险,因为企业很难开展基本活动和支持活动,很难生产出具有差别性特征、又能为目标客户提供价值的低价产品。同时,要想长期正确实施这一策略,企业既需要降低产品成本(成本领先策略要求),又需要提高产品的差别性(差别性策略要求)。

② 凌艳涛,徐静,张华. 基于异质性消费者偏好下的绿色产品垂直差异化设计与定价策略[J]. 管理工程学报,2021,35(6):208-217.

受访者愿意购买绿色电力。与绿色能源相关的其他研究也表明,消费者愿意为绿色产品支付额外的费用。

生产绿色产品的企业不仅承担了社会责任,提升自身的环保形象,同时也能获得更强的市场竞争力。因此,生产绿色产品对公司而言变得越来越重要。认识到市场主体参与者消费趋势的改变,企业也开始转向设计绿色产品以吸引绿色消费者。在生产过程中,企业采用的生产技术类型是影响生产过程、生产效率和原材料利用的决定性因素,它们可以决定企业的环境影响、风险和成本。由于环保产品比传统产品具有更大的环境效益,因此价格往往更高。

绿色产品的生产不单要求生产环节中某个节点是绿色的,还需要生产企业将绿色采购、设计、生产、销售、回收等融入产品经营各环节中,这导致绿色产品的生产成本比那些使用传统方法生产的普通产品更加高。因此,如何设计绿色产品以满足消费者差异化需求已成为企业生产决策的关键点。

2. 中国情景下的绿色产品垂直差异化设计与定价策略

当消费者意愿支付较低时,企业利润为负,绿色产品市场无法存在。随着消费者意愿支付提升至某一临界值,绿色企业可以生产单一种类的绿色产品。当消费者意愿支付持续提升至更高的临界点时,企业可以生产在绿色度方面具有垂直差异化的产品以满足消费者的差异化需求。在绿色度差异化的绿色产品中,产品绿色度越高市场份额占比越大,并且随着消费者意愿支付的进一步提升,每种绿色产品的市场份额都会增加。结果暗示,当企业计划生产绿色产品时,应该对消费者意愿支付做市场调研,根据实际的消费者意愿支付数值制定生产策略。

消费者的绿色满意度提升,会提高绿色企业的市场份额及利润,即消费者更加青睐于购买绿色产品会推动绿色产品业的发展。企业可以通过加强绿色生活方式和绿色产品的宣传来增强消费者的绿色环保意识,并通过树立旗帜消费者,建立示范效应,引导消费者把绿色意识转化成实际行动。

企业的绿色技术研发成本系数提升会降低绿色产品的总体市场份额及总利润。原因在于:当企业绿色技术的研发成本增加时,绿色产品的生产成本会大幅增加,因此售价也会提升,导致消费者购买绿色产品的效用会下降,从而引发需求降低,最终使得企业的利润不断下滑。因此,在生产侧方面,政府可以通过补贴的方式降低企业的绿色技术研发成本。在需求侧方面,企业和政府也可借助宣传等推广方式普及绿色产品的环境价值,从而提升消费者的支付意愿。

3. 思考问题

如何制定多企业竞争下的绿色产品生产策略和定价策略?

Chapter 5 Competitive Behavior

Opening Case[①]

The Competitive History of Huawei

Huawei Technologies Co. Ltd. is a Chinese multinational networking and telecommunications equipment and services company headquartered in Shenzhen, Guangdong. It is the largest telecommunications equipment maker in the world, having overtaken Ericsson in 2012.

Huawei was founded in 1987 by Ren Zhengfei, a former engineer in the People's Liberation Army. At the time of its establishment Huawei was focused on manufacturing phone switches, but has since expanded its business to include building telecommunications networks; providing operational and consulting services and equipment to enterprises inside and outside of China; and manufacturing communications devices for the consumer market. Huawei has over 140,000 employees, around 46% of whom are engaged in research and development (R&D). It has 21 R&D institutes in countries including China, the United States, Canada, UK, Pakistan, France, Belgium, Germany, Colombia, Sweden, Ireland, India, Russia, and Turkey, and in 2013 invested US $5 billion in R&D.

International Expansion

In 1996, Huawei won its first overseas contract, providing fixed-line network products to Hong Kong company Hutchison Whampoa. Later that year, Huawei launched its wireless GSM-based products and eventually expanded to offer CDMA and UMTS. In 1999, the company opened a research and development (R&D) center in Bangalore, India to develop a wide range of telecom software. From 1998 to 2003, Huawei contracted with IBM for management consulting, and underwent significant transformation of its management and product development structure. After 2000, Huawei increased its speed of expansion into overseas markets, having achieved international sales of more than US $100 million by 2000 and establishing an R&D

① 课前案例:华为公司竞争史。

center in Stockholm, Sweden. In 2001, Huawei established four R&D centers in the United States, divested non-core subsidiary Avansys to Emerson for US $750 million and joined the International Telecommunications Union (ITU). By 2002, Huawei's international market sales had reached US $552 million.

In 2004 Huawei continued its overseas expansion with a contract to build a third-generation network for Telfort, the Dutch mobile operator. This contract, valued at more than $US 25 million, was the first such contract for the company in Europe.

In 2005, Huawei's international contract orders exceeded its domestic sales for the first time. Huawei signed a Global Framework Agreement with Vodafone. This agreement marked the first time a telecommunications equipment supplier from China had received Approved Supplier status from Vodafone Global Supply Chain. The agreement established the terms and conditions for the supply of Huawei's solutions to any one of the Vodafone operating companies worldwide. Huawei also signed a contract with British Telecom (BT) for the deployment of its multi-service access network (MSAN) and Transmission equipment for BT's 21st Century Network (21CN), providing BT and the UK telecommunications industry with some infrastructure necessary to support future growth as these companies are multi vendor infrastructure.

In May 2008, Huawei and Optus developed a mobile innovationcentre in Sydney, Australia, providing facilities for engineers to develop new wireless and mobile broadband concepts into "ready for market" products. In 2008, the company embarked on its first large-scale commercial deployment of UMTS/ HSPA in North America providing TELUS's new next generation wireless network and Bell Canada with high-speed mobile access.

Huawei delivered one of the world's first LTE/EPC commercial networks for TeliaSonera in Oslo, Norway in 2009. The company launched the world's first end-to-end 100G solution from routers to transmission system that same year, to help meet the rapid growth of network traffic and enhance router efficiency and reliability.

In July 2010, Huawei was included in the Global Fortune 500 2010 list published by the U. S. magazine Fortune for the first time, on the strength of annual sales of US $21.8 billion and net profit of US $2.67 billion. In late 2010 it was reported that Huawei is planning to invest around US $500 million (Rs 2,200 crore) to set up a telecom equipment manufacturing facility in Tamil Nadu, India and $US 100 million to expand its R&D center in Bangalore.

In October 2012, it was announced that Huawei would move its UK headquarters to Green Park, Reading, Berkshire. The company also, in an effort to increase its prominence in the United States, became the main sponsor of the Jonas Brothers' 2013 summer tour.

In September 2013, Huawei opened a new Canadian office in Regina, Saskatchewan—Huawei had collaborated with the local carrier SaskTel to build its HSPA + and LTE networks. The company also announced that SaskTel would carry its new Ascend Y300 smartphone.

In October 2013, Huawei has been selected by TDC A/S as a sole vendor to modernize the nationwide GSM/UMTS/LTE network in Denmark and provide managed services over a six-year period. The value of the contract is over $700 million over the term of the agreement. As per the latest mandate of The Economist, Huawei is the number one Telecom Vendor in the world.

Investment and Partnerships

Huawei has focused on expanding its mobile technology and networking solutions through a number of partnerships. In March 2003, Huawei and 3Com Corporation formed a joint venture company, 3Com-Huawei (H3C), which focused on the R&D, production and sales of data networking products. The company later divested a 49% stake in H3C for US $880 million in 2006. In 2005, Huawei began a joint venture with Siemens, called TD Tech, for developing 3G/ TD-SCDMA mobile communication technology products. The US $100 million investment gave the company a 49% stake in the venture, while Siemens held a 51% stake. In 2007, after Nokia and Siemens co-founded Nokia Siemens Networks, Siemens transferred all shares it held in TD Tech to Nokia Siemens Networks. At present, Nokia Siemens Networks and Huawei hold 51% and 49% shares of TD Tech respectively.

In 2006, Huawei established a Shanghai-based joint R&D center with Motorola to develop UMTS technologies. Later that year, Huawei also established a joint venture withTelecomVenezuela, called Industria Electronica Orinoquia, for research and development and sale of telecommunications terminals. Telecom Venezuela holds a 65% stake while Huawei holds the remaining 35% stake.

Huawei and American security firm Symantec announced in May 2007 the formation of a joint-venture company to develop security and storage solutions to market to telecommunications carriers. Huawei initially owned 51% of the new company, named Huawei Symantec Inc. while Symantec owned the rest. The joint-venture was based in Chengdu. In March, 2012, Symantec announced the sale of its portion of the joint venture to Huawei.

Grameenphone Ltd. and Huawei won the Green Mobile Award at the GSMA Mobile Awards 2009. In March 2009, the Wimax Forum announced four new members to its Board of Directors including Thomas Lee, the Vice Director of the Industry Standards Department at Huawei.

In 2008, Huawei launched a joint venture with UK-based marine engineering company, Global Marine Systems, to deliver undersea network equipment and related services.

Recent Performance

In April 2011, Huawei announced an earnings increase of 30% in 2010, driven by significant growth in overseas markets, with net profit rising to RMB 23.76 billion (US $3.64 billion; £ 2.23 billion) from RMB 18.27 billion in 2009. In 2010 sales outside China continued to be the main driver of Huawei's business. Overseas revenue rose 34% to RMB 120.41 billion in 2010 from RMB 90.02 billion in 2009, fueled by regions including North America and Russia. Revenues from China rose 9.7% to RMB 64.77 billion, as the country's big telecom operators reduced their investment last year.

Huawei's revenues in 2010 accounted for 15.7% of the $78.56 billion global carrier-network-infrastructure market, putting the company second behind the 19.6% share of Telefon AB L. M. Ericsson, according to market-research firm Gartner.

Huawei is targeting a revenue of $150 million through its enterprise business solutions in India in the next 12 months. It denied using Chinese subsidies to gain global market share after being recently accused by US lawmakers and EU officials of unfair competition at best.

Leadership

Ren Zhengfei is the president of Huawei and has held the title since 1987. Huawei disclosed its list of board of directors for the first time in 2010. Ms. Sun Yafang is board chair. As of 2011, the members of the board are Ms. Sun Yafang, Guo Ping, Xu Zhijun, Hu Houkun, Ren Zhengfei, Xu Wenwei, Li Jie, Ding Yun, Meng Wanzhou, Chen Lifang, Wan Biao, Zhang Pingan, and Yu Chengdong. The members of the Supervisory Board are Liang Hua, Peng Zhiping, Ren Shulu, Tian Feng, and Deng Biao. Richard Yu Chengdong is the Chairman of Huawei Device, its mobile phone division. On 1 July 2013, Huawei Device announced former head of Nokia Colin Giles joined the company as Executive Vice President of Consumer Business.

Ownership

Huawei describes itself as an "employee owned" company, partly as a means of counteracting perceptions of Chinese government involvement. However, the actual ownership structure is opaque and surrounded by a culture of secrecy. According to Caixin magazine, "even long-time employees admit the [shareholding] system is nearly impossible to understand." Employees receive no information about their holdings, and their shares do not entitle them to any voice in management decisions. The company's 50,000 + employees outside China are not given shares. Richard McGregor, author of The Party: The Secret World of China's Communist Rulers, said that the majority of shares are likely owned by Ren Zhengfei and Ren's managers, though the company states Ren directly owns less than 1.5%.

Products and Services

Huawei is organized around three core business segments:

(1) Telecom Carrier Networks, building telecommunications networks and services.

(2) Enterprise Business, providing equipment, software and services to enterprise customers, e. g. Government Solutions etc.

(3) Devices, manufacturing electronic communications devices.

Huawei announced its enterprise business in January, 2011 to provide network infrastructure, fixed and wireless communication, data center, and cloud computing solutions for global telecommunications customers. Huawei has stated that it aims to increase enterprise sales to US $4 billion in 2011 and $15 billion within three to five years.

Telecom Networks

Huawei offers a variety of network technologies and solutions to help telecommunications operators expand the capacity of their mobile broadband networks. Huawei's core network solutions offer mobile and fixed softswitches, plus next-generation home location register and Internet Protocol Multimedia Subsystems (IMS). Huawei assists content service providers looking to migrate from copper to fiber with solutions that support xDSL, passive optical network (PON) and next-generation PON (NG PON) on a single platform. The company also offers mobile infrastructure, broadband access and service provider routers and switches (SPRS). Huawei's software products include service delivery platforms (SDPs), BSSs, Rich Communication Suite and digital home and mobile office solutions.

In 2010, revenues for Telecom Networks were US $18.79 billion.

Global Services

Huawei Global Services provides telecommunications operators with equipment to build and operate networks as well as consulting and engineering services to improve operational efficiencies. These include network integration services such as those for mobile and fixed networks; assurance services such as network safety; and learning services, such as competency consulting.

In 2010, Huawei won 47 managed services contracts to help improve network performance and efficiency for customers, as well as reducing the costs of network operations and maintenance. In 2010 Huawei's global services revenues grew 28.6% to US $4.82 billion.

Ascend Smartphones and Devices

Huawei's Devices division provides white-label products to content-service providers, including USB modems, wireless modems and wireless routers for mobile WiFi, embedded modules, fixed wireless terminals, wireless gateways, set-top boxes, mobile handsets and video products. Huawei also produces and sells a variety of devices under its own name, such as the IDEOS smartphones, tablet PCs and Huawei Smartwatch. Recent products include U8800, U8860, E220, Ascend,U7519, Huawei Mercury M886, Huawei Honor 6 and U8150. On April 15, 2015, Huawei launched Huawei P8 and Huawei P8 Max. In 2010, Huawei Devices shipped 120 million devices around the world. 30 million cell phones, of which 3.3 million units were smartphones, were shipped to markets such as Japan, the United States and Europe.

Competitive Position

Huawei Technologies Co. Ltd., is the world's largest telecom equipment maker and China's largest telephone-network equipment maker. As of 2008, Huawei ranked first in terms of global market share in the mobile softswitches market, tied with Sony Ericsson for lead market share in mobile broadband cards by revenue, ranked second in the optical hardware market, stayed first in the IP DSLAM market, and ranked third in mobile network equipment. In 2009, Huawei was ranked No. 2 in global market share for radio access equipment. In addition, Huawei was the first vendor to launch end-to-end (E2E) 100G solutions, enabling operators to establish enhanced ultra-broadband networks, improving their service and simplifying their network architecture.

According to the World Intellectual Property Organization (WIPO) on 27 January 2009, Huawei was ranked as the largest applicant under WIPO's Patent Cooperation Treaty (PCT), with 1,737 applications published in 2008. Overall, the total number of international patent filings under WIPO's PCT for 2008 represents the highest number of applications received under the PCT in a single year and China improved its ranking by one place, to become the sixth largest user of the PCT, with 6,089 filings. As of February 2011, Huawei has applied for 49,040 patents globally and has been granted 17,765 to date. In 2014, Huawei became the world's No. 1 applicant for international patents in 2014, with 3,442 patents.

Sales

Huawei's global contract sales for 2006 reached US $11 billion (a 34% increase from 2005), 65% of which came from overseas markets. By the end of 2008, global contract sales of Huawei Technologies, China's largest telecoms gear maker, jumped 46 percent to US $23.3 billion. Huawei experienced sales exceeding US $30 billion in 2009, and global sales increased by 24 percent to 185.2 billion yuan in 2010.

Recognition

Huawei Technologies was one of six telecom industry companies included in the World's Most Respected 200 Companies list compiled by Forbes magazine in May 2007. In December 2008, BusinessWeek magazine included Huawei in their inaugural list of "The World's Most Influential Companies".

In 2010 Fast Company ranked Huawei the fifth most innovative company in the world. The same year, Huawei received three honors at the Global Telecom Business Innovation Awards including "Green base station innovation", "Wholesale network innovation" and "Consumer voting innovation" awards with Vodafone, BT and TalkTalk, respectively. In 2010 Frost & Sullivan recognized Huawei as the 2010 SDM Equipment Vendor of the Year and in the contact center application market with the 2010 Asia Pacific Growth Strategy Leadership Award. On 29 July 2010, Huawei was recognized by British Telecom with Best in Class 21CN Solution Maturity, Value, Service and Innovation award, for its innovation and contribution in 21CN and Next Generation Access project. Also in 2010 The Economist recognized Huawei with its Corporate Use of Innovation Award. In May 2011 Huawei won two awards at the LTE World Summit 2011 for "Significant Progress for a Commercial Launch of LTE by a Vendor" and "Best LTE Network Elements." As of May 2011, Huawei has deployed over 100 SingleRAN commercial networks, which are capable of evolving into LTE, and of those that have deployed SingleRAN networks, more than 40 operators have announced the launch or the imminent launch of distinct LTE services.

Huawei has been described as "perhaps China's most globally successful company". In 2014, Huawei was the first Chinese company to join Interbrand's "Best Global Brands" at the 94th most valuable brand at $4.3 billion.

Sponsorship

Huawei sponsors Bundesliga club Borussia Dortmund. On 15 September 2013, Huawei were announced as the new shirt sponsors of A-League club Wellington Phoenix F. C. as well as the sponsor of Liga de Fútbol Profesional (LFP) in Spain.

On 17 January 2014, Arsenal F. C. announced that Huawei will become their official "Global Smartphone Partner".

In March 2014, Huawei becomes the shirt sponsor of Rayo Vallecano for two La Liga matches against Real Madrid and Athletic Bilbao.

In April 2014, Huawei became the "Official Partner" of Paris Saint-Germain for the next three seasons.

Huawei debuted to the field of Cricket in April 2014 by becoming the principal sponsor of Royal Challengers Bangalore, a domestic cricket team that plays in the Indian Premier League.

Ghana Football Association has announced Huawei as its latest sponsor for the Black Stars ahead of the 2014 FIFA World Cup finals in Brazil. The one-year sponsorship deal is worth US $100,000 plus products.

On 12 September 2014, Galatasaray S. K. (football) announced that Huawei will become their journey sponsor for one-year period in Turkish National Süper Lig.

Since October 2014 Huawei has been the main sponsor of South African Premier Soccer League club Ajax Cape Town.

On 4 January 2015 Huawei was announced as the main sponsor of the current champion of the Colombian First Division Tournament, Independiente Santa Fe, for the next two years (2015—2017).

As of 12 February 2015, Huawei was announced as another sponsor for Mexico's Liga MX, Club América. They're on negotiation to being the main sponsor for the following season in Mexico, replacing Grupo Bimbo on the front part of the shirt, as of right now they'll provide cellphone equipment to the team members and will be part of the celebration for the centenary for the club.

Corporate Social Responsibility

As part of its international support for technology and telecommunications education and training, Huawei has contributed funding and equipment to a number of universities and training centers in countries such as Kenya, India, Indonesia, Bangladesh, and Nigeria. In the U. S., since 2008, Huawei has sponsored MIT's Communications Futures Program, a research collaboration that studies the future of the telecommunications industry.

In 2010, Huawei joined the Broadband Commission for Digital Development, formed by the ITU and UNESCO to support broadband deployment to developing nations. In the same year, Huawei joined the Green Touch consortium, an industry group that aims to make communications networks 1,000 times more energy efficient than they are today.

In June 2011, Huawei signed a five-year agreement to contribute donated services, equipment and technical expertise worth over US $1.4 million to Carleton University, in Ottawa, Canada, to establish a research lab dedicated to cloud computing technology and services. The same month, Huawei published its 2010 Corporate Social Responsibility (CSR) Report.

Introduction: The competitive landscape of the twenty-first century will be characterized by increasing globalization, advanced technological development, and other factors that will lead to an environment that is more dynamic and charged with rivalry. Firms will act and react in a dance of sorts, but one involving very high stakes—even survival. This chapter introduces terms and concepts relevant to the conversation about competitive behavior in a variety of markets.

Competitive Dynamics

A strategy's success is determined not only by the firm's initial competitive actions, but also by how well it anticipates competitors' responses to them and by how well the firm anticipates and responds to its competitor's initial actions.

Some important definitions:

(1) Firms operating in the same market with similar products targeting similar customers are competitors.

(2) Competitive rivalry is the ongoing set of competitive actions and competitive responses occurring between rivals as they compete against each other for an advantageous market position.

(3) Competitive behavior is the set of competitive actions and competitive

responses the firm takes to build or defend its competitive advantages and to improve its market position.

(4) Firms competing against each other in several product/geographic markets are in multimarket competition.

(5) All competitive behavior—that is, the total set of actions and responses taken by all firms competing within a market—is called competitive dynamics.

Firms must learn to compete differently if they are to achieve strategic competitiveness in the twenty-first century competitive landscape. To provide an idea of what this means, new ways of competing may include the following:

(1) bringing new goods and services to market more quickly.

(2) the use of new technologies (e. g. , Amazon. com).

(3) diversifying the product line (e. g. , Barnes and Noble into music as a catalyst for growth).

(4) shifting product emphasis (e. g. , U-haul's focus on accessory sales).

(5) consolidation (e. g. , the merger of Hewlett Packard and Compaq).

(6) combining online selling with physical stores (e. g. , Sears's acquisition of Lands' End).

The focus of this chapter is on competitive dynamics, the series of competitive actions and competitive responses among firms competing within a particular industry. The implication that should be strongly stated is that the strategic management process is dynamic, not static.

5.1 A Model of Competitive Rivalry①

Competitive rivalry exists when firms jockey with one another to pursue an advantageous market position. When one or more firms competing in an industry feels pressure to act or perceives an opportunity to improve their competitive position, competitive rivalry occurs as various firms initiate a series of actions and responses.

Research findings showing that intensified rivalry within an industry results in decreased average profitability for firms competing in it supports the importance of understanding these effects. ②

Viewing the model leads to a number of observations:

---

① 竞争对抗模型。

② 研究表明,一个行业内竞争的加剧导致参与该行业竞争的公司的平均利润下降。

(1) Interfirm rivalry or competitive dynamics begin with an assessment of competitors' awareness and motivation to attack and/or respond to competitive moves. ①

(2) Market commonality and resource similarity are affected by a firm's awareness, and motivation affects the likelihood of attack or response. ②

(3) The likelihood of attack and response result in competitive outcomes, with outcomes moderated by a firm's ability to take strategic actions or responses. ③

(4) Feedback from competitive outcomes will affect future competitive dynamics by affecting the nature of a firm's awareness, motivation, and ability for action/response. ④

Competitive rivalry exists because of competitive asymmetry, which describes the fact that firms differ from one another in terms of their resources, capabilities, core competencies, and the opportunities and threats in their competitive environments and industries. It is important that firms see that competition results in mutual interdependence among firms in the industry as each firm tries to establish a sustainable competitive advantage.

(1) As firms strive to achieve strategic competitiveness and above-average returns, they must recognize that strategies are not deployed in isolation from rival's actions and responses.

(2) The strategic management process represents firms taking a series of actions, fending off counter-actions or responses and developing responses of their own.

5.2 Competitor Analysis⑤

A competitor analysis is the first step in predicting the extent and nature of rivalry with each competitor. Appropriate features of this kind of analysis are described below.

---

① 企业间竞争或竞争动态始于评估竞争者攻击或响应竞争行为的意识和动机。

② 市场的共性和资源的相似性受公司意识的影响,并且动机会影响攻击或响应的可能性。

③ 攻击和响应的可能性导致竞争性结果,而结果则受公司采取战略行动或响应的能力的影响。

④ 来自竞争结果的反馈会影响公司的意识、动机和行动能力(响应)的性质,从而影响未来的竞争动态。

⑤ 竞争对手分析。

5.2.1 Market Commonality[①]

Market commonality is represented by the extent to which firms compete in the same markets. And market commonality is increasing as more and more firms compete internationally.

If firms overlap in a number of markets—which is sometimes referred to as multipoint competition—this results in a situation where firms compete against each other simultaneously in multiple geographic or product markets[②]. This can have a significant impact on competitive dynamics (e. g. , expanding into a new market that the competitor has entered to ensure that the rival does not tap a market opportunity that could then be used to support competition in core markets)[③].

In a number of industries (e. g. , airlines, chemicals, pharmaceuticals, and consumer foods) the largest domestic firms compete in many of the same markets. Thus there is high market commonality. This means that each has awareness and motivation to respond to competitive interaction.

Interestingly, high levels of commonality reduce the likelihood of competitive interaction. For firms that are in many common markets, there generally is competitive peace. However, when one of these firms makes a competitive move, the others are compelled to respond rapidly and aggressively.

5.2.2 Resource Similarity[④]

Resource similarity is the extent to which a firm's tangible and intangible resources are comparable to a competitor's in terms of both type and amount. Firms with similar types and amounts of resources are likely to have similar strengths and weaknesses and to use similar strategies.

In contrast to market commonality, assessing resource similarity can be difficult, particularly when critical resources are intangible (e. g. , brand name, knowledge, trust, capacity to innovate) rather than tangible (e. g. , access to raw materials, ability to borrow capital).

---

① 市场共性。

② 如果企业在多个市场中重叠(有时称为多点竞争),则会导致企业在多个地区或产品市场中同时竞争。

③ 这可能会对竞争动态产生重大影响(例如,扩展到竞争对手进入的新市场,以确保竞争对手不会利用该市场机会来支持核心市场的竞争)。

④ 资源相似性。

In most cases, dissimilar resources may increase the likelihood of an attack while firms with similar resources (overlap between their resource portfolios) will be less likely to attack because resource similarity increases the likelihood of retaliation.

Coca-Cola and Pepsi's decision to target the fast-growing market for bottled water provides an example of how resource dissimilarity may cause potential competitors to be overlooked, especially by an industry's dominant firms. This means that competitive responses of firms such as Perrier Group to protect its key bottled water brands may be delayed due to resource dissimilarity.

5.3 Drivers of Competitive Actions①

Awareness② refers to whether or not the attacking or responding firm is aware of the competitive market characteristics such as the market commonality and the resource similarity of a potential attacker or respondent.

When managers are not aware of these factors or assess them inaccurately, industry overcapacity or excessive competition may result. For example, this may be a partial explanation for the recent decline in Levi Strauss' core market as the firm appeared to be unaware of changes in teenagers'interests as competition for their business intensified.

Market commonality affects the firm's perceptions and resulting motivation. For example, all else being equal, the firm is more likely to attack the rival with whom it has low market commonality than the one with whom it competes in multiple markets. The primary reason is that there are high stakes involved in trying to gain a more advantageous position over a rival with whom the firm shares many markets.

Motivation③ is represented by the incentives that a firm has to either initiate an attack or to respond when attacked.

Resource dissimilarity also influences competitive actions and responses between firms, in that the greater the resource imbalance between the acting firm and competitors or potential responders, the greater will be the delay in response by the firm with a resource disadvantage.

Ability④ relates to each firm's resources and the flexibility they provide. Without

① 竞争行为的驱动力。
② 意识。
③ 动机。
④ 能力。

available resources (such as financial capital and people), the firm lacks the ability to attack a competitor or respond to its actions. However, similar resources suggest similar abilities to attack and respond.

5.4 Competitive Rivalry①

Competitive rivalry is the ongoing set of competitive actions and responses occurring between competing firms for an advantageous market position. Because the ongoing competitive action/response sequence between a firm and a competitor affects the performance of both firms, it is important for companies to carefully study competitive rivalry to successfully use their strategies.

Strategic and Tactical Actions②

Firms use both strategic and tactical actions when forming their competitive actions and competitive responses in the course of engaging in competitive rivalry③.

(1) A competitive action is a strategic or tactical action the firm takes to build or defend its competitive advantages or improve its market position④.

(2) A competitive response is a strategic or tactical action the firm takes to counter the effects of a competitor's competitive action⑤.

(3) A strategic action or a strategic response is a market-based move that involves a significant commitment of organizational resources and is difficult to implement and reverse⑥.

(4) A tactical action or a tactical response is a market-based move that is taken to fine-tune a strategy; it involves fewer resources and is relatively easy to implement and reverse⑦.

(5) Hyundai Motor Co.'s expenditures on research and development and plant expansion to support the firm's desire to be one of the world's largest carmakers by

---

① 竞争对抗。

② 战略和战术行动。

③ 在参与竞争性对抗的过程中,企业在采取竞争行为和竞争响应时会同时使用战略和战术行动。

④ 竞争行为是企业为建立或捍卫其竞争优势或改善其市场地位而采取的战略或战术行动。

⑤ 竞争响应是公司为应对竞争对手的竞争行为而采取的战略或战术措施。

⑥ 战略行动或战略响应是一种基于市场的举动,涉及大量组织资源投入,难以实施和逆转。

⑦ 战术行动或战术响应是一种基于市场的行为,用于战略的调整。它涉及的资源较少,并且相对容易实现和逆转。

2010 are strategic actions[①].

(6) Tactical actions are easily reversed-pricing decisions are often taken by these firms to increase demand in certain markets during certain periods[②].

In mid-2007, Auchan had 6,775 stores and was projected to generate revenues in excess of \$350 billion. Approximately 40 percent of this revenue is being generated outside of the United States as Auchan continues to expand internationally. Analysts believe that Auchan's business model will prove successful in some emerging markets even though the firm struggles with adequate profitability in some developed markets such as Germany and Japan.

Europe's Carrefour, Costco Wholesale, and Target are Auchan's major competitors, although a number of other companies (including Kohl's, J. C. Penney, and BJ's Wholesale Club) also compete against the retailing giant. As a tactical action, Auchan prices some products to increase overall sales revenue and to attract customers to its stores in hopes that they will purchase other items as well. Aggressive pricing works (for Auchan and others such as Costco Wholesale using the practice) when reduced prices generate sales revenues in excess of those generated without the price cuts, and when customers buy other higher-margin items while shopping. Both Auchan and Costco now offer gasoline filling stations to attract customers to their stores. The same pricing tactics are utilized as an enticement to draw customers into their stores to hopefully purchase other items.

As a tactical action, aggressive pricing is used with virtually all products that Auchan sells. Toys and electronics (i. e., flat panel televisions, PCs, and telephones) are priced aggressively during holiday seasons. More recently, Auchan aggressively priced appliances in order to compete against Best Buy, Home Depot, and Lowe's in this product category. For the back-to-school season, Auchan often cuts prices anywhere from 10 percent to 50 percent on as many as 16,000 school-related items.

Firms must carefully evaluate the effectiveness of all of their competitive actions and competitiveresponses. Some feel that Auchan's emphasis on low prices is preventing the firm from allocating sufficient resources to remodel aging stores and to upgrade the quality of its merchandising mix. Competitors Kohl's and Costco appear to be attracting some of Auchan's customers by offering more appealing mixes of

---

① 现代汽车公司在研发和企业扩张上投入巨资，希望公司 2010 年能成为世界最大的汽车制造商之一，这种做法就是战术行为。

② 战术行为可以轻松逆转：某些特定时期中，企业为了提高市场需求，经常采用不同的定价策略。

merchandise and a marginally more pleasant shopping experience that modernized facilities provide. Thus, Auchan must carefully assess the degree to which its tactical action of aggressive pricing is allowing it to successfully engage competitors in marketplace competitions.

Students should be reminded that the cost of utilizing a pricing tactic may be more extensive than the profit forgone. The real cost in this case is not having funding available to maintain, improve, and expand current infrastructure and product mix in order to retain current customer levels. Auchan has established itself as a target at which competition is aiming. No single firm can challenge Auchan head-on, but each accepts Auchan as the price leader in its respective market, and will employ tactics to protect its respective turf.

5.5 Likelihood of Attack①

In addition to market commonality, resource similarity, and the drivers of awareness, motivation, and ability, other factors affect the likelihood a competitor will use strategic actions and tactical actions to attack its competitors. Three of these factors—first-mover incentives, organizational size, and quality—are described below.

5.5.1 First-Mover Incentives②

First movers are the firms that take an initial competitive action, either strategic or tactical. First movers are firms that have the resources, capabilities, and core competencies that enable them to gain a competitive advantage through innovative and entrepreneurial competitive actions③.

By being early, the first mover hopes to④:

(1) earn above-average returns until competitors respond effectively⑤.

(2) gain customer loyalty, thus creating a barrier to entry by competitors⑥.

---

① 攻击的可能性。

② 先行者动机。

③ 先行者是首先采取战略或战术竞争行动的企业。先行者是具有资源、能力和核心竞争力的企业，这些资源、能力和核心能力使他们能够通过创新和创业竞争行动获得竞争优势。

④ 先行者起步早，他们希望能够——

⑤ 在竞争者做出响应之前，获得高于平均的收益。

⑥ 提高客户忠诚度，为竞争者入市制造壁垒。

(3) gain market share that can be difficult for competitors to take in the future①.

Consider the success of Harley-Davidson in large motorcycles (cruisers). In the 1980s Harley-Davidson set the standard for low, heavyweight motorcycles and has successfullydefended its position by emphasizing its reputation and brand name.

The firm trying to predict its rivals' competitive actions might conclude that they will take aggressive strategic actions to gain first movers' benefits. However, while a firm's competitors might be motivated to be first movers, they may lack the ability to do so. First movers tend to be aggressive and willing to experiment with innovation and take higher, yet reasonable, levels of risk. To be a first mover, the firm must have readily available the resources to significantly invest in R&D as well as to rapidly and successfully produce and market a stream of innovative products.

Organizational slack is what makes it possible for firms to have the ability (as measured by available resources) to be first movers. Slack is the buffer or cushion provided by actual or obtainable resources that aren't currently in use. Thus, slack is liquid resources that the firm can quickly allocate to support the actions (e. g., R&D investments and aggressive marketing campaigns) that lead to first mover benefits.

There also are dangers or disadvantages to being a first mover②.

(1) It is difficult to accurately estimate the returns that will be earned from introducing product innovations③.

(2) The first mover's cost to develop a product innovation can be substantial, reducing the slack available to support further innovation④.

(3) Lack of product acceptance over the course of the competitor's innovations may indicate less willingness in the future to accept the risks of being a first mover⑤.

Second movers are firms that respond to a first mover's competitive action, typically through imitation⑥. Doing so allows the second mover to⑦:

(1) avoid both the mistakes and the huge spending of the pioneers (first movers)⑧.

(2) have time to develop processes and technologies that are more efficient than

---

① 抢占市场份额,增加竞争者未来占额难度。

② 做先行者同样存在难度或风险。

③ 很难准确估算引进产品革新所带来的收益。

④ 先行者用于产品革新的成本较高,占用了进一步革新所需的费用。

⑤ 竞争者革新过程中,如果客户对产品接受度不高,未来则更不愿意接受先行者风险。

⑥ 跟随者指响应先行者竞争行为的企业,典型的手段是模仿。

⑦ 跟随者通过模仿,可以——

⑧ 避免先行者的错误及巨大的投资。

those used by the first mover①.

(3) respond quickly to first movers' successful, innovation-based market entries②.

(4) rapidly and meaningfully interpret market feedback to respond quickly, yet successfully to the first mover's successful innovations③.

An example of industry dynamics—and how a second mover can succeed—is provided by looking at the competitive dynamics of the athletic shoe industry④.

(1) New Balance is a second mover in the athletic shoe industry⑤.

(2) It effectively competes against industry leaders Nike and Reebok by focusing on the needs of a well-defined market segment.

(3) New Balance products are not particularly innovative compared to industry leader, Nike.

(4) New Balance is able to succeed by doing a better job of satisfying the needs of baby boomers, whose ages are significantly higher than those of Nike's and Reebok's core customer groups, 42, compared to 25 and 33, respectively.

(5) New Balance offers a new model every 17 weeks, compared to six weeks for most rivals.

(6) New Balance's success seems to come not from rapid introductions of innovative new products, but by offering high-quality products at moderate prices and by making them available in multiple widths (ranging from AA to EEEE), recognizing that many people do not have "average" feet.

Late movers are firms that respond to a competitive action, but only after considerable time has elapsed after the first mover's action and the second mover's response⑥.

Typically, a late response is better than no response at all, although any success

---

① 有时间开发比先行者更为有效的程序和技术。

② 对先行者以革新为基础的成功入市迅速做出响应。

③ 迅速准确地解读市场反馈,以便迅速有效地对先行者的成功革新做出响应。

④ 行业动态的一个例子是运动鞋行业的竞争动态,也是跟随者成功的案例。

⑤ (1) 新百伦是运动鞋行业的追随者。(2) 新百伦专注细分市场的需求,与行业领头者耐克及锐步竞争成功。(3) 新百伦产品与耐克相比,并不特别具备创新性。(4) 新百伦更好地满足了婴儿潮一代人的需求,这代人的年龄层为42岁,明显高于耐克的核心客户的年龄:25岁;也高于锐步核心客户的年龄:33岁。(5) 新百伦每17周推出一个新款,而多数对手每6周推出新款。(6) 新百伦的成功并非来自频繁推出创新性新产品,而是认识到并非所有人的脚型都"一样",因此推出价格适中的优质产品,并且有多种鞋型(从AA型到EEEE型)可供选择。

⑥ 后进者是对竞争行为做出响应的企业,但是这种响应发生在先行者行为和跟随者响应相当长的时间之后。

achieved from the late competitive response tends to be slow in coming and considerably less than that achieved by first and second movers①.

As late movers are the last to respond to the first and second movers' actions, late movers tend to be poor performers and often are weak competitors. For example, Avon was a late mover in e-commerce and Dell was a late mover in providing Internet access②.

5.5.2 Organizational Size③

An organization's size affects the likelihood that it will take competitive actions as well as the types of actions it will take and their timing④. Small firms are more likely to, and quicker to, launch competitive actions⑤.

Large firms are likely to initiate more competitive actions as well as strategic actions during a given time period. Thus, the competitive actions a firm will likely encounter from larger competitors will be different than the competitive actions it will encounter from smaller competitors⑥.

Large organizations often have slack resources to launch a larger number of total competitive actions, and thus do. However, smaller firms have the flexibility needed to launch a greater variety of competitive actions.

Auchan appears to be an example of a large firm that has the flexibility required to take many types of competitive actions. Analysts believe that Auchan's tactical actions are critical to its success and show a great deal of flexibility (such as a quick advertising change for 2007 back-to-school sales, after disappointing spring, 2007 sales). In other words, Auchan's competitive actions will be a combination of the tendencies shown by small and large companies.

5.5.3 Quality

Product quality shapes the competitive dynamics in many industries. In fact,

---

① 通常,迟到的响应好过没有响应,虽然迟到的竞争响应入市速度慢,成就远不如先行者和追随者。

② 由于后进者最后对先行者和追随者行为做出响应,后进者通常市场表现不佳,竞争力不强。例如,雅芳是电子商务的后进者,戴尔是互联网接入的后进者。

③ 组织规模。

④ 组织的规模会影响采取竞争行为的可能性,也会影响其采取的行为及时机。

⑤ 小型企业通常采取竞争行为可能性更大,反应也更迅速。

⑥ 大型企业更可能在给定时间内,采取竞争性更强及更具战略意义的行为。因此,大型竞争者采用的竞争行为与小型竞争者的竞争行为有所不同。

product quality is no longer a competitive issue but a necessary or mandatory product attribute if firms expect to successfully implement any of the generic business strategies discussed in Chapter 3—low cost, differentiation, focus, or integrated cost leadership/differentiation. Quality involves meeting or exceeding customer expectations in the products and/or services offered.

The following observations may prove useful in presenting this section:

(1) The necessity of quality is illustrated by competition in the automobile industry and the uphill battle of U. S. automakers to produce cars with a quality level comparable to those produced by the Japanese.

(2) While U. S. automakers appear to have reached quality parity, they should expect that Japanese automakers will initiate strategic responses to their competitive actions. In fact, many observers expect the Japanese to use their core competencies to develop a source of competitive advantage other than quality. In turn, this will stimulate U. S. (and European) automakers to develop and implement competitive responses.

(3) In the long run, it costs less to make quality products or to offer quality services than it does to make or offer defective ones (because of the costs related to repairing defects or correcting service errors).

While quality is necessary, it is not a sufficient product attribute for firms to achieve strategic competitiveness. An acceptable level of quality merely provides firms with the opportunity to compete. Products and services must continue to meet customer preferences.

Quality is as important in the services sector as it is in manufacturing. For the importance of quality to permeate the entire organization (and affect all of its processes and value-creating activities), a dedication to quality must come from the organization's top-level executives.

This is what has happened at Dell Computer as top management, especially Michael Dell, is obsessed with maintaining high levels of product quality and continuous quality improvements. At Dell, a total quality management process is found throughout the firm's activities and processes.

Quality affects competitive rivalry.

(1) The firm studying a competitor with poor quality products can predict that the competitor's costs are high and that its sales revenue will likely decline until the quality issues are resolved.

(2) The firm can predict that the competitor is unlikely to be aggressive in terms

of taking competitive actions, given that its quality problems must be corrected in order to gain credibility with customers.

(3) Once corrected, the competitor will likely act by emphasizing additional dimensions of competition.

To improve quality or to maintain a focus on it, firms often become involved with total quality management, which is a "managerial innovation that emphasizes an organization's total commitment to the customer and to continuous improvement of every process through the use of data-driven, problem-solving approaches based on empowerment of employee groups and teams." Through TQM, firms seek to (1) increase customer satisfaction, (2) cut costs, and (3) reduce the amount of time required to introduce innovative products to the marketplace.

TQM

TQM combines W. Edward Deming's and Joseph Juran's teachings on statistical process control (SPC is a technique used to continually upgrade the quality of goods or services that a firm produces) with group problem-solving processes and Japanese values related to quality and continuous improvement.

A key attribute of SPC is the early detection and elimination of variations in the processes used to manufacture a good or service (compared to waiting until a product is completed).

It is interesting—and, at the same time, discouraging—to note that Japanese firms adapted and implemented Deming's and Juran's quality management techniques long before they were recognized as important by U. S. firms. This lag by U. S. firms explains how Japanese firms were able to achieve a competitive advantage based on product quality that forced U. S. firms to play catch up.

The principal goals of TQM are increasing customer satisfaction with the firm's goods and/or services, compressing product introduction time (time-to-market) and reducing costs.

Critical to successfully implementing Deming's framework is recognizing that the firm (and all of its employees) must continuously strive to improve the quality of the firm's processes as well as that of its goods and services.

Newer methods of TQM use benchmarking and emphasize organizational learning for firms attempting to gain competitive advantage. Benchmarking facilitates TQM by developing information on best practices that can guide the firm's own TQM efforts.

Quality Dimensions of Goods and Services

The quality dimensions of products and services differ slightly from each other. As presented, the quality dimensions of products are more objective or measurable, relating to:

(1) how the product performs and how it conforms with pre-established standards.

(2) what features it has.

(3) its flexibility, durability, conformance, and serviceability.

(4) how it looks or feels and an overall perception of quality.

In contrast, the quality dimensions of services are more subjective, dealing with:

(1) timeliness, courtesy, and convenience.

(2) accuracy, completeness, and consistency.

5.6 Likelihood of Response

Once a competitive action has been taken, its success generally is determined by the likelihood and nature of the competitive response.

In general, a firm is likely to respond to a competitor's action when

(1) the action leads to better use of the competitor's capabilities to gain or produce stronger competitive advantages or an improvement in its market position,

(2) the action damages the firm's ability to use its capabilities to create or maintain an advantage, or

(3) the firm's market position becomes less defensible.

To predict how a competitor is likely to respond to competitive actions, firms should consider:

(1) market commonality and resource similarity.

(2) awareness, motivation, and ability.

(3) type of competitive action, reputation and market dependence.

5.6.1 Type of Competitive Action

Remember, competitive actions are significant competitive moves taken by a firm that are designed to gain a competitive advantage in a market, with the type of competitive action taken being based on the firm's strategy. Competitive actions can be classified based on the scope or breadth and significance of the action.

The likelihood of a competitive response to an action depends on the type of action taken—strategic or tactical—and the potential effect on competitors.

Because strategic actions require the use or dedication of specific organizational resources, are more difficult to implement successfully, are more time consuming, and are difficult (and often costly) to reverse, it is more likely that tactical actions will be implemented and responded to more often.

Because tactical actions require fewer organizational resources and are relatively easy to implement and reverse, their effects on the competitive situation are more immediately felt.

Some examples of strategic actions include:

(1) Continental's decision to initiate flights into Lima, Peru.

(2) Bank One's implementation of an Internet banking company.

Tactical actions are taken to fine-tune a strategy. They involve fewer and more general organizational resources and are relatively easy to implement and reverse, if necessary. Fare increases (decreases) in the airline industry represent tactical actions. They require few organizational resources (other than communicating new prices), are relatively easy to implement, and can be reversed. Tactical actions also are generally more quickly responded to by competitors than are strategic actions.

It can be instructive to compare the rapid response by airlines to competitors' tactical actions (such as fare reductions) to American Airline's acquisition of another airline company and its $1 billion purchase of gates at JFK airport to respond to Continental's efforts to gain market share (strategic actions).

5.6.2 Actor's Reputation

To predict the likelihood of a competitor's response to a current or planned action, the firm studies the responses that that competitor has taken previously when attacked, in that past behavior is assumed to be a reasonable predictor of future behavior.

Competitors are more likely to respond to either strategic or tactical actions that are taken by a market leader. For example, competitive actions taken by Home Depot are almost certain to incite a response from Lowe's.

Some likely effects of reputation are the following:

(1) Actions initiated by firms with a previous history of success also will be more likely to result in quick reactions and imitation.

(2) Actions taken by firms with reputations for risk-taking and for initiating complex and unpredictable actions are less likely to be responded to.

(3) Actions taken by price predators (firms who cut prices to capture market

share and then raise prices) are seen as having a negative effect on competitors and their actions receive only minimal response and imitation.

5.6.3 Dependence on the Market

Market dependence denotes the extent to which a firm's revenues/profits are derived from a particular market.

Firms that are highly concentrated in—or dependent on—an industry (or market) in which a competitive action has been taken are more likely to respond than are firms who do business in multiple industries and markets.

5.7 Competitive Dynamics

Whereas competitive rivalry concerns the ongoing actions and responses between a firm and its competitors for an advantageous market position, competitive dynamics concerns the ongoing actions and responses taking place among all firms competing within a market for advantageous positions.

To explain competitive dynamics, it is important to understand the effects of varying rates of competitive speed in different markets (called slow-cycle, fast-cycle, and standard-cycle markets, defined below) on the behavior (actions and responses) of all competitors within a given market. Competitive behaviors as well as the reasons or logic for taking them are similar within each market type, but differ across market type. Thus, competitive dynamics differ in slow-cycle, fast-cycle, and standard-cycle markets. The sustainability of the firm's competitive advantages differs across the three market types.

5.7.1 Slow-Cycle Markets

Slow-cycle markets are those in which the firm's competitive advantages are shielded from imitation, often for long periods of time and where imitation is costly. Thus, competitive advantages are sustainable in slow-cycle markets.

Building a unique competitive advantage that is proprietary leads to competitive success in a slow-cycle market. This type of advantage is difficult for competitors to understand. Copyrights, geography, patents, and ownership of an information resource are examples of what leads to unique advantages.

Once a proprietary advantage is developed, the firm's competitive behavior in a slow-cycle market is oriented to protecting, maintaining, and extending that advantage.

Providing some examples may help students understand what has been involved in establishing and defending a one-of-a-kind competitive advantage. The following are some possibilities:

(1) IBM's historical dominance of the mainframe computer industry.

(2) Boeing's dominant position in larger, commercial jet aircraft (at least until the Airbus super-jumbo jet hits the market).

(3) Microsoft's dominant position in the market for PC operating system software (though diminished somewhat by a recent swell of new competitors).

(4) Auchan's use of local market monopolies as it established its dominant position in discount retailing by setting up stores in small, rural communities.

Gradual Erosion of a Sustained Competitive Advantage

A firm operating in a slow-cycle market may be able to retain its competitive advantage over time.

(1) Returns from the competitive action increase during the early, launch years of the strategy.

(2) When returns level out, the firm exploits its position.

(3) Competitors counterattack or launch strategies that cause the first firm's bases for competitive advantage to erode. As a result, returns are competed away.

5.7.2 Fast-Cycle Markets

Fast-cycle markets are markets in which the firm's competitive advantages aren't shielded from imitation and where imitation happens quickly and somewhat inexpensively through reverse engineering and technology diffusion. Competitive advantages aren't sustainable in fast-cycle markets.

The technology often used by fast-cycle competitors isn't proprietary, nor is it protected by patents as is the technology used by firms competing in slow-cycle markets. For example, only a few hundred parts readily available on the open market are required to build a PC. Patents protect only a few of these parts, such as microprocessor chips.

Fast-cycle markets are more volatile than slow-cycle and standard-cycle markets. Prices fall quickly in these markets, so companies need to profit quickly from their product innovations (e.g., rapid declines in the prices of microprocessor chips produced by Intel and Advanced Micro Devices continuously reduces their prices to end users).

Imitation of many fast-cycle products is relatively easy, as demonstrated by Dell and Gateway, along with a host of local PC vendors. All of these firms have partly or largely imitated IBM's initial PC design to create their products.

The focus of fast-cycle competition is competitive disruption, an approach where competition is based on one set of resources and then shifted to another—in other words, using price as a first step toward sustaining a competitive advantage, then shifting to quality, then speed, then innovation, and so on. The principle is that the primary basis of the competitive advantage is shifted as the firm disrupts, and changes, the rules of the game.

Firms in fast-cycle markets avoid "loyalty" to any of their products, preferring to cannibalize their own before competitors learn how to do so through successful imitation. This emphasis creates competitive dynamics that differ substantially from what is witnessed in slow-cycle markets. Instead of concentrating on protecting, maintaining, and extending competitive advantages, these companies focus on learning how to rapidly and continuously develop superior advantages.

Obtaining Temporary Advantages to Create Sustained Advantage

As illustrated, one way in which firms might sustain a competitive advantage is to move continuously from advantage to advantage. This is accomplished by moving from one source of advantage to another, never allowing competitors to catch up.

Examples of firms that have successfully followed the incremental approach to sustain competitive advantage are Vodafone in telecommunications services and Cisco Systems in telecommunications systems.

The following has been prescribed as the incremental or step-by-step approach to managing competitive advantages in fast-cycle markets.

(1) Disrupt the status quo—a firm should identify new opportunities to meet customer needs, thereby shifting or changing the basis of competition.

(2) Create a temporary advantage—the temporary advantage should be based on improved knowledge of customers' needs, innovative application of technology, and an attempt to define the future basis of customer satisfaction.

(3) Seize the initiative—move aggressively and rapidly, forcing competitors to play catch up; taking a proactive approach while leaving competitors to be reactive.

(4) Sustain the momentum—continue to develop new sources of advantage; don't

wait for competitors to catch up; stay one step ahead.

As discussed earlier, the new competitive landscape requires that firms ① introduce more new products, ② develop broader product lines, and ③ provide more rapid product upgrades.

5.7.3 Standard-Cycle Markets

Standard-cycle markets are those in which the firm's competitive advantages are moderately shielded from imitation and where imitation is moderately costly. Competitive advantages are partially sustainable in standard-cycle markets, but only when the firm is able to continuously upgrade the quality of its competitive advantages.

The competitive actions and responses that form a standard-cycle market's competitive dynamics find firms seeking large market shares, trying to gain customer loyalty through brand names, and carefully controlling their operations to consistently provide the same usage experience for customers without surprises.

Because of large volumes, the size of mass markets, and the need to develop scale economies, the competition for market share is intense in standard-cycle markets. P&G and Unilever are direct competitors—they share multiple markets, have similar types and amounts of resources, and follow similar strategies. For example, they both compete aggressively for market share in laundry detergents, where tiny fractions make a huge difference at the bottom line.

Innovation has a substantial influence on competitive dynamics as it affects the actions and responses of all companies competing within a slow-cycle, fast-cycle, or standard-cycle market.

本章课程思政学习专题

中国家电行业的竞争策略组合①

1. 动态竞争

一直以来,在动态竞争研究领域,最基本的研究对象是企业的竞争行动。竞争行动及其回应被定义为由企业发起的一种特别的、可检测到的市场行动,这些行动会侵蚀竞争对手的市场绩效或减少其预期的市场回报。事实上,动态竞争研

① 邓新明,罗欢,龙贤义,等.高管团队异质性、竞争策略组合与市场绩效:来自中国家电行业的实证检验[J].南开管理评论,2021,24(4):103-115.

究方法的核心视角是在一个真实的竞争情境中调查企业行为。进攻—回应对偶视角成为调查中的基本单元。然而,当人们尝试分析企业在面对不同竞争者而采取的竞争策略时,针对某特定竞争者的进攻或回应行为分析就失去了其意义。因此,考虑更长时间和更多方面的行动或策略的序列/组合是一个更受关注的趋势。研究者开始从单个行为的聚焦发展到将企业一段时期所发动的竞争行为集合,即竞争策略组合进行整体研究。迥异于传统以对偶层次为主体的分析方式,竞争策略组合所代表的是一种思考竞争策略的全新方法,它让动态竞争研究范畴超越了单纯的行动—回应双边模型视角,使从整个竞争行动的集合视角提供一个关于企业间竞争的更加整体的"知识图景"成为可能。

2. 中国家电上市企业竞争态势

企业间竞争日益激烈,当某个企业发动某个行动时,其他企业都争相模仿和学习,并且整个行业竞争随着时间推演呈现阶段性且愈发成熟。起初,当家电行业刚刚起步且初具规模时,家电企业的市场竞争行为仍停留在"价格战"的阶段,大量而单一的行为很容易被对手企业模仿,焦点企业的竞争优势也难以持久。后来,随着家电企业规模不断增大,行业内企业数量不断增加,竞争越发激烈,竞争行动内容也从单纯的价格战慢慢过渡到营销、研发、进入新行业、慈善公益等复杂多样的行动组合。中国家电行业的竞争态势变化是其他行业(除了寡头垄断行业)竞争演变的缩影,行业内企业数量且规模不断增加,产品的更新换代速度加快,相应的企业竞争行动也从单一走向复杂多样。因此,参与动态竞争的企业需要在商战中不断学习,不断积累竞争经验,根据行业竞争形势的变化,不断调整自己的竞争策略。现实情况中,跟得上行业竞争变化的企业总能凭借着敏锐的市场嗅觉取得理想的竞争地位和不错的市场绩效水平。

参与动态竞争的企业的竞争策略组合需要与企业的竞争阶段相对应。在企业处于竞争复杂性低水平时,多数企业处于竞争的起步阶段,资源配置不合理并且竞争经验不足,提高竞争行为的复杂度会使市场绩效下降,但当企业处于竞争复杂性高水平时,越复杂的竞争行动组合对市场绩效越有利。企业需要根据自身所处的竞争阶段发动复杂性不同的竞争行动。如果企业追求短期绩效的提高,单一而惯常的行动组合能满足需求,但会面临着未来投资者和顾客流失、绩效下降的状况。从动态竞争的战略视角分析,企业需要根据自身的资源和能力制定复杂的行动,竞争复杂性不仅在于行动数量多,还包括行动多样、变化和新奇,这里更强调后者而非前者。2014 年 TCL 发动的行动数量约 32 个,但市场绩效却低于同期美的约 6%,虽然美的行动数量仅 6 个,在数量方面不占优势,但其行动新奇远高于 TCL。同年,海信的行动数量与美的相同,但行动多样性和新奇远低于美的,相应的市场绩效仅为美的电器的 18%。因此,对于实力雄厚的大企业,通过增加行动数量提高竞争复杂性,当然也需要注重行动的种类多样,行动的时间变化等;

对于实力弱的小企业,不要硬碰硬而是要智取,通过发动某一个或某几个全新的行动来增加竞争复杂性,达到出其不意的效果,获得竞争优势。

3. 思考问题

试以其他行业中的企业为例,进行动态竞争组合策略分析。

Chapter 6 Corporate-Level Strategy

Opening Case[①]

The Changing Business of BYD

BYD Co Ltd is a Chinese manufacturer of automobiles and rechargeable batteries based in Shenzhen, Guangdong province. It has two major subsidiaries, BYD Automobile and BYD Electronic[②].

Hailed for its innovations, BYD has grown to become a major manufacturer of rechargeable batteries, most notably mobile phone batteries.

BYD topped the 2010 Bloomberg Businessweek Tech 100 list, a list of large, fast-growing tech companies.

The name BYD is an acronym derived from the phrase "build your dreams".

Founded in the February 1995 and listed on the Hong Kong Stock Exchange on July 31, 2002, BYD Co Ltd began as a rechargeable-battery factory competing in the Chinese market against Japanese imports.

BYD grew quickly; within ten years capturing more than half the world's mobile-phone battery market and becoming the largest Chinese manufacturer (and in the top four worldwide) of all types of rechargeable batteries. Replacing work done by machines with cheap, local labor lowered costs, and the company began expanding beyond batteries, adding automobiles and mobile phone components.

A year after the 2002 acquisition of Tsinchuan Automobile Co Ltd, BYD Automobile Co Ltd was born. One of many Chinese automakers, in 2010 it was the sixth largest in terms of sales volume.

Seeking to utilize BYD battery production resources, in addition to gasoline-powered models, BYD sells a full hybrid, the F3DM, and all-electric K9 buses[③].

---

① 课前案例:比亚迪的多变业务。

② 比亚迪是中国一家汽车及充电电池的生产商,总部在广东深圳。比亚迪有两家子公司,比亚迪汽车及比亚迪电子。

③ 比亚迪为了利用电池生产资源,不仅销售汽油动力汽车,还销售混合动力车 F3DM 以及纯电动客车 K9。

Introduction

Chapter 6 takes this a step further by standing back to consider strategy at a higher level—corporate strategy. The concern here is for the performance benefits that are derived from putting together an effective "portfolio of businesses"—that is, putting businesses together in a way that makes sense and can generate synergies between units.

Corporate-level Strategy

A business-level or competitive strategy—actions a firm should take to compete in a single industry or product market—and the actions and responses that affect the competitive dynamics of a single industry or product market①.

In contrast, when a firm diversifies its operations by operating business in several industries, corporate level strategy becomes a primary focus②. This means that a diversified firm has two levels of strategy: business-level (or competitive) and corporate-level (or company-wide), the latter of which entails selecting a strategy that focuses on the selection and management of a mix of businesses.

Corporate-level strategies detail actions taken to gain a competitive advantage through the selection and management of a mix of businesses competing in several industries or product markets. Primary concerns of corporate-level strategy are③:

(1) What businesses should the firm be in?④

(2) How should the corporate office manage its group of businesses?⑤

(3) How can the corporation as a whole add up to more than the sum of its business parts?⑥

The ultimate measure of the value of a firm's corporate-level strategy is that the businesses in the firm's portfolio are worth more under current management (and by following the firm's corporate-level strategy) than they would be under different ownership or management.

---

① 公司层战略或竞争战略指企业在单一产业或产品市场采取的竞争措施,这种竞争措施会对单一产业或产品市场的竞争动态产生影响。

② 当公司通过在多个行业中经营业务来实现经营多元化时,公司层战略将成为主要焦点。

③ 公司层战略关注的主要问题是——

④ 企业应参与哪个行业?

⑤ 企业管理者如何管理业务?

⑥ 如何使企业整体大于部分业务之和?

6.1 Levels of Diversification①

Diversified firms vary according to two factors:②

(1) the level of diversification③.

(2) connection or linkages between and among business units④.

Levels and Types of Diversification⑤

Levels and types of diversification defined and discussed in more detail in the next sections of this chapter are:

Low levels of diversification⑥

(1) Single business⑦.

(2) Dominant business⑧.

Moderate to high levels of diversification⑨

(1) Related-constrained diversification⑩.

(2) Related-linked diversification (mixed related and unrelated)⑪.

Very high levels of diversification⑫

Unrelated diversification⑬.

6.1.1 Low Levels of Diversification

Firms that follow single or dominant-business strategies have low levels of diversification⑭. A single business is a firm where more than 95 percent of its revenues

---

① 多元化层次。
② 根据下述两个因素,企业多元化程度不同。
③ 多元化的层次。
④ 业务单位之间的联系或关联。
⑤ 多元化的层次和种类。
⑥ 低层次多元化。
⑦ 单一经营。
⑧ 主导经营。
⑨ 中高层次多元化。
⑩ 紧密相关多元化。
⑪ 相关连结型多元化(相关型与无关型相结合)。
⑫ 高层次多元化。
⑬ 无关多元化。
⑭ 单一经营或主导经营的企业多元化层次低。

are generated by the dominant business[①].

Firms such as the Wrigley Co. are examples of single-business firms. Wrigley Co. has dominated the global gum-related industry as the largest manufacturer of chewing gum, specialty gums, and gum bases. Its brands, Doublemint, Spearmint and Juicy Fruit, led the market.

A dominant business is a firm that generates between 70 and 95 percent of its sales within a single business area.

6.1.2 Moderate and High Levels of Diversification

A related-diversified firm is one that earns at least 30 percent of its revenues from sources outside of the dominant business and whose units are related to each other—e.g., by the sharing of resources and by product, technological, and distribution linkages.

Related-constrained firms also earn at least 30 percent of their revenues from the dominant business, and all business units share product, technological, and distribution linkages. Kodak, Procter & Gamble, and Campbell Soup Company are related-constrained firms[②].

Mixed related and unrelated or related-linked firms, such as Johnson and Johnson and General Electric, generate at least 30 percent of their total revenues from the dominant business, but there are few linkages between key value-creating activities[③].

Unrelated-diversified (or highly diversified) firms do not share resources or linkages. Firms that pursue unrelated diversification strategies—often known as conglomerates—include United Technologies, Samsung, and Textron[④].

While there are more unrelated diversified firms in the U. S. than in most other countries, conglomerates (firms following unrelated diversification strategies) dominate the private sector economy in Latin America and in several emerging economies (such as China, South Korea, and India).

Many firms that have at one time pursued unrelated diversification strategies are

---

① 单一经营指企业超过95%的收益来自主导经营。

② 紧密相关多元化的企业至少30%的收益来自主导经营,其所有的经营单位分享产品、技术及分销链条。柯达、宝洁及金宝汤公司均是紧密相关多元化企业。

③ 相关经营或无关经营、混合经营企业至少30%收益源自主导经营,但主要价值创造活动之间几无联系,如强生及通用电气。

④ 无关多元化(高度多元化)企业不分享资源或关系,采用无关多元化战略(通常称作混合多元化)的企业有:联合技术公司、三星以及德事隆集团。

restructuring to focus on a less diversified mix of businesses, a move that may reflect:

(1) an inability to manage high levels of diversification.

(2) recognition that a lower level of diversification would improve the match between the firm's core competencies and environmental opportunities and threats.

6.2 Reasons for Diversification[①]

Firms may implement diversification strategies to enhance or increase the strategic competitiveness of the overall organization, and thus the value of the firm increases.

Value can be created through either related or unrelated diversification if the strategies enable the firm's mix of businesses to increase revenues and/or decrease costs when implementing business-level strategies.

Firms may implement diversification strategies that are either value neutral or result in devaluation of the firm. They may attempt to diversify

(1) to neutralize a competitor's market power.

(2) to reduce managers' employment risk (i.e., risk of the CEO being unemployed when a dominant-business firm fails as compared to this risk when a single business fails when it is only one part of a diversified firm).

(3) to increase managerial compensation because of the positive relationships between diversification, firm size, and compensation.

Reasons for Diversification

Firms follow diversification strategies for many reasons. These can be grouped into three broad sets of motives[②]:

Motives to enhance strategic competitiveness[③]:

(1) economies of scope (related diversification) through activity-sharing and the transfer core competencies[④].

(2) market power motives (related diversification) by vertical integration or blocking competitors via multipoint competition[⑤].

(3) financial economies motives (unrelated diversification) to improve efficiency

---

① 多元化的原因。

② 企业采用多元化战略的原因有很多,可以归类为以下三大类动机。

③ 提高战略竞争力的动机。

④ 通过行为资源共享及核心能力转让实现范围经济(相关多元化)。

⑤ 通过纵向一体化或与竞争者多点竞争获得市场支配力(相关多元化)。

of capital allocation through an internal capital market or by restructuring the portfolio of businesses①.

Motives that are value-neutral with respect to strategic competitiveness②:

(1) to avoid violations of antitrust regulations③.

(2) to take advantage of tax incentives④.

(3) to overcome low performance⑤.

(4) to reduce the uncertainty of future cash flows⑥.

(5) to reduce overall firm risk⑦.

(6) to exploit tangible resources⑧.

(7) to exploit intangible resources⑨.

Managerial or value-reduction motives⑩:

(1) to diversify managerial employment risk⑪.

(2) to increase managerial compensation⑫.

Value-creating Strategies of Diversification: Operational and Corporate Relatedness

Firms seek to create value from economies of scope through two basic kinds of operationaleconomies: sharing activities and transferring skills (corporate core competencies). However, the levels of the two of these will lead to different corporate strategies with different advantages associated with each.

6.3 Value-Creating Diversification⑬

Firms implement related diversification strategies in order to achieve and exploit

---

① 金融经济动机(无关多元化)通过内部资本市场或重组业务领域以提高资金划拨的效率。

② 在战略竞争上价值中立的动机。

③ 避免违反反垄断规制。

④ 利用税收优惠。

⑤ 克服低效能。

⑥ 降低未来现金流的不确定性。

⑦ 减少企业的整体风险。

⑧ 开发有形资源。

⑨ 开发无形资源。

⑩ 管理动机或降值动机。

⑪ 增加管理者就业的风险种类。

⑫ 增加管理者薪酬。

⑬ 价值创造多样化。

economies of scope and build a competitive advantage by building on existing resources, capabilities, and core competencies①.

For firms that operate in multiple industries or product markets, economies of scope represent cost savings attributed to entering an additional business and sharing activities or using capabilities and core competencies developed in another business that can be transferred to a new business without significant additional costs②.

The difference between activity sharing and core competence sharing is based on how different resources are used jointly to create economies of scope③:

(1) To create economies of scope, tangible resources, such as plant and equipment or other business-unit physical assets, often must be shared. Less tangible resources, such as manufacturing know-how, also can be shared④.

(2) Know-how transferred between separate activities with no physical or tangible resource involved, is a transfer of a corporate-level core competence, not an operational sharing of activities⑤.

A key to creating value through sharing essentially separate activities is to share know-how or skills rather than physical or tangible resources⑥.

6.4 Diversification⑦

6.4.1 Operational Relatedness⑧

Because all of its businesses share product, technological, and distribution linkages, activity sharing is common among related-constrained diversified firms, such

---

① 企业实施相关的多样化战略,旨在通过在已有资源、能力及核心竞争力的基础上,开发并达成范围经济,建立竞争优势。

② 对于参与多个行业或产品市场的企业而言,投入新的业务、共享行为资源或运用其他业务中发展出来的核心能力导致成本下降,因此企业转向其他业务时,不需要大量的额外成本,便形成了范围经济。

③ 行为资源共享与核心能力共享的差别在于为了创造范围经济,以何种方式整合不同资源。

④ 为了创造范围经济,应共享有形资源,如厂房设备或业务相关的实物资产,无形资源也应共享,如生产技术。

⑤ 不同活动之间的技术转移不涉及实物或有形资源,是公司层核心能力的转移,而非实际的行为资源共享。

⑥ 通过本质不同行为之间的共享来创造价值,关键在于共享技术或技能,而非共享有形或实物资源。

⑦ 多元化。

⑧ 经营层面相关性。

as Procter & Gamble[①].

P&G's paper towel and disposable diaper units can share many activities due to their common characteristics:

(1) Each business uses paper products as a key input, so they are likely to share key facets of procurement and inbound logistics, as well as primary manufacturing activities.

(2) Because all three businesses produce consumer products that are sold in similar (if not the same) outlets, they will likely share outbound logistics, distribution channels, and possibly sales forces.

Recall from the discussion of the primary and support activities in a firm's value chain that primary activities (such as inbound logistics, outbound logistics, and operations) might have several shared activities. Firms that are able to develop core competencies through effective (and efficient) sharing of primary activities will achieve a competitive advantage[②]. Examples of activity sharing may include the following:

(1) Inbound logistics[③]: inventory delivery systems, warehouse facilities, quality assurance.

(2) Operations[④]: assembly facilities, quality control systems, maintenance operations.

(3) Outbound logistics[⑤]: sales force and service management.

(4) Support activities[⑥]: procurement, technology development.

Firms also must recognize that, while activity sharing is intended to reduce costs through achieving economies of scope, there are incremental costs related to sharing activities (costs that are created by sharing). These costs must be recognized and taken into account when planning activity sharing or scope economies may not result[⑦].

Activity sharing can also result in new risks since closer linkages between business units create tighter interrelationships and/or interdependencies[⑧]. For example, if two

---

① 由于其所有业务都共享产品、技术和分销联系,因此在相关多元化公司(如宝洁)中,共享活动很常见。

② 能够通过有效(和高效)分享主要活动来发展核心竞争力的公司将获得竞争优势。

③ 内向物流。

④ 生产操作。

⑤ 外向物流。

⑥ 辅助活动。

⑦ 企业还必须认识到,虽然共享活动旨在通过实现范围经济来降低成本,但与共享活动相关的成本(由共享产生的成本)是递增的。当规划活动共享或范围经济可能无法实现时,必须确认并考虑这些成本。

⑧ 共享活动还可能导致新的风险,因为业务部门之间更紧密的联系会产生更紧密的相互依存关系。

business units share production facilities and sales in one unit's products decline to the point that revenues no longer cover the costs of shared production, then each business unit's ability to achieve strategic competitiveness may be adversely affected.

Regardless of the risks that accompany activity sharing, research indicates that activity sharing—or the potential for activity sharing—can increase the value of the firm. Some findings are summarized here:

(1) Acquiring firms in the same industry—a horizontal acquisition—where sharing of activities and resources is implemented results in improved performance and higher returns to shareholders.

(2) Selling off units where resource sharing is a possible source of economies of scope results in lower returns to shareholders than does selling off business units unrelated to the firm's core business.

(3) Firms with more related units have less risk.

6.4.2 Corporate Relatedness①

Over time, most firms develop intangible resources that can become a foundation for core competencies that are competitively valuable. In diversified firms, these core competencies generally are made up of managerial and technical knowledge, experiences, and expertise.

There are at least two ways the related linked diversification strategy helps firms to create value②:

(1) any costs related to developing the competence have already been incurred.

(2) competencies based on intangible resources, such as marketing know-how, are less visible and therefore are more difficult for competitors to understand and imitate.

Other firms have focused on transferring a variety or resources/capabilities across businesses in their control.

(1) Virgin has transferred its marketing skills across travel, cosmetics, music, drinks, and other retail businesses.

(2) Thermo Electron has employed its entrepreneurial skills in starting up a

---

① 公司层面相关性。

② 相关多元化战略至少通过两种方式帮助企业创造价值:(1) 与发展能力相关的任何费用已经发生(不必额外进行研发投入)。(2) 基于无形资源(如营销诀窍)的能力不那么明显,因此竞争对手更难理解和模仿。

number of new ventures and maintaining a new venture network.

(3) Honda has developed and transferred across its businesses its expertise in small and now larger engines for a number of vehicle types—from motorcycles and lawnmowers to its range of automotive products.

One way that firms can facilitate the transfer of competencies between or among business units is to move key personnel into new management positions in the receiving unit. However, research suggests that transferring expertise often does not lead to performance improvement①.

6.4.3 Market Power②

Firms also may implement related diversification strategies in an attempt to gain market power③.

(1) Market power exists when a firm is able to sell its products at prices above the existing competitive level or decrease the costs of its primary activities below the competitive level, or both.

(2) Market power through diversification may be gained through multipoint competition, a condition where two or more diversified firms compete in the same product areas or geographic markets.

Firms also might gain market power by following a vertical integration strategy, which exists when a company produces its own inputs (backward integration) or owns its own distribution system (forward integration)④.

A vertical integration strategy may be motivated by a firm's desire to strengthen its position in its core business relative to competitors by increasing its market power.

Vertical integration enables a firm to increase market power by:

(1) developing the ability to save on its operations.

(2) avoiding market costs.

(3) improving product quality.

(4) protecting its technology from imitation by rivals.

(5) having strong ties between their assets for which no market prices exist.

---

① 企业促进业务单位之间或业务单位之间能力转移的一种方法是将关键人员调到接收单位的新管理职位。然而,研究表明,专业知识的转移通常不会导致绩效的提高。

② 市场权力(支配力)。

③ 企业也可能实施相关的多元化战略,以获得市场支配力。

④ 企业也可能通过遵循垂直整合战略获得市场支配力,这种战略存在于公司生产自己的投入(后向整合)或拥有自己的分销系统(前向整合)时。

However, like other strategies that create value and aid the firm in achieving strategic competitiveness, vertical integration may not be the perfect answer because of risks and costs that accompany it①.

(1) Outside suppliers may be able to provide inputs at a lower cost (and, possibly also of a higher quality).

(2) The costs of coordinating vertically integrated activities may exceed the value of the control realized.

(3) Vertical integration may result in the firm losing strategic competitiveness if the internal unit does not keep up with changes in technology.

(4) To vertically integrate, the firm may need to build a facility with capacity that exceeds the ability of its internal units to absorb, forcing the selling unit to sell to outside users in order to achieve scale economies.

Many manufacturing firms no longer pursue vertical integration. In fact, deintegration is the focus of most manufacturing firms, such as Intel and Dell, and even among large automobile companies, such as Ford and General Motors, as they develop independent supplier networks. Solectron Corp., a contract manufacturer, represents a new breed of large contract manufacturers that is helping to foster this revolution in supply-chain management. Such firms often manage their customers' entire product lines, and offer services ranging from inventory management to delivery and after-sales service.

E-commerce allows vertical integration to turn into "virtual integration", permitting closer relationships with suppliers and customers through electronic means of integration. This lets firms reduce transaction costs while boosting supply-chain management skills and tightening inventory control. ②

6.5 Unrelated Diversification③

Firms implementing unrelated diversification strategies hope to create value by realizing financial economies, which are cost savings realized through improved

① 然而,与其他创造价值和帮助企业实现战略竞争力的战略一样,垂直整合可能不是完美的答案,因为垂直整合会带来风险和成本。

② 电子商务允许纵向一体化转变为“虚拟一体化”,允许通过电子一体化手段与供应商和客户建立更密切的关系。这让企业在提高供应链管理技能和加强库存控制的同时降低交易成本。

③ 非相关多元化。

allocations of financial resources based on investments inside or outside the firm. [①]

Financial economies are realized through internal capital allocations (that are more efficient than market-based allocations) and by purchasing other companies and then restructuring their assets.

6.5.1 Efficient Internal Capital Market Allocation[②]

Although capital generally is efficiently distributed in a market economy through the capital markets, large diversified firms may be able to distribute capital more efficiently to divisions and thus create value for the overall organization[③]. This generally is possible because:

(1) Corporate offices have more detailed and accurate information on actual division performance and future prospects.

(2) Investors have limited access to internal information and generally can only estimate division performance.

One implication of increased access to information is that the internal capital market may be able to allocate resources between investment opportunities more accurately (and at more adequate levels) than the external capital market. [④] There are several reasons for this:

(1) Information disclosed to capital markets through annual reports may not fully disclose negative information, reporting only positive prospects while meeting all regulatory disclosure requirements.

(2) External capital sources have limited knowledge of what is taking place within large, complex firms.

(3) While owners have access to information, full and complete disclosure is not guaranteed.

(4) An internal capital market may enable the firm to safeguard information related to its sources of competitive advantage that otherwise might have to be disclosed. Through disclosure, the information could become available to competitors

---

① 实施非相关多元化战略的公司希望通过实现财务经济性来创造价值,这是通过基于公司内外投资的财务资源优化配置实现的成本节约。

② 内部资本市场的有效分配。

③ 虽然在市场经济中,资本通常通过资本市场进行有效分配,但大型多元化企业能够更有效地将资本分配给各部门,从而为整个组织创造价值。

④ 增加信息获取的一个含义是,内部资本市场可能比外部资本市场更准确地(在更充分的水平上)在投资机会之间分配资源。

who might use the information to duplicate or imitate the firm's sources of competitive advantage.

Other advantages of internal capital markets:

(1) Corrective actions may be more efficiently structured and underperforming management can be more effectively disciplined through the internal capital market than through external capital market mechanisms. Thus, the internal capital market is more capable of taking specific, finely-tuned corrective actions compared to the external market.

(2) If external intervention is required, only drastic alternatives generally are available, such as forcing the firm into bankruptcy or forcing the removal of top-level managers.

(3) With an internal capital market, the corporate office can adjust managerial incentives or can suggest strategic changes to make the desired corrections.

Research suggests that in efficient capital markets, the unrelated diversification strategy may be discounted. Stock markets have applied what some have called a "conglomerate discount" reflected in the valuation of diversified manufacturing conglomerates at 20 percent less, on average, than the value of the sum of their parts.

The Achilles heel of the unrelated diversification strategy is that conglomerates in developed economies have a fairly short life cycle because financial economies are more easily duplicated than are the gains derived from operational relatedness and corporate relatedness.① This is less of a problem in emerging economies, where the absence of a "soft infrastructure" (e. g., effective financial intermediaries, sound regulations, and contract laws) supports and encourages use of the unrelated diversification strategy. In fact, in emerging economies such as those in India and China, diversification increases performance of firms from large diversified business groups.

6.5.2 Restructuring of Assets②

A restructuring approach to creating value in an unrelated diversified firm involves the buying and selling of other companies (and their assets) in the external market.

Following the asset sale and layoffs, under-performing divisions (those acquired in the purchase) are sold to other firms and remaining divisions are placed under strict

① 非相关多元化战略的致命弱点是,发达经济体的企业集团生命周期相当短,因为金融经济体比运营关联性和公司关联性带来的收益更容易复制。

② 资产重组。

budgetary controls accompanied by the reporting of cash inflows and outflows to the corporate office.

Success in implementing unrelated diversification strategies usually requires that firms[①]:

(1) focus on firms in mature, low technology industries.

(2) avoid service businesses because of their client- or sales-orientation.

6.6 Value-Neutral Diversification[②]

As mentioned earlier, not all firms diversify to increase the value of the overall firm. Some attempts at diversification are implemented to prevent the value of the firm from decreasing.

6.6.1 Incentives to Diversify[③]

In most instances managers have a choice regarding the level of diversification that their firm should implement. In addition, both the external and internal environments are sources of incentives or reasons that managers might use to justify diversification choices.

Antitrust Regulation and Tax Laws[④]

In the 1960s and 1970s, government policies—in the form of antitrust enforcement and tax laws—provided U. S. firms with incentives to diversify the mix of businesses controlled by the firm. As a result of these policies, the vast majority of mergers during the period represented unrelated diversification. They were classified as conglomerate mergers.

Conglomerate mergers (unrelated diversification) were encouraged in large part by the Celler-Kefauver Act which discouraged horizontal and vertical mergers. That is, federal legislation (and enforcement by the U. S. Department of Justice) discouraged market power boosting via related diversification. As one measure of the effectiveness of official "discouragement", almost 80 percent of mergers during the 1973—1977

---

① 成功实施无关多元化战略通常需要公司:(1) 关注成熟、低技术行业的公司。(2) 避免从事服务性企业业务,因为它们以客户或销售为导向。

② 价值中立多元化。

③ 多元化动机。

④ 反垄断法规和税法。

period were conglomerate mergers.

During the 1980s, enforcement of antitrust laws slackened and firms chose to implement horizontal merger strategies (or mergers with firms in the same line of business).

At the same time, investment bankers aggressively promoted merger and acquisition activity to the extent that many acquisitions were classified as unfriendly or as hostile takeovers.

Firms that had diversified (in an unrelated fashion) in the 1960s and 1970s began to implement strategies to refocus their firms, and an era of restructuring began.

When firms generate more cash than they are able to profitably reinvest in the firm's primary activities, the excess funds, or "free cash flows", should be returned to shareholders in the form of dividends. However, during the 1960s and 1970s, dividends were taxed more heavily than ordinary personal income. (Dividends are taxed twice: once when the firm pays taxes on its operating income and a second time when net income is paid out to shareholders in the form of dividends as shareholders pay a tax on dividends received at their personal income tax rate).

In 1986, the perspective shifted once again, as the Tax Reform Act of 1986 reduced the top personal income tax rate from 50 percent to 28 percent. Capital gains rules were changed so that capital gains would be taxed at the ordinary personal income tax rate, and personal interest deductibility was eliminated.

These changes in federal tax laws, which affected individual tax rates for dividends and capital gains (with the former decreasing and the latter increasing), have created an incentive for shareholders to favor reduced levels of diversification (after 1986) unless funded by tax-deductible debt.

The recent changes recommended by the Financial Accounting Standards Board (FASB), regarding the elimination of the "pooling of interests" method for accounting for the acquired firm's assets and the elimination of the write-off for research and development in process, reduce some of the incentives to make acquisitions, especially related acquisitions in high-technology industries.

Although there was a loosening of federal regulations in the 1980s and a retightening in the late 1990s, a number of industries have experienced increased merger activity due to industry-specific deregulation activity, including banking, telecommunications, oil and gas, and electric utilities.

Low Performance

When firms are able to earn above-average or superior returns in a single business, they have little incentive to diversify. However, low performance may provide an incentive for diversification as a low-performing firm may become more risk-seeking in an effort to improve overall firm performance①.

In response to low returns (or poor performance), firms often choose to seek greater levels of diversification. At some point, however, poor performance slows the pace of diversification, often resulting in restructuring divestitures of businesses to lower the level of firm diversification.

The Curvilinear Relationship between Diversification and Performance

In search of even higher performance, related-diversified firms may continue to diversify, but elect to acquire unrelated businesses.

When a firm's core competencies do not create value in unrelated businesses, firm performance decreases.

Daimler Chrysler had to deal with the challenges that were created partly by its failed diversification efforts. The firm faced the task of reversing this strategy, which started with the sale of its electronics operation, divesting a 34 percent stake in Cap Gemini (a French software services company), and liquidating Fokker (a Dutch aircraft manufacturer). The firm also eliminated a layer of upper-level executives and shaped a culture of responsibility and entrepreneurship, with innovation (using cross-functional project teams) as the force supporting the new culture.

Uncertain Future Cash Flows

Firms also may implement diversification strategies when their products reach maturity (in the product life cycle) or are threatened by external factors that the firm cannot overcome. Thus, firms may view diversification as a survival strategy②.

In the 1960s and 1970s, railroads diversified because of the threat from the trucking industry to reduce demand for rail transportation.

Uncertainty can be derived from supply, demand, and distribution sources. ③ For example, at one time PepsiCo acquired Quaker Oats to fortify its growth with Gatorade and healthy snacks, on the projection that these products would experience greater

---

① 当公司能够在一项业务中获得高于平均水平或更高的回报时,他们几乎没有动力进行多元化经营。然而,低绩效可能会催生多元化动机,因为低绩效公司可能会变得更加追求风险,以努力提高公司的整体绩效。

② 当其产品达到成熟期(在产品生命周期内)或受到公司无法克服的外部因素的威胁时,公司也可以实施多元化战略。因此,企业可能将多元化视为一种生存战略。

③ 不确定性来自供应、需求和分销来源。

growth rates than Pepsi's soft drinks.

Uncertainty can derive from supply sources or demand conditions①. ENEL, Italy's state-owned electricity company, has diversified broadly in recent years to cope with anticipated deregulation across Europe, which may mean that ENEL will have to cede 30 percent of its generating capacity to new rivals with cheaper electricity production. Thus, since ENEL's future sources of revenue are threatened, ENEL is using corporate-level diversification to compete in multiple segments of the utility market.

To adapt to decreases in government defense spending in Russia, Reuben Central Design Bureau (the celebrated submarine designer) used a diversification strategy. With its world class design engineers, it continued its marine business while expanding into other areas—e. g., developing a high-speed rail system, a floating sea launch for rocket companies, real estate development, a restaurant chain, and a tea business, among others. The Bureau's diversification strategy has allowed it to survive in the chaotic Russian economic environment.

Synergy and Firm Risk Reduction②

As you will recall from the discussion earlier in this chapter, firms that diversify in pursuit of economies of scope take advantage of linkages between primary value-creating activities to realize synergy from sharing. ③

Synergy exists when the value created by business units working together exceeds the value the units create when working independently.

These linkages—and the inter-relatedness or interdependencies that result—produce joint profitability between business units, and the flexibility of the firm to respond may be constrained, increasing the risk of failure④.

To eliminate this risk, firms may do one of two things⑤:

(1) operate in more certain environments to reduce the level of technological change and choose not to pursue potentially profitable, yet unproven product lines.

(2) constrain or reduce the level of activity-sharing, thus foregoing the potential

---

① 不确定性可能来自供应来源或需求条件。

② 协同效应与企业风险降低。

③ 追求范围经济的多元化企业利用主要价值创造活动之间的联系,实现共享的协同效应。

④ 这些联系以及由此产生的相互关联性或相互依赖性在业务部门之间产生了共同的盈利能力,企业应对的灵活性可能受到限制,从而增加了失败的风险。

⑤ 为了消除这种风险,公司可以做以下两件事之一:(1) 在更特定的环境中运营,以降低技术变革的水平,并选择不追求潜在盈利但未经验证的产品线。(2) 限制或降低共享活动水平,从而放弃协同效应的潜在好处。

benefits of synergy.

However, these decisions could lead to further diversification

(1) to diversify into industries where more certainty exists.

(2) to additional, but unrelated diversification.

Research suggests that a firm using a related diversification strategy is more careful in bidding for new businesses, whereas a firm pursuing an unrelated diversification strategy may be more likely to overprice its bid, because an unrelated bidder may not have full information about the acquired firm. However, firms using either a related or an unrelated diversification strategy must understand the consequences of paying large premiums.

6.6.2 Resources and Diversification[①]

In addition to having incentives to diversify, a firm also must possess the correct mix of resources—tangible, intangible, or financial—that makes diversification feasible. However, remember that resources create value when they are rare, valuable, costly to imitate, and non-substitutable. In other words, resources that do not have these characteristics can be more easily duplicated (or acquired) by competitors. Thus, it may not be possible to create value using such resources.[②]

This implies that acquisitions purchased at market prices using a firm's "free cash flow", such as Anheuser-Busch's purchase of the St. Louis Cardinals baseball team, acquisition of the Campbell Taggart's bakery business, and $400 million investment in the development and operation of Eagle Snacks, were not likely to create value exceeding average returns because of the flexibility (or mobility) and common nature of liquid assets. As a result of poor performance, Anheuser-Busch sold off Campbell Taggart and closed its Eagle Snacks business. However, it continues to use its free cash flows to support some of its other businesses.

The excess capacity of tangible resources may be used to justify diversification, especially when the firm sees opportunities for activity sharing. However, value-creation may be possible only in related diversification. Remember, using tangible resources also creates interrelationships through its activity linkages in production,

---

① 资源与多元化。

② 除了拥有多元化的激励外,企业还必须拥有有形、无形或金融资源的正确组合,使多元化成为可能。然而,请记住,当资源稀有、有价值、模仿成本高且不可替代时,它们就会创造价值。换句话说,不具备这些特征的资源更容易被竞争对手复制(或获得)。因此,使用这些资源可能无法创造价值。

marketing, procurement, and technology, and these interdependencies often reduce firm flexibility and may, in fact, increase the risk of failure.

Ideally, as discussed earlier, a firm's intangible resources—because they are less visible and less understood by competitors—should be used to facilitate and create value from diversification.

6.7 Value-Reducing Diversification: Managerial Motives to Diversify[①]

Some managers may be motivated to diversify their firms even if there are no incentives, and a lack of resources can constrain inclinations toward diversification. Managers' motives for diversification include the following[②]:

(1) Diversification may enable managers to reduce employment risk (the risks related to the loss of their jobs or a reduction in compensation) because by diversifying the firm (i. e., by adding a number of additional businesses), managers may be able to diversify their employment risk, as long as profitability does not decline greatly as a result of the diversification.

(2) Diversification allows managers to increase their compensation because of positive correlations between diversification, firm size, and executive compensation (which is based on the logic that large firms are more difficult to manage).

If properly structured and used, governance structures—such as the firm's board of directors, performance monitoring, executive compensation limits, and the market for corporate control—may provide the means to exert control over managers' tendencies to overdiversify because of self-interest motives.[③]

However, if a firm's internal governance structure is not strong (or functions imperfectly), managers may diversify the firm beyond the optimal level. As a result, the overall firm may fail to earn average returns.

When the internal governance structure fails to restrain managers from over-diversifying (and performance declines), external governance mechanisms, such as

---

① 降低价值多元化:管理人员的多元化动机。

② 管理者支持多元化的动机包括:(1)多元化可使管理者降低就业风险(与失去工作或薪酬降低相关的风险),因为通过企业多元化(即通过增加一些额外的业务),管理者可以分散其就业风险,只要盈利能力不因多元化而大幅下降。(2)由于多元化、公司规模和高管薪酬之间存在正相关关系(基于大公司更难管理的逻辑),多元化允许管理者增加薪酬。

③ 如果结构和使用得当,公司董事会、绩效监控、高管薪酬限额和公司控制权市场等治理结构可能会提供控制管理者因自利动机而过度多元化倾向的手段。

the takeover market, may come into play.

In the takeover market (also known as the market for corporate control), improved levels of diversification (and improved performance) are achieved by replacing incumbent or current managers and restructuring the firm. However, managers may be able to avoid takeovers through defensive tactics, such as golden parachutes, poison pills, greenmail, or increasing the firm's leverage ratio.

In spite of the preceding comments, most managers take positive strategic actions (such as those related to diversification) that result in overall firm profitability and contribute to the strategic competitiveness of the firm.

In addition to the internal and external governance mechanisms discussed, managers also may be provided with incentives to limit firm diversification to optimal levels by a concern for their personal reputations in the labor market and the related market for managerial talent (also known as the market for managers).

One signal that the firm may be overdiversified is when operating diversified businesses reduces, rather than improves, the overall performance of the firm.

Summary Model of the Relationship between Firm Performance and Diversification

A firm's diversification strategy is determined by three inter-related factors,

(1) economies of scope,

(2) resources and incentives,

(3) managerial motives.

In turn, the relationship between diversification strategy and firm performance is moderated by:

(1) external governance mechanisms,

(2) internal governance mechanisms.

The success with which the diversification strategy is implemented.

Diversification strategies can be used to enhance a firm's strategic competitiveness and enable it to earn above-average returns. However, positive outcomes from diversification are possible only when the firm achieves the appropriate level of diversification, given its resources, capabilities, and core competencies, and taking into account the external environmental opportunities and threats. ①

---

① 然而,只有在考虑到公司的资源、能力和核心竞争力,并考虑到外部环境的机会和威胁,达到适当的多元化水平时,多元化才能产生积极的结果。

本章课程思政学习专题

中国民营企业核心能力与多元化战略选择①

1. 中国民营企业多元化战略

改革开放以来,民营企业成为中国经济增长的重要引擎,最新数据表明全国税收的50%、60%的GDP、70%以上的技术创新、80%以上的城镇就业以及90%以上的企业数量来自民营经济,如何确保民营企业的健康发展成了整个国民经济发展的关键。华为、格兰仕、海底捞以及BAT等企业早期聚焦于国内甚至根植于某个行业或区域,最后不断成长为全国性甚至国际知名企业。然而与民营企业的快速崛起并不一致,学术界对其如何进行发展路径选择却知之甚少。现实中既有海底捞、老干妈等走出本地全国经营的企业,也不乏在地市县雄霸一隅多业务经营的"商业帝国"。本研究尝试从发展战略角度诠释中国情境中这些风格迥异的商业模式选择,从更深层次理解民营企业发展甚至中国经济增长的根源和过程。

与国有企业或国外成熟的私营企业相比,大部分年轻的民营企业具有明显的创业期特征。为了克服早期的新生期劣势,国内市场成了最初和最为重要的选择。然而国内不同地区间存在较大的制度差异,面对不同的制度环境和商业机会,选择扎根本地还是采用全国经营的区域多元化战略,以及选择单一产品战略还是多产品发展的产品多元化战略,成了决定民营企业经营范围的首要问题。作为最富有活力和创新精神的市场经济主体,民营企业通常选择研发或政治关联两种核心能力来实现发展。然而对于不同类型多元化战略的影响,以及不同的制度环境如何影响其作用,现有文献却关注较少。传统研究也很少同时考察研发与政治关联能力对于多元化的影响,政治关联往往被视作内部制度环境的一部分而忽视了其内在的核心能力。多元化不仅是产品多元化或国际化代表的区域多元化,内部制度差异较大国家的区域多元化也同等重要。近年来个别国外研究也指出多元化的复杂性远超早期学者的预计,需要重新进行审视,甚至对传统结论提出质疑。

2. 多元化战略选择机理

通过资源观与制度观融合视角,将民营企业发展的政治关联与研发能力之争转向了两者的影响过程和作用情境研究,避免了极端化的刻板归类,认为都是企业发展的必备能力并呈现在不同战略选择之中,两种能力的优劣需要结合所关注的组织结果和作用情境。主要结论包括:第一,民营企业的两种核心能力对于企业不同维度的多元化存在着不同的直接效应。研发能力促进了区域多元化而对

---

① 曾萍,汪金爱,吕迪伟.中国民营企业核心能力与多元化战略选择研究[J].科研管理,2022,43(3):89-98.

产品多元化存在一定的抑制作用,政治关联能力的直接效应并不显著,其作用存在更为复杂的影响机制。第二,民营企业政治关联能力反向调节研发能力对区域和产品多元化的影响,较高的政治关联能力使得企业更加本地化和多产品经营。为了弥补制度风险,获得稀缺资源以便降低市场不确定性,很多民营企业都会通过政治关联能力弥补市场制度的不足。但随着政治关联能力的上升,企业被本地资源所束缚,扎根本土以多产品满足本地不同的消费偏好。第三,随着制度环境的不断成熟,市场化制度削弱了政治关联能力的影响,综合考察时研发促进了区域多元化但却聚焦在较窄的产品线。市场制度在一定程度上保证了民营企业心无旁骛,通过挖掘研发能力赢得全国市场。另外,政治关联能力具有极高的成本和风险,随着中国法治进程的不断完善和反腐行动的深入,一旦政治关联受损,扎根本土的多元化企业可能在多个产品领域都面临着毁灭性风险。

3. 思考问题

中国民营企业多元化战略选择对企业发展有何启示?

Chapter 7 Merger and Acquisition Strategies

Opening Case①

Mergers and Acquisitions Conducted by Lenovo

Lenovo works to integrate the management of each newly acquired company into its larger culture. Lenovo has a dedicated mergers and acquisitions team that tracks the progress of these integrations②. Lenovo has an annual meeting where the management of newly acquired companies meet with its top 100 executives. In these meetings, held in English, Lenovo explains its global strategy and how new executives fit in.

Lenovo acquired IBM's personal computer business in 2005, including the ThinkPad laptop and tablet lines③. Lenovo's acquisition of IBM's personal computer division accelerated access to foreign markets while improving both its branding and technology④. Lenovo paid US $1.25 billion for IBM's computer business and assumed an additional US $500 million of IBM's debt. This acquisition made Lenovo the third-largest computer maker worldwide by volume⑤.

In regards to the purchase of IBM's personal computer division, Liu Chuanzhi said, "We benefited in three ways from the IBM acquisition. We got the ThinkPad brand, IBM's more advanced PC manufacturing technology and the company's international resources, such as its global sales channels and operation teams. These three elements have shored up our sales revenue in the past several years."

IBM acquired an 18.9% shareholding in Lenovo in 2005 as part of Lenovo's purchase of IBM's personal computing division. Since then, IBM has steadily reduced its holdings of Lenovo stock. In July 2008, IBM's interest in Lenovo fell below the 5% threshold that mandates public disclosure.

---

① 课前案例:联想的并购案例。

② 联想尝试将每个新并购公司的管理并入自身版图。联想有专业的并购团队,对整个并入过程进行追踪。

③ 2005 年,联想并购了 IBM 的个人电脑业务,包括 ThinkPad 及平板电脑生产线。

④ 联想并购 IBM 的个人电脑业务,提升了自身品牌形象,改进了技术,同时加快了进入国外市场的进程。

⑤ 联想花费 12.5 亿美元购入 IBM 的个人电脑业务,同时承担了 IBM 5 亿美元的债务。因为此次并购,联想成为全球销量第三的电脑生产商。

IBM's Intel based server lines, including IBM System x and IBM Blade Center were sold to Lenovo in 2014. Lenovo says it will gain access to more enterprise customers, improve its profit margins, and develop a closer relationship with Intel, the maker of most server processors, through its acquisition of IBM's x86-based server business. On 1 October 2014, Lenovo closed its acquisition of IBM's server division, with the final price put at $2.1 billion. Lenovo said this acquisition came in at a price lower than the previously announced $2.3 billion partially because of a change in the value of IBM inventories.

The deal has been already approved by Europe, China and the United States. The US Department of Treasury CFIUS (Committee on Foreign Investment in the United States) was reportedly the last hurdle for Lenovo since the US has the strictest policies. According to Timothy Prickett-Morgan from Enterprise Tech, the deal still awaits "approval of regulators in China, the European Commission, and Canada".

After closing, Lenovo said that its goal was to become the world's largest maker of servers. Lenovo also announced plans to start integrating IBM's workforce. The acquisition added about 6,500 new employees to Lenovo. Lenovo said that it has no immediate intent to cut jobs. Lenovo said that positions in research and development and customer-facing roles such as marketing would be "100% protected" but expected "rationalization" of its supply chain and procurement.

Lenovo said that its x86 servers will be available to all its channel partners. Lenovo plans to cut prices on x86 products in order to gain market share.

Lenovo sold its smartphone and tablet division in 2008 for US $100 million in order to focus on personal computers and then paid US $200 million to buy it back in November 2009. As of 2009, the mobile division ranked third in terms of unit share in China's mobile handset market. Lenovo invested CN ¥100 million in a fund dedicated to providing seed funding for mobile application development for its LeGarden online app store. As of 2010, LeGarden had more than 1,000 programs available for the LePhone. At the same time, LeGarden counted 2,774 individual developers and 542 developer companies as members.

Lenovo entered the smartphone market in 2012 and quickly became the largest vendor of smartphones in Chinese mainland. Entry into the smartphone market was paired with a change of strategy from "the one-size-fits-all" to a diverse portfolio of devices. These changes were driven by the popularity of Apple's iPhone and Lenovo's desire to increase its market share in Chinese mainland. Lenovo passed Apple to become the No. 2 provider of smartphones to the Chinese market in 2012. However, due to there being about 100 smartphone brands sold in China, this second only equated to a 10.4% market share.

In May 2012, Lenovo announced an investment of US $793 million in the construction of a mobile phone manufacturing and R&D facility in Wuhan, China.

NEC

On January 27, 2011, Lenovo formed a joint venture to produce personal computers with Japanese electronics firm NEC. The companies said in a statement that they would establish a new company called Lenovo NEC Holdings, to be registered in the Netherlands. NEC received US $175 million in Lenovo stock. Lenovo was to own a 51% stake in the joint venture, while NEC would have 49%. Lenovo has a five-year option to expand its stake in the joint venture.

This joint venture was intended to boost Lenovo's worldwide sales by expanding its presence in Japan, a key market for personal computers. NEC spun off its personal computer business into the joint venture. As of 2010, NEC controlled about 20% of Japan's market for personal computers while Lenovo had a 5% share. Lenovo and NEC also agreed to explore cooperating in other areas such as servers and tablet computers.

Roderick Lappin, chairman of the Lenovo-NEC joint venture, told the press that the two companies will expand their co-operation to include the development of tablet computers.

In April 2014, Lenovo purchased a portfolio of patents from NEC related to mobile technology. These included over 3,800 patent families in countries around the world. The purchase included standards-essential patents for 3G and LTE cellular technologies and other patents related to smartphones and tablets.

Medion

In June 2011, Lenovo announced that it planned to acquire control of Medion, a German electronics manufacturing company. Lenovo said the acquisition would double its share of the German computer market, making it the third-largest vendor by sales (after Acer and Hewlett-Packard). The deal, which closed in the third quarter of the same year, was the first in which a Chinese company acquired a well-known German company.

This acquisition will give Lenovo 14% of the German computer market. Gerd Brachmann, chairman of Medion, agreed to sell two-thirds of his 60 percent stake in the company. He will be paid in cash for 80 percent of the shares and will receive 20 percent in Lenovo stock. That would give him about one percent of Lenovo.

CCE

In September 2012, Lenovo agreed to acquire the Brazil-based electronics company Digibras, which sells products under the brand-name CCE, for a base price of 300 million reals (US $148 million) in a combination of stock and cash. An additional payment of 400 million reals was made dependent upon performance benchmarks. Prior to its acquisition of CCE, Lenovo already established a $30 million factory in Brazil, but Lenovo's management had felt that they needed a local partner to maximize regional growth. Lenovo cited their desire to take advantage of increased sales due to the 2014 World Cup that would be hosted by Brazil and the 2016 Summer Olympics and CCE's reputation for quality. Following the acquisition, Lenovo announced that its subsequent acquisitions would be concentrated in software and services.

Stoneware

In September 2012, Lenovo agreed to acquire the United States-based software company Stoneware, in its first software acquisition. The transaction was expected to close by the end of 2012; no financial details have been disclosed. Lenovo said that the company was acquired in order to gain access to new technology and that Stoneware is not expected to significantly affect earnings. More specifically, Stoneware was acquired to further Lenovo's efforts to improve and expand its cloud-computing services. For the two years prior to its acquisition, Stoneware partnered with Lenovo to sell its software. During this period Stoneware's sales doubled. Stoneware was founded in 2000. As of September 2012, Stoneware is based in Carmel, Indiana and has 67 employees.

LenovoEMC

Lenovo and EMC formed LenovoEMC as a joint venture to offer network attached storage (NAS) solutions. LenovoEMC's products were formerly offered under the Iomega brand name. After the formation of LenovoEMC, Iomega ceased to exist as business unit. LenovoEMC's products are designed for small and medium-sized that do not have the budgets for enterprise-class data storage. LenovoEMC is part of a broader partnership between the two companies announced in August 2012[①]. This partnership also includes an effort to develop x86-based servers and allowing Lenovo to act as an OEM for some EMC hardware. Lenovo is expected to benefit from the relatively high profit margins of the NAS market. LenovoEMC is part of Lenovo's Enterprise Products Group.

Motorola Mobility

On 29 January 2014, Google announced it would sell Motorola Mobility to Lenovo for US $2.91 billion in a cash-and-stock deal. When Google and Lenovo first announced the acquisition of Motorola, they said the purchase would be funded with $660 million in cash, $750 million in Lenovo stock, and a $1.5 billion promissory note due in three years. As of February 2014, Google owns about 5.94% of Lenovo's stock. The deal includes smartphone lines like the Moto X and Moto G and the Droid Turbo. Lenovo also got the future Motorola Mobility product roadmap. Google will retain the Advanced Technologies & Projects unit and all but 2,000 of the company's patents. Lenovo will receive royalty free licenses to all the patents retained by Google.

Yang Yuanqing stated that "the acquisition of such an iconic brand, innovative product portfolio and incredibly talented global team will immediately make Lenovo a strong global competitor in smartphones". Yang also said, "Don't be scared by the $1 billion-a-year loss. We will improve that even from day one. Google is very good at software, ecosystems and services. But we are stronger in the manufacturing of devices." Yang said that Lenovo would make Motorola profitable within six quarters.

Lenovo has stated that Motorola was purchased in large part due to its long-standing relationships with cellular network operators in the United States and the United Kingdom. Lenovo previously had difficulty breaking into the United Kingdom due to the high proportion of customers who sign contracts and receive phones from carriers. A Lenovo executive said, "There are lots of reasons why we bought Motorola but primarily because it has a history of distribution in the UK. Motorola has long and established relationships with routes to market in North America and the UK, where people are tied to their network operator."

Lenovo received approval from the European Union for its acquisition of Motorola

---

① 联想与易安信(EMC)成立 LenovoEMC,开发网络附加储存(NAS)解决方案。LenovoEMC 的产品过去是以艾美加的品牌销售，LenovoEMC 成立后,艾美加业务部门停止经营。LenovoEMC 的产品定位是没有企业级数据存储预算的中小型企业。2012 年 8 月,联想与易安信宣布开展更广泛合作，LenovoEMC 只是其中一部分。

in June 2014. In a statement the European Union said, "The Commission concluded that the proposed acquisition would not raise competition concerns in relation to smart mobile devices (smartphones and tablets), given the limited market position of the parties and the presence of other strong suppliers in the market." At the time of the EU approval Lenovo said it was on track to win final approval of the merger in the United States.

The acquisition was completed on 30 October 2014. Motorola Mobility will remain headquartered in Chicago, and continue to use the Motorola brand, but Liu Jun—president of Lenovo's mobile device business, became the company's chairman.

Nok Nok Labs

Lenovo invested in Nok Nok Labs, a firm dedicated to improving computer security by eliminating the use of passwords in favor of voice recognition, fingerprint scanning, and other technologies. Lenovo has at least one seat on Nok Nok's board. Both Nok Nok and Lenovo were founding members of the FIDO (Fast IDentity Online) Alliance, a group of over 100 companies including Google, Microsoft and PayPal that wants to create a new cyber security ecosystem. The companies behind the initiative aim to stop users from creating easily guessed passwords, often used for multiple sites, that make it easy for hackers to steal information and seize control of social media accounts. The most common passwords are still "123456" and "password".

Introduction: With continued merger and acquisition activity, this chapter is very important.

The Increased Trend toward Cross-Border Acquisitions

Many firms, not only from developed countries, but also from emerging economies, are increasingly becoming involved in merger and acquisition activities. In the latter half of the twentieth century, acquisition became a prominent strategy used by major corporations to achieve growth and meet competitive challenges. Even smaller and more focused firms began employing acquisition strategies to grow and to enter new markets. However, acquisition strategies are not without problems, as some acquisitions fail.

Interestingly, much of the acquisition activity by European and Japanese firms have been driven by currency valuations, especially relative to the United States, as the dollar is much lower in value than either the euro or the Japanese yen currencies compared to the 1990s. Emerging economies, such as India, have become quite aggressive in overseas transactions as well. India's Tata Group won the bid for British steel maker Corus Group PLC for $13.2 billion.

In summary, the number of cross-border deals continues to increase, leading many emerging-country firms to pursue acquisitions in developed countries, especially in the United States, the United Kingdom, and elsewhere in Europe. These developed economies have more open policies that allow emerging-country economies to make inroads, especially in mature globalizing businesses such as steel and aluminum, or basic services including managing airports and railroads.

In the latter half of the 20th century, acquisition became a prominent strategy used by major corporations to achieve growth and meet competitive challenges. Even smaller and more focused firms began employing acquisition strategies to grow and to enter new markets. However, acquisition strategies are not without problems; a number of acquisitions fail. Thus, the chapter focuses on how acquisitions can be used to produce value for the firm's stakeholders.

7.1 The Popularity of Merger and Acquisition Strategies①

Acquisitions have been a popular strategy among U. S. firms for many years. Some believe that this strategy played a central role in the restructuring of U. S. businesses during the 1980s, 1990s, and into the twenty-first century.

Increasingly, acquisition strategies are becoming more popular with firms in other nations (e. g., those of Europe). In fact, about 40 to 45 percent of the acquisitions in recent years have been made across country borders (i. e., where a firm headquartered in one country acquires a firm headquartered in another country).

Merger and acquisition trends:

(1) There were five waves of mergers and acquisitions in the 20th century, the last two in the 1980s and 1990s.

(2) There were 55,000 acquisitions valued at $1.3 trillion in the 1980s.

(3) Acquisitions in the 1990s exceeded $11 trillion in value.

(4) World economies (especially the U.S. economy) slowed in the new millennium, reducing M&As completed.

(5) Mergers and acquisitions peaked in 2000 at about $3.4 billion and fell to about $1.75 billion in 2001.

(6) The global volume of announced acquisition agreements was up 41 percent

① 并购战略的盛行。

from 2003 to \$1.95 trillion for 2004, the highest level since 2000, and the pace in 2005 was significantly above the level of 2004.

(7) Although the frequency of acquisitions has slowed, their number remains high.

(8) In the latest acquisition boom between 1998 and 2000, acquiring firm shareholders experienced significant losses relative to the losses in all of the 1980s.

A firm may make an acquisition to do the following①:

(1) increase its market power because of a competitive threat②.

(2) enter a new market because of an available opportunity③.

(3) spread the risk due to the uncertain environment④.

(4) shift its core business into more favorable markets (e.g., because of industry or regulatory changes)⑤.

Evidence suggests that at least for acquiring firms, acquisition strategies may not result in desirable outcomes. Studies have found that shareholders of acquired firms often earn above-average returns from an acquisition, while shareholders of acquiring firms are less likely to do so. In approximately two-thirds of all acquisitions, the acquiring firm's stock price falls immediately after the intended transaction is announced, indicating investors' skepticism about the likelihood that the acquirer will be able to achieve the synergies required to justify the premium.

Mergers, Acquisitions, and Takeovers: What Are the Differences?⑥

Before starting the discussion of the reasons for acquisitions, problems related to acquisitions, and long-term performance, three terms should be defined because they will be used throughout this chapter and Chapter 10.

A merger is a transaction where two firms agree to integrate their operations on a relatively co-equal basis because they have resources and capabilities that together may create a stronger competitive advantage⑦.

An acquisition is a transaction where one firm buys a controlling or 100 percent interest in another firm with the intent of making the acquired firm a subsidiary

---

① 企业进行并购,可能是为了——

② 增加市场支配力,从而避免市场威胁。

③ 获得新机会,进入新市场。

④ 分摊不确定环境的风险。

⑤ 将核心业务转移至利好市场(行业或政策变化所致)。

⑥ 合并、收购、接管:有何区别?

⑦ 合并是指两个企业的能力和资源合并后,可以产生更大的竞争优势,因此在相对平等的基础上,将双方业务合并。

business within its portfolio①.

While most mergers represent friendly agreements between the two firms, acquisitions sometimes can be classified as unfriendly takeovers②. A takeover is an acquisition—and normally not a merger—where the target firm did not solicit the bid of the acquiring firm and often resists the acquisition (a hostile takeover)③.

7.2 Reasons for Acquisitions④

Oracle, SAP, and Microsoft compete in the database management software arena. SAP holds approximately 22 percent of the market share while Oracle and Microsoft each hold 10 and 5 percent respectively. Competitive intensity between these three players is becoming more intense as they target customer firms that have not integrated their firms' business units using databases. Once a software provider is selected by a targeted firm, it becomes relatively costly for that firm to switch to another platform. Because of these significant switching costs, Oracle is utilizing a horizontal acquisition strategy in order to pursue growth. The logic applied is that each acquisition has an established customer-base that will likely be retained because of the high switching costs incurred to switch platforms. In addition, the products offered by the acquired firm's sales force will be expanded to include Oracle's catalog, and Oracle's sales staff will have an expanded catalog to offer current Oracle customers.

Oracle's acquisition strategy began when Oracle's CEO, Larry Ellison, decided that the corporate-software industry had matured and needed consolidation. A series of acquisitions led to Oracle's 50 percent revenue increase to \$17.7 billion in the fiscal year ending May 2007. The acquisitions also enabled Oracle to develop a refined set of industry focuses with applications in retail, financial services, utilities, communications, and government service.

In addition, Oracle acquired three organizations specializing in retail software. These acquisitions allowed Oracle to win thirty new retail customers in 2006 and 2007, including Auchan, Nordstrom, and Perry Ellis International. Perry Ellis International expects to save more than \$20 million a year in improved just-in-time inventory

---

① 收购指一家企业购入另一家公司的全部或大部分股份,并将其转变为成自己的子公司。

② 在大多数的合并中,企业之间是友好协商关系;但有时,收购则可被归为不友好的接管。

③ 接管是收购(通常不是合并)的一种,目标公司并非主动选择被收购,常常反对收购(即恶意接管)。

④ 进行收购的原因。

controls, improved merchandising efficiency, and software that helps to adapts its pricing by store and region efficiently through the application of the newly integrated Oracle software applications.

Comparatively, SAP is ahead in specific industry applications. It has applications in twenty-six industries compared to Oracle's five. Also, beyond large corporations in specific industries, both companies are pursuing growth in small- to medium-sized enterprises.

In a vertical merger, CVS Corporation, a drugstore chain, purchased pharmacy-benefits manager (PBM) Caremark RX, Inc., for \$21 billion in 2007. The combined company will have \$75 billion in annual sales, far higher than any other competitor, including Walgreens and comparable PBMs such as Medco Health. In this vertical acquisition CVS is purchasing a powerful customer that negotiates on behalf of large companies and their health insurance providers. One of the incentives for this vertical merger is that PBMs have put pressure on drugstores by negotiating prices on behalf of their clients and forcing firms into mail-order plans for prescription drugs. The merger will help CVS obtain large deals with big companies by offering significant discounts to employees for CVS private-label products. When Auchan began charging much lower prices for generic drugs in many of their stores, drugstores and PBM firms felt additional pressure for mergers. Walgreens, a large competitor of CVS, also plans to increase its PMB business, but it has not signaled whether it will use an acquisition process.

Students should be able to differentiate between horizontal and vertical acquisitions and the reasons for each. The above examples of both vertical and horizontal acquisitions are well explained. You may want to defer discussion of this article until you visit the later one on DaimlerChrysler. The above acquisitions have achieved operational and financial goals. The DaimlerChrysler merger did not achieve intended goals and can be considered a failure. Perceived synergies never came to fruition, and differences in markets were too great to overcome. How did Oracle, SAP, and CVS overcome these common snags?

7.2.1 Increased Market Power①

A primary reason for acquisitions is that they enable firms to gain greater market power. Acquisitions to meet a market power objective generally involve buying a

① 提升市场支配力。

supplier, a competitor, a distributor, or a business in a highly related industry.

While a number of firms may feel that they have an internal core competence, they may be unable to exploit their resources and capabilities because of a lack of size.①

Horizontal Acquisitions②

When a competitor in the same industry is acquired, a firm has engaged in a horizontal acquisition. Horizontal acquisitions increase a firm's market power by exploiting cost-based and revenue-based synergies③.

Research suggests that horizontal acquisitions of firms with similar characteristics result in higher performance than when firms with dissimilar characteristics combine their operations. Examples of important similar characteristics include strategy, managerial styles, and resource allocation patterns.

Horizontal acquisitions are often most effective when the acquiring firm integrates the acquired firm's assets with its assets, but only after evaluating and divesting excess capacity and assets that do not complement the newly combined firm's core competencies.

Vertical Acquisitions④

A vertical acquisition has occurred when a firm acquires a supplier or distributor, which is positioned either backward or forward in the firm's cost/activity/value chain⑤.

Related Acquisitions⑥

When a target firm in a highly related industry is acquired, the firm has made a related acquisition⑦.

During the 1960s and 1970s, both horizontal and related acquisitions were discouraged as they were regularly challenged by agencies of the federal government. The ability of firms to make horizontal acquisitions increased in the 1980s because of

---

① 许多企业认为自身具有核心能力,但由于规模限制而无法开发资源与能力。

② 横向收购。

③ 企业收购行业中的竞争对手,便称为横向收购。通过开发成本及收益的协同效应,横向收购可提高企业的市场支配能力。

④ 纵向收购。

⑤ 企业收购位于其成本链(或行为链、价值链)前端或后端的供货商或经销商,称为纵向收购。

⑥ 相关收购。

⑦ 收购目标是行业高度相关企业的,称为相关收购。

changes in the interpretation and enforcement of anti-trust laws and regulations by the courts and the Justice Department.

It is important to note that acquisitions intended to increase market power are subject to regulatory review, as well as to analysis by financial markets.

7.2.2 Overcoming Entry Barriers①

Barriers to entry represent factors associated with the market and/or firms operating in the market that make it more expensive and difficult for new firms to enter the market.

It may be difficult to enter a market dominated by large, established competitors. Such markets may require:

(1) investments in large-scale manufacturing facilities that enable the firm to achieve economies of scale so that it can offer competitive prices.

(2) significant expenditures in advertising and promotion to overcome brand loyalty toward existing products.

(3) establishing or breaking into existing distribution channels so that goods are convenient to customers.

When barriers to entry are present, the firm's best choice may be to acquire a firm already having a presence in the industry or market. In fact, the higher the barriers to entry into an attractive market or industry, the more likely it is that firms interested in entering will follow acquisition strategies②.

Entry barriers firms face when trying to enter international markets are often great. Commonly, acquisitions are used to overcome entry barriers in international markets. It is important to compete successfully in these markets since global markets are growing faster than domestic markets③. Also, five of the emerging markets (China, India, Brazil, Mexico, and Indonesia) are among the fastest growing economies in the world.

Cross-Border Acquisitions④

Acquisitions between companies with headquarters in different countries are called

---

① 克服进入壁垒。

② 出现进入壁垒时,企业的最优选择是收购已经进入行业或市场的企业。实际上,进入吸引力市场遇到的壁垒越大,企业选择收购策略的可能性越高。

③ 企业进入国际市场时通常遇到巨大的壁垒。一般情况下,企业利用收购来消除国际市场上的进入壁垒。国际市场比国内市场的发展速度快,因此,在国际市场竞争成功很重要。

④ 跨境收购。

cross-border acquisitions①.

Historically, U. S. firms have been the most active acquirers of companies outside their domestic market. However, in the global economy, companies throughout the world are choosing this strategic option with increasing frequency. In recent years, cross-border acquisitions have represented as much as 40 percent of the total number of acquisitions made annually.

Some trends in cross-border acquisitions②:

(1) Because of relaxed regulations, the amount of cross-border activity among nations within the European community also continues to increase③.

(2) Many large European corporations have approached the limits of growth within their domestic markets and thus seek growth in other markets④.

(3) Many European and U. S. firms participated in cross-border acquisitions across Asian countries that experienced a financial crisis due to significant currency devaluations in 1997, and this facilitated the survival and restructuring of many large Asian companies such that these economies recovered more quickly than they would have otherwise⑤.

Acquisitions represent a viable strategy for firms that wish to enter international markets because these:

(1) may be the fastest way to enter new markets.

(2) provide more control over foreign operations than do strategic alliances with a foreign partner.

7.2.3 Cost of New Product Development and Increased Speed to Market⑥

Acquisitions also may represent an attractive alternative to developing new products internally because of the cost and time required to start a new venture and achieve a positive return.

Also of concern to firms' managers is achieving adequate returns from the capital

---

① 收购对象总部设在不同国家的，称为跨国收购。

② 跨国收购新趋势。

③ 由于政策宽松，欧共体国家之间的跨国收购行为将持续增长。

④ 欧洲许多大型企业在国内市场已达发展极限，因此寻求其他的市场发展。

⑤ 1997 年，亚洲国家由于货币贬值严重，发生金融危机，许多欧洲及美国企业跨国收购了亚洲企业，亚洲许多大型企业因此得以重组生存，经济恢复比不接受收购快得多。

⑥ 新产品开发成本和上市速度的加快。

invested to develop and commercialize new products—an estimated 88 percent of innovations fail to achieve adequate returns. Perhaps contributing to these less-than-desirable rates of return is the successful imitation of approximately 60 percent of innovations within four years after the patents are obtained. Because of outcomes such as these, managers often perceive internal product development as a high-risk activity.

Internal development of new products is often perceived by managers to be costly and to represent high risk investments of firm resources. While sometimes costly, it may be in the firm's best interest to acquire an existing business because of the following[①]:

(1) The acquired firm has established sales volume and customer base, thus yielding predictable returns[②].

(2) The acquiring firm gains immediate market access[③].

In addition to representing attractive prices, large pharmaceutical firms have used acquisitions to supplement products in the pipeline with projects from undervalued biotechnology companies; thus, this is one way to appropriate new products.

7.2.4 Lower Risk Compared to Developing New Products[④]

As discussed earlier, internal product development processes can be risky, in that entering a market and earning an acceptable return on investment requires significant resources and time. All the same, acquisition outcomes can be estimated easily and accurately (as compared to the outcomes of an internal product development process), causing managers to view acquisitions as carrying lowering risk.

Not long ago, P&G acquired premium dog and cat food manufacturer Iams Co. to support the launch of its pet products into supermarket chains and mass merchandisers such as Auchan. Having assessed the potential of Iams in the marketplace, P&G managers were confident they would achieve positive results through their strategy; thus, they may have considered entry into the premium pet-food market through acquisition to be less risky than entering the market via internal product development.

Because acquisitions recently have become such a common means of avoiding risky internal ventures, they could become a substitute for innovation, which has a

---

① 有时,收购已有业务的成本虽然高,但符合企业的最高利益,原因如下。

② 目标企业已建立销售规模及客户群,因此会产生可预测回报。

③ 收购企业可立刻获得市场准入。

④ 与开发新产品相比,风险更低。

serious downside (e. g. , the decline of Cisco systems).

Although they often enable firms to offset the risk of internal ventures and of developing new products, acquisitions are not without risks of their own. Acquisition-related risks will be discussed later in this chapter.

7.2.5 Increased Diversification①

It should be easier for firms to develop new products and/or new ventures within their current markets because of market-related knowledge, but firms that desire to enter new markets may find that current product-market knowledge and skills are not transferable to the new target market.

Acquisitions also may have gained in popularity as a related or horizontal diversification strategy (enabling rapid moves into related markets, or to expand market power) and as an unrelated diversification strategy because of the changes in regulatory interpretation and enforcement of anti-trust laws discussed in Chapter 6.

Using acquisitions to diversify a firm is the quickest and often the easiest way to change its portfolio of businesses—e. g. ,Goodrich evolved from a tire maker to a top-tier aerospace supplier through 40 + acquisitions.

Firms must be careful when making acquisitions to diversify their product lines because horizontal and related acquisitions tend to contribute more to strategic competitiveness, and thus they are more successful than diversifying acquisitions.

Remember, related diversification seeks lower costs through economies of scope, synergy, and resource sharing, while unrelated diversification hopes to realize financial economies and better internal resource allocation among diverse businesses.

7.2.6 Reshaping the Firm's Competitive Scope②

To reduce intense rivalry's negative effect on financial performance, a firm may use acquisitions as a way to restrict its dependence on a single or a few products or markets.

The following are examples of auto manufacturers that have gone through acquisitions to reduce dependence of too few businesses:

(1) General Motors acquired Electronic Data Systems and Hughes Aerospace to lessen its dependence on the domestic automobile market (where its market share had

---

① 提高多元化程度。
② 重塑企业的竞争范畴。

declined from approximately 50 percent in 1980 to less than 30 percent 10 years later) and escape intense competition with Japanese automakers. However, GM later sold these businesses to focus its efforts on its core automobile business.

(2) DaimlerChrysler considered expanding into financial and computer services, aftermarket sales, and electronics and satellite systems to pursue more desirable operating margins in areas that are more attractive than are alliances or acquisitions in car manufacturing.

(3) Ford management considered making the company the world's leading consumer services business that specializes in the automotive sector by tapping all sectors in after-sales markets, including repairs, replacement parts, and product servicing. To evaluate its success in reshaping the firm's competitive scope through diversification, Ford would measure its performance against world-class consumer firms, regardless of industry (i. e., rather than using the traditional yardsticks of rival automakers).

7.2.7 Learning and Developing New Capabilities[①]

Some acquisitions are made to gain capabilities that the firm does not possess—e. g., acquisitions used to acquire a special technological capability. Acquiring other firms with skills and capabilities that differ from its own helps the acquiring firm to learn new knowledge and remain agile, but firms are better able to learn these capabilities if they share some similar properties with the firm's current capabilities.[②]

One of Cisco System's primary goals in its early acquisitions was to gain access to capabilities that it did not currently possess through its commitment to learning. The firm developed an intricate process to quickly integrate the acquired firms and their capabilities (knowledge) after an acquisition is completed.

Reasons for Acquisitions and Problems in Achieving Success

To summarize, the seven reasons that firms (and managers) implement acquisition strategies are to:

(1) increase market power,

(2) overcome entry barriers,

---

① 学习并发展新能力。

② 一些收购是为了获得公司不具备的能力,例如,用于获得特殊技术能力的收购。收购具有不同于自身技能和能力的其他公司有助于收购公司学习新知识并保持灵活性,但如果这些公司与公司当前的能力有一些相似的特性,那么它们能够更好地学习这些能力。

(3) reduce the cost of new product development and increase speed to market,

(4) lower risk compared to developing new products,

(5) increase diversification,

(6) avoid excessive competition,

(7) learn and develop new capabilities.

The seven reasons for poor performance of acquisitions or problems faced in attempts to achieve success are:

(1) integration difficulties,

(2) inadequate evaluation of target,

(3) large or extraordinary debt,

(4) inability to achieve synergy,

(5) too much diversification,

(6) managers overly focused on acquisitions,

(7) too large.

7.3 Problems in Achieving Acquisition Success①

Research suggests that perhaps 20 percent of all mergers and acquisitions are successful, approximately 60 percent produce disappointing results, and the last 20 percent are clear failures. Successful acquisitions generally involve a well-conceived strategy in selecting the target, the avoidance of paying too high a premium, and employing an effective integration process.

A number of problems accompany an acquisition strategy. Acquisition-related problems will be discussed in this section are:

(1) difficulties in integrating the two firms after the acquisition is completed.

(2) paying too much for the target (acquired) firm or inappropriately or inadequately evaluating the target.

(3) the cost of financing the acquisition, related to large or extraordinary debt.

(4) overestimating the potential for gains from capabilities and/or synergy.

(5) excessive or too much diversification.

(6) management being preoccupied or overly focused on acquisitions.

(7) the combined firm becoming too large.

① 成功并购的障碍。

7.3.1 Integration Difficulties[①]

Integration problems or difficulties that firms often encounter can take many forms. Among them are:

(1) melding disparate corporate cultures,

(2) linking different financial and control systems,

(3) building effective working relationships (especially when management styles differ),

(4) problems related to differing status of acquired and acquiring firms' executives.

The importance of integration success should not be underestimated. Without successful integration, a firm achieves financial diversification, but little else[②]. Consider these points.

(1) The post-acquisition integration phase may be the single most important determinant of shareholder value creation (or value destruction) in mergers and acquisitions.

(2) Managers should understand the large number of activities associated with integration processes.

Several years ago, Intel acquired Digital Equipment's semiconductors division. On the day Intel began to integrate the acquired division into its operations, six thousand deliverables were to be completed by hundreds of employees working in dozens of countries.

It is important to maintain the human capital of the target firm after the acquisition to preserve the organization's knowledge. Turnover of key personnel from the acquired firm can have a negative effect on the performance of the merged firm.

Following are some example of firms and the steps they took to preserve human capital through the acquisition process.

(1) When AllliedSignal acquired Honeywell, the firm set an aggressive timetable to merge their operations into a $24 billion industrial powerhouse in six months, despite the great diversification involved. This required a team to develop and implement the integration.

---

① 整合困难。

② 不应低估整合成功的重要性。如果没有成功的整合,一家公司只能实现财务多元化,而其他的方面几乎没有变化。

(2) Rapid integration is one of the guidelines that DaimlerChrysler uses for successful firm integration in a global merger or acquisition. Managers are encouraged to deal with unpopular issues immediately and honestly so employees will be able to anticipate the effects the integration is likely to have on them.

(3) Cisco Systems is quick to integrate acquisitions with its existing operations. Focusing on small companies with products and services related closely to its own, some believe that the day after Cisco acquires a firm, employees in that company feel as though they have been working for Cisco for decades.

7.3.2 Inadequate Evaluation of Target①

Due diligence is a process through which a firm evaluates a target firm for acquisition. In an effective due-diligence process hundreds of items are examined in areas as diverse as the financing for the intended transaction, differences in cultures between the acquiring and target firm, tax consequences of the transaction, and actions that would be necessary to successfully meld the two workforces.

Due diligence is commonly performed by investment bankers, accountants, lawyers, and management consultants specializing in that activity, although firms actively pursuing acquisitions may form their own internal due-diligence team.

For the reasons below, firms often pay too much for acquired businesses:

(1) Acquiring firms may not thoroughly analyze the target firm, failing to develop adequate knowledge of its true market value.

(2) Managers' overconfidence may cloud the judgment of acquiring firm managers.

(3) Shareholders (owners) of the target must be enticed to sell their stock, and this usually requires that acquiring firms pay a premium over the current stock price.

(4) In some instances, two or more firms may be interested in acquiring the same target firm. When this happens, a bidding war often ensues and extraordinarily high premiums may be required to purchase the target firm.

Some acquirers over-paying for target firms include the following:

(1) British retailer Marks & Spencer paid $750 million for Brooks Brothers of the United States, but the acquisition was still unsuccessful after more than ten years of integration.

(2) Sony paid a 28 percent premium for CBS Records and a 60 percent premium

① 目标评价不充分。

for Columbia Pictures.

(3) Bridgestone paid a 60 percent premium for Firestone, and its winning bid was 38 percent higher than a competing bid from Pirelli.

(4) National City Corporation agreed to acquire First of America for a price that was 3.8 times book value and 22.9 times First's estimated 1998 earnings—National City's stock fell 5.9 percent.

(5) First Union Corp. paid 5.3 times book value when it acquired CoreStates Financial Corp.

(6) Federated paid \$10 per share for Broadway Department Stores when Broadway's stock was selling for \$2 per share, a 400 percent premium in a transaction valued at \$1.6 billion to acquire Broadway's prime West Coast real estate locations.

An example of effective due diligence was DaimlerChrysler's 1999 decision not to acquire NissanMotor Company. DaimlerChrysler wanted Nissan to expand its access to global auto markets, especially those in Southeast Asia. But the target had \$22 billion in debt, which caused concern among DaimlerChrysler executives and derailed the acquisition.

7.3.3 Large or Extraordinary Debt①

In addition to overpaying for targets, many acquirers must finance acquisitions with relatively high-cost debt②.

In the 1980s, investment bankers developed a new financing instrument for acquisitions, the junk bond. Junk bonds represented a new financing option in which risky investments were financed with money (debt) that provided a high return to lenders (bond holders). Junk bonds offer relatively high rates, some as high as 18 to 20 percent during the 1980s.

Junk bonds are considered by many to be a new financing option, not because they are new, but because they represented the first instances in which non-investment grade (below a B rating) securities were used to raise funds by companies whose securities were normally rated as investment grade.

A number of well-known and well-respected finance scholars argue in favor of firms utilizing significantly high levels of leverage because debt discourages managers from misusing funds (for example, by making bad investments) because debt (and

① 巨额或特别的债务。

② 除了为目标支付过高的价格外,许多收购方还必须为债务成本相对较高的收购提供融资。

interest) repayment eliminates the firm's "free cash flow."

7.3.4 Inability to Achieve Synergy①

Acquiring firms also face the challenge of correctly identifying and valuing any synergies that are expected to be realized from the acquisition. This is a significant problem because, to justify the premium price paid for target firms, managers may overestimate both the benefits and value of synergy②.

To achieve a sustained competitive advantage through an acquisition, acquirers must realize private synergies and core competencies that cannot easily be imitated by competitors. Private synergy refers to the benefit from merging the acquiring and target firms that is due to the unique assets that are complementary between the two firms and not available to other potential bidders for that target firm.

As pointed out earlier, the average return to acquiring firm shareholders is near zero, and many of these lead to negative returns for acquiring firm shareholders.

Firms experience transaction costs when using acquisition strategies to create synergy. Direct costs include legal fees and charges from investment bankers. Managerial time to evaluate target firms and then to complete negotiations and the loss of key managers and employees post-acquisition are indirect costs.

7.3.5 Too Much Diversification③

In general, firms using related diversification strategies outperform those using unrelated diversification strategies. However, conglomerates (i. e., those pursuing unrelated diversification) can also be successful.

In the drive to diversify the firm's product line, many firmsoverdiversified during the 60 s, 70 s, and 80 s.

Information processing requirements are greater for a related diversified firm (compared to its unrelated counterparts) due to its need to efficiently coordinate the linkages and interdependencies upon which value-creation through activity sharing depends④.

---

① 无法实现协同。

② 收购公司还面临着正确识别和评估预期从收购中实现的任何协同效应的挑战。这是一个重大问题,因为为了证明为目标公司支付的溢价是合理的,管理者可能高估了协同效应的好处和价值。

③ 多样化程度过高。

④ 对于相关多元化公司(与无关多元化公司相比)来说,信息处理要求更高,因为它需要有效地协调通过活动共享创造价值所依赖的联系和相互依赖关系。

In addition to increased information processing requirements and managerial expertise, overdiversification may result in poor performance when top-level managers emphasize financial controls over strategic controls.

Financial controls may be emphasized when managers feel that they do not have sufficient expertise or knowledge of the firm's various businesses. When this happens, top-level managers are not able to adequately evaluate the strategies and strategic actions that are taken by division or business unit managers. As a result,

(1) When they lack a rich understanding of business units' strategies and objectives, top-level managers tend to emphasize the financial outcomes of strategic actions rather than the appropriateness of the strategy itself.

(2) This forces division or business unit managers to become short-term performance-oriented.

(3) The problem is more serious when manager compensation is tied to short-term financial outcomes.

(4) Long-term, risky investments (such as R&D) may be reduced to boost short-term returns.

(5) In the final analysis, long-term performance deteriorates.

Acquisitions can have a number of negative effects. They may result in greater levels of diversification (in products, markets, and/or industries), absorb extensive managerial time andenergy, require large amounts of debt, and create larger organizations. As a result, acquisitions can have a negative impact on investments in research and development and thus on innovation. ①

Reducing the emphasis on R&D and on innovation may result in the firm losing its strategic competitiveness unless the firm operates in mature industries in which innovation is not required to maintain competitiveness.

7.3.6 Managers Overly Focused on Acquisitions②

If firms follow active acquisition strategies, the acquisition process generally requires significant amounts of managerial time and energy.

For the acquiring firm this takes the form of:

① 收购可能会产生一些负面影响。它们可能导致更大程度的多样化(在产品、市场和/或行业方面),耗费大量管理时间和精力,需要大量债务,并创建更大的组织。因此,收购可能会对研发投资产生负面影响,从而对创新产生负面影响。

② 管理者过度关注收购。

(1) searching for viable candidates.

(2) completing effective due diligence.

(3) preparing for negotiations with the target firm.

(4) managing the integration process post-acquisition.

The desire to merge is like an addiction in many companies: Doing deals is much more fun and interesting than fixing fundamental business problems.

Due diligence and negotiating with the target often include numerous meetings between representatives of the acquirer and target, as well as meetings with investment bankers, analysts, attorneys, and in some cases, regulatory agencies. As a result, top-level managers of acquiring firms often pay little attention to long-term, strategic matters because of time (and energy) constraints.

7.3.7 Too Large Scale[①]

Firms can reach economies of scale by growing. But, after a certain size is achieved, size can become a disadvantage as firms reach a point where they suffer from what is called "diseconomies of scale". This implies that problems related to excess growth may be similar to those that accompany overdiversification.[②]

Other actions taken to enable more effective management of increased firm size include increasing or establishing bureaucratic controls, represented by formalized supervisory and behavioral controls such as rules and policies that are designed to ensure consistency across different units' decisions and actions.

On the surface (or in theory), bureaucratic controls may be beneficial to large organizations. However, they may produce overly-rigid and standardized behavior among managers. The reduced managerial (and firm) flexibility can result in reduced levels of innovation and less creative (and less timely) decision making.

7.4 Effective Acquisitions

Research has identified attributes that appear to be associated consistently with successful acquisitions:

(1) when a firm's assets are complementary (highly related) with the acquired

---

① 规模过大。

② 企业可以通过增长达到规模经济。但是，当企业达到一定规模后，规模可能会成为一个劣势，因为企业会遭受所谓的"规模不经济"。这意味着与过度生长相关的问题可能与过度分化相关的问题相似。

firm's assets and create synergy and, in turn, unique capabilities, core competencies, and strategic competitiveness.

(2) when targets were selected and "groomed" through earlier working relationships (e.g., strategic alliances).

(3) when the acquisition is friendly, thereby reducing animosity and turnover of key employees.

(4) when the acquiring firm has conducted due diligence.

(5) when management is focused on research and development.

(6) when acquiring and target firms are flexible/adaptable (e.g., from executive experience with acquisitions).

(7) when integration quickly produces the desired synergy in the newly created firm, allowing the acquiring firm to keep valuable human resources in the acquired firm from leaving.

Attributes of Successful Acquisitions

Successful acquisitions generally are characterized by the following attributes and results:

(1) target and acquirer having complimentary assets and/or resources which results in a high probability of achieving synergy and gaining competitive advantage.

(2) making friendly acquisitions to facilitate integration speed and effectiveness and reducing any acquisition premium.

(3) target selection and negotiation processes which result in the selection of targets having resources and assets that are complimentary to the acquiring firm's core business, thus avoiding overpayment.

(4) maintaining financial slack to make acquisition financing less costly and easier to obtain.

(5) maintaining a low to moderate debt position which lowers costs and avoids the trade-offs of high debt and lowers the risk of failure.

(6) possessing flexibility and skills to adapt to change to facilitate integration speed and achievement of synergy.

(7) continuing to invest in R&D and emphasizing innovation to maintain competitive advantage.

7.5 Restructuring[①]

Restructuring refers to changes in the composition of a firm's set of businesses and/or financial structure.

From the 1970s into the 2000s, divesting businesses from company portfolios and downsizing accounted for a large percentage of firms' restructuring strategies. Restructuring is a global phenomenon.

During this period, restructuring can take several forms:

(1) downsizing, primarily to reduce costs by laying off employees or eliminating operating units.

(2) downscoping to reduce the level of firm unrelatedness.

(3) leveraged buyouts to restructure the firm's assets by taking it private.

Sometimes firms use a restructuring strategy because of changes in their external and internal environments. For example, opportunities sometimes surface in the external environment that are particularly attractive to the diversified firm in light of its core competencies. In such cases, restructuring may be appropriate.

7.5.1 Downsizing[②]

Once thought to be an indicator of organizational decline, downsizing is now recognized as a legitimate restructuring strategy and has been one of the most common restructuring strategies adopted by U. S. firms.

Downsizing represents a reduction in the number of employees, and sometimes in the number of operating units, but may or may not represent a change in the composition of the businesses in the firm's portfolio[③].

In the late 1980s, early 1990s, and early 2000s, thousands of jobs were lost in private and public organizations in the United States. One study estimates that 85 percent of Fortune 1000 firms have used downsizing as a restructuring strategy. Moreover, Fortune 500 firms terminated more than one million employees, or 4 percent of their collective workforce, in 2001 and into the first few weeks of 2002. This trend

---

① 重组。

② 裁员。

③ 裁员意味着减少一些雇员数量，有时减少一些运营单位，但并不一定表示企业的投资组合会发生变化。

continued in many industries. For instance, in 2007, Citigroup signaled that it cut 15,000 jobs and up to five percent of its workforce over time, in the process taking a $1 billion charge.

Firms use downsizing as a restructuring strategy for different reasons. The most frequently cited reason is that the firm expects improved profitability from cost reductions and more efficient operations.

Downscoping①

Compared to downsizing, downscoping has a more positive effect on firm performance.

Downscoping refers to the divestiture, spin-off, or other means of eliminating businesses that are unrelated to the firm's core business. In other words, downscoping refocuses the firm on its core businesses②.

While downscoping often includes downsizing, the former is targeted so that the firm does not lose key employees from core businesses (because such losses can lead to the loss of core competencies)③.

As indicated by the discussion ofoverdiversification earlier in the chapter, reducing the diversity of businesses in the portfolio enables top-level managers to manage the firm more effectively because

(1) the firm is less diversified as a result of downscoping.

(2) top-level managers can better understand the core and related businesses.

There are many examples of downscoping strategies. Two of these with which the students are likely to be familiar are the following:

(1) General Motors' successful spin-off of EDS.

(2) PepsiCo's spin-off of its fast-food businesses (e. g. , Taco Bell, Pizza Hut, & KFC).

U. S. firms use downscoping as a restructuring strategy more frequently than do European companies. However, there has also been an increase in downscoping by Asian and Latin American firms as they adopt Western business practices.

Research has shown that refocusing is not usually successful unless the firm has

---

① 缩小范围。

② 缩小范围指的是转让、剥离资产或其他对企业非核心业务的减少。换句话说,缩小范围使企业重新聚焦在它的核心业务身上。

③ 缩小范围通常包含了裁员。前者是最终目标,因而在裁员时企业不会流失掉核心业务中的关键员工(因为这些员工的流失会带来核心竞争力的下降)。

adequate resources to have the flexibility to formulate the necessary strategies to compete effectively.

7.5.2 Leveraged Buyouts[①]

A leveraged buyout (LBO) refers to a restructuring action, whereby the management of the firm and/or an external party buys all of the assets of the business, largely financed with debt, and thus takes the firm private[②].

Often, LBOs are used as a restructuring strategy to correct for managerial mistakes or because managers are making decisions that primarily serve their personal interests rather than those of shareholders[③].

In other words, a firm is purchased by a few (new) owners using a significant amount of debt (in a highly leveraged transaction) and the firm's stock is no longer traded publicly. [④]

In general, the new owners restructure the private firm by selling a significant number of assets (businesses) both to downscope the firm and to reduce the level of debt (and significant debt costs) used to finance the acquisition.

A primary intent of the new owners is to improve the firm's efficiency. This enables them to sell the firm (outright to another owner or by a public stock underwriting), thus capturing the value created through the restructuring. It is not uncommon for those buying a firm through an LBO to restructure the firm to the point that it can be sold at a profit within a five- to eight-year period.

There are three types of leveraged buyouts: management buyouts (MBO), employee buyouts (EBO), and whole-firm buyouts where another firm takes the firm private (LBO). Research has shown that management buyouts can also lead to greater entrepreneurial activity and growth[⑤].

---

① 杠杆收购。

② 杠杆收购(LBO)指的是一种重组行为,即公司管理层和/或外部方购买企业的所有资产,主要由债务融资,从而将公司私有化。

③ 通常,杠杆收购被用作一种重组战略,以纠正管理失误,或者因为管理者的决策主要是为了个人利益而不是股东利益。

④ 换句话说,一家公司是由少数(新)所有者使用大量债务(在高杠杆交易中)购买的,该公司的股票不再公开交易。

⑤ 杠杆收购有三种类型:管理层收购(MBO)、员工收购(EBO)和另一家公司将公司私有化的全公司收购(LBO)。研究表明,管理层收购还可以带来更大的创业活动和增长。

7.5.3 Restructuring Outcomes

Downsizing often does not lead to higher firm performance; in fact, research has shown that downsizing contributed to lower returns for both U. S. and Japanese firms. The stock markets in the firms' respective nations evaluated downsizing negatively. Investors concluded that downsizing would have a negative effect on companies' ability to achieve strategic competitiveness in the long term. Investors also seem to assume that downsizing occurs as a consequence of other problems in a company①.

In free-market based societies, downsizing has generated a host of entrepreneurial opportunities for individuals to operate their own businesses. In fact, as discussed in Chapter 13, start-up ventures in the United States are growing at three times the rate of the national economy.

Downsizing tends to result in a loss of human capital in the long term. Losing employees with many years of experience with the firm represents a major loss of knowledge. As noted in Chapter 3, knowledge is vital to competitive success in the global economy. Thus, in general, research evidence and corporate experience suggest that downsizing may be of more tactical (or short-term) value than strategic (or long-term) value.

Downscoping generally leads to more positive outcomes in both the short and the long term than does downsizing or engaging in a leveraged buyout. Downscoping's desirable long-term outcome of higher performance is a product of reduced debt costs and the emphasis on strategic controls derived from concentrating on the firm's core businesses. In so doing, the refocused firm should be able to increase its ability to compete.

While whole-firm LBOs have been hailed as a significant innovation in the financial restructuring of firms, there can be negative trade-offs.

(1) the resulting large debt increases the financial risk of the firm.

(2) the intent of the owners to increase the efficiency of the bought-out firm and then sell it within five to eight years can create a short-term and risk-averse managerial focus.

(3) these firms may fail to invest adequately in R&D or take other major actions designed to maintain or improve the company's core competence.

---

① 公司所在国家的股票市场对裁员持负面评价。投资者得出结论,裁员将对公司实现长期战略竞争力的能力产生负面影响。投资者似乎还认为裁员是公司其他问题的结果。

Restructuring and Outcomes

(1) Downsizing reduces labor costs, but the long-term results are a loss of human capital and lower performance.

(2) Downscoping reduces debt costs and emphasizes strategic controls, which result in higher performance.

(3) Leveraged Buyouts provide an emphasis on strategic controls but increases debt costs; the long-term outcome is an increase in performance, but also greater firm risk.

本章课程思政学习专题

跨国并购对创新绩效的影响①

1. 跨国并购影响创新绩效

实施跨国并购已成为中国企业探索海外技术源、利用自身技术优势的重要渠道。通过充分并购整合国外优质的技术、营销、管理等方面的知识,一大批企业的创新绩效得到了极大提升。如吉利在并购沃尔沃之后获得了对方的全部知识产权,企业创新步入发展快车道;三一重工在并购混凝土泵制造商普茨迈斯特后获得了代表顶尖技术的"德国制造",迅速成长为国内最强、世界第5的工程机械制造商。然而,也存在一大批企业在实施跨国并购之后并没有实现当初的创新设想,甚至是使得企业负债累累。如上汽在并购韩国双龙之后的整合过程中不断遭到来自双龙工会的抵制,使得当初设想中的技术合作、技术引进毫无踪影。

中国企业跨国并购创新绩效的巨大反差促使理论上有必要深入探索跨国并购的创新机制。关于跨国并购与创新关系的理论解释经历了资源观到资源整合视角的转变过程。基于资源观的学者认为,并购能够帮助企业快速获取外部新技术和互补创新资源,进而推动企业创新。然而,这一派的观点并没有获得实证上的广泛支持,大量研究发现并购对创新无影响、甚至是具有负向影响。这一矛盾性的结果使得学者们认识到从跨国并购完成到创新绩效提升之间存在一个复杂的中间过程,并且开始从并购后资源整合的角度试图打开并购影响创新的中间黑箱,关注重点由表及里逐渐转移至并购所带来的整合机会、并购企业的整合能力以及并购整合过程。

事实上,由于来源国在政治环境、经济体系、关于决策制定的规则与价值观等

① 吴航,陈劲. 跨国并购影响创新绩效的中介机制:制度复杂性战略响应视角[J]. 科学学与科学技术管理,2020,41(11):31-47.

多方面的差异，使得跨国企业在并购后的资源整合过程中不可避免地会遭受由于母国与东道国制度逻辑冲突所带来的影响，这种制度逻辑冲突导致的制度复杂性情境使得并购企业在整合过程中步履维艰。例如，上汽在并购整合韩国双龙的过程中仍遵循国内的运营思路，强调通过减员增效、收缩战线等计划来应对双龙的发展困局，这种“精兵简政”的中国式制度改革遭遇了双龙工会的极力抵制，导致“韩国公司中国化”的计划彻底成为泡影。因此，如何应对并购整合过程中的制度复杂性直接决定了并购整合的成败和最终创新目标能否实现。鉴于此，本研究认为制度复杂性战略响应视角为解释跨国并购影响创新绩效的中介机制提供了合适的理论切入点。

2. 中国企业跨国并购影响创新绩效的作用机制

中国企业的跨国并购仍处于发展的早期阶段。在并购的早期阶段，通过重复的利用性活动能够不断精炼企业在产品开发、营销和物流等方面的惯例，使得创新活动更为聚焦，进而提升企业的创新效率；然而，当利用性的跨国并购进入成熟阶段，重复的知识利用和信息搜索活动的负面效应不断显现，同质性文化的形成和多元化技巧的丧失使得并购企业越来越简单和失去创新的动力。

跨国企业需要积极响应整合过程中的制度复杂性，才能实现创新绩效的提升，而并购动机的差异会导致战略响应方式的不同。具体来说：①探索性并购导向的跨国企业主要通过制度适应的方式来响应制度复杂性，进而获得合法性认可和创新绩效提升。从理论上讲，探索导向的并购企业在遭遇制度冲突时可以选择制度适应或制度共创任何一种战略响应方式，然而由于共同创造新制度相比适应对方制度而言需要更多的资源投入和制度创新经验，因此跨国企业倾向于选择更为容易的制度适应来推动整合过程中的知识转移和创新合作。②利用性并购导向的跨国企业主要通过制度共创的方式来响应制度复杂性，进而增进并购双方的相互信任和深度交流，最终达到提升创新绩效的目的。与探索性并购不同，利用性并购的跨国企业是为了在国外利用自己的所有权优势，而原有所有权优势的形成又是根植于原先的制度环境，因此在响应制度复杂性时就不能简单地选择制度适应的方式，而是需要选择这样一种战略响应方式：既保留原有的制度特征、又与目标方的制度属性兼容。此时，共创新制度相比制度适应更为可行，在保留原有制度特征的同时又获得了目标方的深度认可和信任，对于后期的知识分享和创新合作极为有利。

3. 思考问题

试分析不同类型的跨国并购与企业特征、组织因素和环境条件的匹配关系。

Chapter 8 International Strategy

Opening Case①

Shanghai Automotive Industry Corporation: Reaching for Global Markets

The Shanghai Automotive Industry Corporation (SAIC) is one of China's leading automotive companies. The firm manufactures cars, tractors, motorcycles, trucks, buses, and automotive parts. SAIC has had highly successful joint ventures with General Motors and Volkswagen to produce GM and VW automobiles for the growing Chinese automobile market. The majority of SAIC's sales in the 1990s and 2000s have come from these joint ventures. In fact, driving in any major city in China shows the popularity of the GM (e. g. , Buick) and VW autos in that country. In addition to these joint ventures, SAIC also owns almost 51 percent of the Korean automaker, SSangyong, and the intellectual property rights to the Rover 25 and 75 models, as well as the K-series engine. SAIC started manufacturing the Rover 75 (redesigned for the Chinese market) in 2007.

SAIC learned much from its partnerships, and with the licensed technology, it decided to launch and promote its own branded vehicles. The Chinese government is emphasizing the importance of Chinese companies to develop their own brands partly because foreign brands are controlling many of the Chinese markets. Additionally, for these firms to become successful globally competitive companies, they need their own brands. In keeping with this goal, Chinese executives have a favorite term, zizhu pinpai, meaning self-owned brand. Actually, zizhu means to be one's own master. In 2007, SAIC began selling its own automobile brand, named the Roewe, in Chinese markets.

SAIC is currently among the top three automobile companies in China, and it has a goal of becoming among the top ten global auto competitors. To do so, it has a goal of entering and competing effectively in the U. S. auto market, which is the largest automobile market in the world.

SAIC has a very lofty goal. The automotive market in the United States is the

① 课前案例:上海汽车工业总公司:进军全球市场。

largest market in the world, but all major automobile companies compete there. This undertaking will represent a major challenge to SAIC as evidenced by Hyundai's failed attempt to make inroads in the US auto market despite major improvements in quality and lower prices than comparable cars.

Chinese exposure to the global auto market has been minimal, and very few Chinese cars are exported to the United States. Although the market share of U. S. automakers has been falling for the last several years, most of the gains in market share have been obtained by Japanese auto manufacturers, especially Toyota. Chinese exports are expected to reach 500,000 autos in 2007, but most are targeted for South America, Southeast Asia, and Eastern Europe. Yet, analysts predict Chinese automakers' success in global markets, including the United States, over time, and SAIC is likely to be one of the leaders.

This case raises two very basic questions, specifically, why does SAIC feel that it can succeed in the United States automobile market when other ex-US firms have been unsuccessful? And, will American buyers consider spending significant dollars on Chinese produced automobiles in light of a barrage of Chinese product recalls? Would your students buy a Chinese automobile? What major challenges face SAIC managers in expansion to the United States? Will these hurdles rise or fall as time goes on? These are some of the basic issues that must be address when considering international strategic decisions.

Please note that the Strategic Focus articles in Chapter 8 specifically address SAIC's partners/competitors referenced in this Opening Case. You may do well to read the first Strategic Focus describing General Motors and the second that targets Toyota before discussing the above SAIC case.

Chapter Introduction: This chapter examines opportunities facing firms as they seek to develop and exploit core competencies by diversifying into global markets. In addition, it addresses different problems, complexities, and threats that might accompany use of the firm's international strategies. Although national boundaries, cultural differences, and geographical distances all pose barriers to entry into many markets, significant opportunities draw businesses into the international arena. A business that plans to operate globally must formulate a successful strategy to take advantage of these global opportunities. Furthermore, to mold their firms into truly global companies, managers must develop global mind-sets. Especially in regard to managing human resources, traditional means of operating with little cultural diversity and without global sourcing are no longer effective. These themes are all emphasized in the chapter.

Although national boundaries, cultural differences, and geographical distances all pose barriers to entry into many markets, significant opportunities draw businesses into the international arena.

(1) Global firms must formulate a successful strategy to take advantage of international opportunities.

(2) Managers must develop global mind-sets.

(3) Operating with little cultural diversity and without global sourcing is no longer effective.

(4) Global firms must develop relationships with suppliers, customers, and partners, and then learn from these.

Opportunities and Outcomes of International Strategy①

The following opportunities and outcomes of international strategy are illustrated:

(1) Firms should first identify international opportunities related to increasing market size, return on investment, economies of scale and learning, and location-related advantages②.

(2) Once international opportunities have been identified, firms must develop international strategies based on firm resources and capabilities③.

(3) A mode of entry should be selected to take advantage of the firm's core competencies④.

(4) A firm's ability to realize strategic competitiveness is tempered by management's ability to manage effectively and efficiently a complex organization with locations in multiple countries and the economic and political risks that accompany firm internationalization⑤.

(5) The strategic outcomes from the process can include better performance and more innovation⑥.

---

① 国际化战略的机遇及成果。

② 企业应首先明确与加大市场规模、投资回报、规模经济及区域优势等相关的机遇。

③ 一旦明确了国际机遇,企业应当根据自身资源与能力开发国际战略。

④ 应选择能利用企业核心能力的方式进入市场。

⑤ 企业实现战略竞争力的能力会因为管理层的管理能力而弱化,管理层是否能有效管理位于不同国家的复杂组织,以及应对企业国际化时遇到的经济和政治等风险,均会影响战略竞争力的实现。

⑥ 企业国际化的战略成果包括更好的业绩及更多的创新。

8.1 Identifying International Opportunities: Incentives to Use an International Strategy[①]

International strategy refers to selling products in markets outside of the firm's domestic market to expand the market for their products[②]. This is explained by Vernon's adaptation of the product life cycle concept formulated to explain internationalization[③].

(1) A firm introduces an innovation (new product) in its domestic market[④].

(2) Product demand develops in other countries and exports are provided from domestic operations[⑤].

(3) As demand increases, foreign rivals produce the product; then, firms justify investing in production abroad[⑥].

(4) As products become standardized, firms relocate production to low-cost countries[⑦].

Some firms implement an international strategy to secure critical resources, such as petroleum reserves (for the oil industry), bauxite (for the manufacture of aluminum), or rubber (for tire manufacturing)[⑧].

Traditional motives persist, but other emerging motives also drive international expansion[⑨].

(1) Pressure has increased for global integration of operations, driven mostly by universal product demand.

(2) In some industries, technology drives globalization because the economies of scale necessary to reduce costs to the lowest level often require an investment greater than that needed to meet domestic market demand.

(3) New large-scale, emerging markets, such as China and India, provide a

---

① 明确国际化的机遇:采用国际化战略的动机。

② 国际战略指企业为了扩大产品市场,在国内市场以外的市场进行产品销售。

③ 弗农提出了产品生命周期概念来解释国际化现象,这个概念可以解释国际战略。

④ 企业将创新(新产品)引入国内市场。

⑤ 其他国家产品需求增长,国内市场出口。

⑥ 需求不断增加,国外竞争对手开始生产,接着,企业开始投资在国外生产。

⑦ 产品标准化之后,企业将生产线转移至低成本国家。

⑧ 一些企业实施国际化战略是为了节约关键资源,例如原油行业中的石油、铝制品生产中的铝土矿、轮胎制造中的橡胶等。

⑨ 在传统的理由之外,一些新的动机也驱动着企业进行国际化扩张。

strong internationalization incentive because of the potential demand in them.

Companies seeking to expanding operations in Europe, as elsewhere, need to understand the pressure on them to respond to local, national, or regional customs, especially where goods or services require customization because of cultural differences or effective marketing to entice customers to try a different product.

(1) Firms adapt products to local tastes as they move into new national markets.

(2) Local repair/service capabilities are another factor that increases desire for local country responsiveness.

(3) Transportation costs of large products and their parts may preclude a firm's suppliers from following the firm into an international market.

(4) Employment contracts and labor forces differ. Host governments demand joint ownership and frequently require a high percentage of local procurement, manufacturing, and R&D. These issues increase the need for local investment.

Accompanying these traditional and emerging reasons for international expansion, other opportunities available to firms through an international strategy include①:

(1) increasing the size of potential markets,

(2) achieving greater returns on capital and/or investment in new product/process developments,

(3) gaining economies of scale, scope, or learning,

(4) gaining location-based competitive advantage.

Firms expanding into international markets must recognize that many countries have characteristics that are unique and may differ significantly from the traditional European markets into which U. S. firms have expanded. Thus, firms must recognize this and:

(1) be capable of managing multiple risks—e. g. , financial, economic, political risks,

(2) be aware of increased pressure for local country or regional responsiveness, especially where cultural differences require customization of goods or services,

(3) weigh the potential advantages of enhancing the firm's strategic competitiveness relative to the costs of meeting managerial challenges and product/geographic diversification requirements in international markets.

---

① 伴随国际扩张的或传统或新兴的原因,企业可以通过国际化获得一些其他的机会。

8.1.1 Increased Market Size①

Expanding internationally enables firms to increase greatly the size of the potential market for their products. This may be of critical importance if the domestic market is too small to support scale-efficient manufacturing facilities (e. g. , the pharmaceutical firms' push into China)②.

The size of a particular international market affects a firm's willingness to invest in R&D to build advantages in that market, with larger markets tending to provide higher returns and lower risk. ③

The strength of the science base in a country also can affect a firm's foreign R&D investments, so most firms prefer to invest more heavily in those countries with the scientific knowledge and talent that produce more effective new products and processes from their R&D.

8.1.2 Return on Investment④

When firms make large investments in such items as plants and equipment and/or research and development, they may need to search beyond their domestic market to be able to earn an adequate return on their investment. ⑤

To illustrate, aircraft manufacturers—Boeing and Airbus Industries (a European entity)—must be able to sell in international as well as domestic markets if they are to be strategically competitive and achieve satisfactory returns on their enormous investment.

As the pace of technology development accelerates—and products become obsolete much faster—firms must be able to recoup R&D investments as quickly as possible.

This may be a good place to discuss reverse engineering. Reverse engineering is where a firm takes apart a competing product, learns the technology, and then develops a similar product that mirrors or imitates the new technology and successfully

---

① 扩大市场规模。

② 进行国际化扩张可以使企业显著增加产品潜在市场的规模。这一点对那些国内市场太小无法支持生产规模效益的企业尤为重要。例如,制药公司向中国的扩展。

③ 某一国际市场的规模会影响到企业在该市场进行研发投资以建立优势的意愿。更大的市场规模趋向于带来更高的回报和更低的风险。

④ 收回投资成本。

⑤ 当公司在厂房和设备和/或研发等项目上进行大规模投资时,他们可能需要在国外市场寻找机会,以便能够获得足够的投资回报。

meets customer preferences. In other words, imitation and reverse engineering may shorten the time during which an innovative firm can profit from its innovation. Because of this, innovative firms often seek international markets so that they can increase their opportunities to recoup significant capital investment and R&D expenditures.

8.1.3 Economies of Scale and Learning①

By expanding the size and scope of their markets, firms may be able to achieve economies of scale in manufacturing (and in other operations, such as marketing, research and development, and distribution) by standardizing products across national borders and spreading fixed costs over a larger sales base.

Economies of scale are critical in the global auto industry. Honda has been a largely successful firm with substantial competencies in the manufacture of engines; however, it has sometimes struggled to compete against larger and more resource-rich auto makers (e. g. , Ford and GM). To have a chance to survive, Honda achieved economies of scale in the development and application of its engines (e. g. , by providing engines for many applications [e. g. , lawnmowers, weed trimmers, snowmobiles] and forming an alliance with GM to produce engines). Thus, Honda may excel as an independent engine manufacturer.

Firms may also be able to exploit core competencies in international markets through resource and knowledge sharing between units across country borders. This sharing generates synergy, which helps the firm produce higher-quality goods or services at lower cost. In addition, working across international markets provides the firm with new learning opportunities②.

Strategic Focus③

Does General Motors' Survival Depend on International Markets?④

In order for this Strategic Focus to have maximum value, students should have read and discussed the Opening Case about Shanghai Industry Corporation (SAIC).

---

① 规模经济与学习。

② 企业还可以通过跨国单位之间的资源和知识共享,利用国际市场的核心竞争力。这种共享产生的协同效应,有助于企业以更低的成本生产出更高质量的商品或服务。此外,跨国市场的工作为公司提供了新的学习机会。

③ 战略重点。

④ 通用汽车的生存,是否依赖于国际市场?

These two cases complement each other.

For 76 years, General Motors (GM) was the global industry sales leader, but in 2007, Toyota became the world's largest automaker. In addition to market share deterioration, GM has been struggling to earn positive returns in recent years. It finally returned to profitability in 2007 after experiencing several years of significant losses. Many of GM's problems stem from its competitive capabilities in the North American market, where Toyota and other foreign auto makers have made substantial gains. Interestingly, GM's return to profitability is not due to success in its North American operations as it continues to lose money there. Its recent profits have come from GM's international operations, especially sales in the Chinese market. China surpassed Japan to become the second largest vehicle market in the world. GM has the second highest market share in the Chinese market behind Volkswagen.

GM's sales in China come from a 50 – 50 joint venture with the Shanghai Automotive Industry Corporation (SAIC) named Shanghai General Motors. In 2006, this joint venture manufactured more than 400,000 passenger automobiles. GM predicts that Shanghai General Motors will produce 1 million passenger cars by 2010. Of course, the Chinese market for autos continues to grow and is expected to eventually become the largest auto market in the world. GM's competitive advantage is clear because Toyota sold slightly more than 275,000 cars in China during the same period. Thus, GM has made large investments in Asia to offset Toyota's gains elsewhere.

Even as GM is experiencing success in Asia and is hoping for more in Latin America, it faces many challenges in the next decade. Importantly, its partner in China may become a critical competitor. The transfer to technology and managerial capabilities to SAIC through the joint venture has helped it to develop its own branded auto that will compete with the GM Buicks sold in China. But equally critical is SAIC's intentions to introduce its cars into the Untied States market. As a result, GM must employ effective strategies to maintain its current competitive advantages in China and other Asian markets and it must also try to stem the tide of lost market share in other markets (e.g., the United States and Western Europe).

GM has a real dilemma with its China exposure. This situation might best be referred to as double jeopardy. SAIC is currently a partner in one of GM's few bright spots, but has developed the capability to become an intense competitor in both China and the United States. And GM has been SAIC's mentor. What sort of international strategy should GM implement to protect its recently developed China turf as well as protect its United States' market from interlopers? Ask students to identify strategic alternatives that GM should consider. Is it reasonable to do nothing to protect its shrinking market share in the United States and rely on its current U. S. competitors to protect the U. S. market?

8.1.4 Location Advantages[①]

Firms also may be able to achieve a comparative advantage and lower the basic costs of their products by locating facilities in low-cost markets for critical raw materials, cheap labor, key suppliers, energy, customers, and/or natural resources[②].

The large and unified market of the European Union is attracting considerable investment from international companies, and European markets and firms are undergoing substantial changes to take advantage of the economies of scale, potential learning, and advantages of location. The common currency and integration of capital markets have reduced financial risks and made available significant amounts of capital that were previously unavailable in the separate country markets. (This may be a good place to discuss the euro and its impact on global business.)

Other factors that may impact location advantages are as follows:

(1) the needs of intended customers,

(2) cultural influences (if there is a strong match between the cultures involved, the liability of foreignness is lower than if there is high cultural distance),

(3) regulation distances which influence the ownership positions of multinational firms as well as their strategies for managing expatriate human resources.

8.2 International Strategies[③]

International strategies available to firms are business-level and corporate-level.

(1) Business-level strategy choices are generic, extending our earlier discussion of cost leadership, differentiation, focus, and integrated cost leadership/differentiation strategies.

(2) Corporate-level strategies are dependent on the complexity and scope of product and geographic diversification, and these includemultidomestic, global, and

① 区位优势。

② 企业还可以通过在关键原材料、廉价劳动力、关键供应商、能源、客户和/或自然资源的低成本市场设立设施,实现比较优势,降低产品的成本。

③ 国际战略。

transnational (hybrid) strategies.

8.2.1 International Business-Level Strategy①

Each business must develop a competitive strategy focused on its own domestic market. Business-level generic strategies are discussed in Chapter 4, but international business-level strategies have some unique features.

(1) In an international business-level strategy, the home country of operation is often the most important source of competitive advantage.

(2) The resources and capabilities established in the home country frequently allow the firm to pursue the strategy into markets located in other countries.

(3) As a firm continues its growth into multiple international locations, research indicates that the country of origin diminishes in importance as the dominant factor.

Determinants of National Advantage②

Four interrelated national or regional factors contribute to the competitive advantage of firms competing in global industries.

(1) Factor conditions or the factors of production.

(2) Demand conditions.

(3) Related and supporting industries.

(4) Firm strategy, structure, and rivalry.

Perhaps the most basic factor in the model, factor conditions or factors of production, refers to the inputs necessary to compete in any industry. These include such factors as labor, land, natural resources, capital, and infrastructure (such as highway, postal, and communications systems).

These factors can be subdivided into four categories:

(1) Basic factors, such as labor and natural resources.

(2) Advanced factors, including digital communications systems and highly-educated work forces.

(3) Generalized factors (required by all industries), such as highway systems and a supply of capital.

(4) Specialized factors that are most valuable in specific uses (e.g., skilled personnel employed at a port who specialize in the handling of bulk chemicals).

---

① 业务层国际战略。

② 国家优势的决定因素。

Nations having both advanced and specialized factors are likely to be characterized by growth in new firms that are strong global competitors.

Ironically, countries often develop advanced and specialized factors because they lack critical basic resources.

(1) Some Asian countries, such as South Korea, lack abundant natural resources but offer a strong work ethic, a large number of engineers, and systems of large firms to create expertise in manufacturing.

(2) Germany developed a strong chemical industry, partially because Hoechst and BASF spent years creating a synthetic indigo dye to reduce their dependence on imports, unlike Britain, whose colonies provided large supplies of natural indigo.

The second factor that determines national advantage is demand conditions, which are characterized by the nature and size of buyers' needs in the home market for the industry's products or services. The size of the segment can create demand sufficient to justify the construction of scale-efficient facilities.

Related and supporting industries are the third factor of the national advantage model. National firms may be able to develop competitive advantage when industries that provide either materials or components, or that support the activities of the primary industry are present.

(1) Italian firms are world leaders in the shoe industry because of the related and supporting industries present in Italy (e. g., a mature leather processing industry and design and manufacture of leather-working machinery).

(2) In Japan, copiers and cameras are related, as are cartoon, consumer electronics, and video game industries.

Growth in certain industries is fostered by the fourth factor—firm strategy, structure, and rivalry. As expected, patterns of firm strategy, structure, and competitive rivalry among firms in an industry vary between nations①.

(1) In Italy, the national pride of the country's designers has spawned strong industries in sports cars, fashion apparel, and furniture.

(2) In the United States, competition among computer manufacturers and software producers has favored the development of these industries.

As described, the four basic factors of Porter's Diamond of Advantage model emphasize the impact or influence of the environmental or structural attributes of a

① 某些行业的增长是由第四个因素——企业战略、结构和竞争推动的。一个行业中的企业战略、结构和竞争对手的模式因国家而异。

nation's economy that may contribute to a national advantage for its firms in specific industries.

In spite of the presence of the four factors and government support, the factors leading to national advantage are likely to result in a firm achieving competitive advantage only when the firm develops and implements strategies that enable it to take advantage of country-specific factors.

8.2.2 International Corporate-Level Strategy①

The type of corporate-level strategy adopted by a firm will have an impact on the selection and implementation of its international business-level strategy.

Some corporate-level strategies provide individual country units with the flexibility to develop country-specific strategies, while others dictate all country business-level strategies from the home office and coordinate activities across units for the purposes of resource-sharing and product standardization.

International corporate-level strategy can be distinguished from international business-level strategy by the scope of operations, in terms of both product and geographic diversification.

International Corporate Strategies

A firm should choose its international corporate strategy based on the need for both local responsiveness and for global integration.

(1) When the need for global integration is high and there is little need for local market responsiveness, the firm should adopt a global strategy.

(2) When the need for global integration is low, but there is great need for local market responsiveness, the firm should adopt a multidomestic strategy.

(3) When there is a great need for both global integration and local market responsiveness, the firm should adopt a transnational strategy.

Multidomestic Strategy②

Multidomestic strategy is one where strategic and operating decisions are decentralized to the strategic business unit in each country in order to tailor products

---

① 公司层国际战略。

② 多国本土化战略。

and services to the local market. ① The multidomestic strategy:

(1) assumes business units in different countries are independent of one another.

(2) contends that markets differ and can be segmented by national borders.

(3) focuses on competition within each country.

(4) suggests products and/or services can be customized to meet individual markets needs or preferences.

(5) assumes economies of scale are not possible because of demand for market-specific customization.

A few years back, Sony's entertainment business changed its strategy from global to multidomestic when it decided to produce films and television programs for local markets around the world through production facilities and television channels in most larger Latin American and Asian countries. In 1999, Sony produced approximately 4,000 hours of foreign-language programs and about 1,700 hours of English-language programs. Sony now has more than 24 channels operating across 62 countries, and some of these channels are highly successful.

The use of multidomestic strategies:

(1) usually expands the firm's local market share because the firm can pay attention to the needs of local buyers.

(2) results in more uncertainty for the corporation as a whole, because of the differences across markets and thus the different strategies employed by local country units.

(3) does not allow for the achievement of economies of scale and can be more costly.

(4) decentralizes a firm's strategic and operating decisions to the business units operating in each country.

Global Strategy②

A global strategy is one where standardized products are offered across country markets and competitive strategy is dictated by the home office. The global strategy:

(1) assumes strategic business units operating in each country are interdependent.

(2) attempts to achieve integration across businesses and national markets, as

① 多国本土化战略是指将战略和运营决策权下放给每个国家的战略业务部门,以便为当地市场量身定制产品和服务。

② 全球化战略。

directed by the home office.

(3) emphasizes economies of scale.

(4) offers greater opportunities to use innovations developed at home or in one country in other markets.

(5) often lacks responsiveness to local market needs and preferences.

(6) is difficult to manage because of the need to coordinate strategies and operating decisions across borders.

(7) requires resource-sharing and an emphasis on coordination across national borders.

U. K. -based temporary energy provider, Aggreko, operates in 48 countries and employs a global strategy. The firm's fleet of equipment is integrated globally, which allows it to shift equipment to different regions of the world to meet specific needs. Its global strategy also allows Aggreko to design and assemble its equipment in-house to meet the needs of its customers.

Transnational Strategy①

A transnational strategy is a corporate strategy that seeks to achieve both global efficiency and local (national market) responsiveness.

(1) It is difficult to achieve because of requirements for both strong central control and coordination to achieve efficiency and local flexibility and decentralization to achieve local responsiveness.

(2) A transnational strategy mandates building of a shared vision and individual commitment through an integrated network to produce a core competence that would result in strategic competitiveness (that competitors would find difficult to imitate).

(3) Effective implementation of a transnational strategy often produces higher performance than does implementation of either the multidomestic or global international corporate-level strategies.

Students sometimes find the transnational strategy difficult to grasp. This has prompted some to refer to this option as an "idealized form", suggesting that this is not possible to achieve in reality. This also suggests, however, that this model represents a worthy goal for the international firm. It is worth asking students if they believe it will ever be possible to be truly transnational and ask what would be needed to make this a reality.

---

① 跨国经营战略。

DaimlerChrysler employed a transnational strategy to design and manufacture the Crossfire, a product that was introduced in 2003 and features a sleek Chrysler design, but 40 percent of its components are from Mercedes Benz. This global integration has facilitated lower costs for the vehicle—components already engineered were adapted from elsewhere and design enhancements produced an attractive car for the U. S. market.

8.3 Environmental Trends[①]

Implementing a transnational strategy is difficult; however, firms are challenged to do so because of these facts:

(1) There is an increased emphasis on local requirements—e. g. , customization to meet government regulations within particular countries or to fit customer tastes and preferences.

(2) Most multinational firms desire coordination and sharing of resources across country markets to hold down costs.

(3) Some products and industries may be more suited than others for standardization across country borders.

Liability of Foreignness[②]

Research shows that firms may focus less on truly global strategies and more on regional adaptation. Even Internet-based strategies now require local adaptation.

Regionalization[③]

A firm competing in international markets must decide whether to compete in all (or many) world markets or to focus its efforts on a specific region or regions. Competing in many markets may enable the firm to achieve economies of scale because of the size of the combined markets, but only if customer preferences in multiple markets do not differ significantly. If customer preferences vary significantly among national markets, a firm might be better served by narrowing its focus to a specific region. A regional focus may enable the firm to better understand cultures, legal and

---

① 环境趋势。
② 外来者劣势。
③ 区域化。

social norms, and other factors that may be important to achieving strategic competitiveness. ①

At this point, it might useful to draw a parallel between competing in multiple national markets and owning businesses in multiple industries. Firms may be better positioned by focusing on a specific region where markets are more similar, thus allowing a degree of integration and resource sharing. In Chapter 7, a similar comment was made regarding disadvantages that often accompanyoverdiversification and the prescribed downscoping to refocus the firm more on related, as opposed to, unrelated diversification.

Regional strategies also are being promoted by groups of countries that have developed trade agreements to enhance the economic power of a region. Examples include the following:

(1) Membership in the European Union (EU) is limited to Western European countries, but it is being expanded to include other Western European countries as well as countries in Central and Eastern Europe.

(2) The North American Free Trade Agreement (NAFTA) is an integration designed to facilitate trade among the U. S., Canada, and Mexico (and it may be expanded to include some South American countries).

(3) South America's Organization of American States (OAS) is a system of country associations that developed trade agreements to promote the flow of trade across country boundaries within their respective regions.

(4) CAFTA is a U. S. trade agreement with Central American nations that is designed to reduce tariffs with five countries in Central America plus the Dominican Republic in the Caribbean Sea.

Most firms enter regional markets sequentially, beginning in markets with which they are more familiar. And they introduce their largest and strongest lines of business into these markets first, followed by their other lines of business once the first lines are successful. They also usually invest in the same area as their original investment location.

---

① 在国际市场上竞争的公司必须决定是在所有(或许多)世界市场上竞争,还是将其精力集中在一个或多个特定区域。由于合并市场的规模,在许多市场中竞争可能使公司实现规模经济,但前提是多个市场中的客户偏好没有显著差异。如果客户偏好在各个国家市场之间存在显著差异,那么将关注点缩小到特定区域可能会更好地为公司服务。区域重点可以使公司更好地了解文化、法律和社会规范以及其他对实现战略竞争力可能很重要的因素。

8.4 International Entry Mode①

Global Market Entry: Choice of Entry Mode②

Five alternative entry modes available to firms for international expansion③:

(1) exporting,

(2) licensing,

(3) strategic alliances,

(4) acquisition,

(5) new, wholly owned subsidiary.

The next section of this chapter discusses characteristics of each mode, including cost/control trade-offs.

8.4.1 Exporting④

A common—but not necessarily the least costly or most profitable—form of international expansion is for firms to export products from the home country to other markets.

(1) Exporters have no need to establish operations in other countries.

(2) Exporters must establish channels of distribution and outlets for their goods, usually by developing contractual relationships with firms in the host country to distribute and sell products.

However, exporting also has disadvantages:

(1) Exporters may have to pay high transportation costs.

(2) Tariffs may be charged on products imported to the host country.

(3) Exporters have less control over the marketing and distribution of their products.

Because of the potentially significant transportation costs and the usually greater similarity of geographic neighbors, firms often export mostly to countries that are closest to its facilities.

Small businesses are the most likely to use exporting. One of the largest problems

---

① 国际市场的进入模式。

② 进入国际市场:进入方式的选择。

③ 企业进行国际化扩张的五种可选模式。

④ 出口。

with which small businesses must deal is currency exchange rates, a challenge for which only large businesses are likely to have specialists.

8.4.2 Licensing[①]

Through licensing, a firm authorizes a foreign firm to manufacture and sell its products in a foreign market[②].

(1) The licensing firm (licensor) generally is paid a royalty payment on every unit that is produced and sold.

(2) The licensee takes the risks, making investments in manufacturing and paying marketing/distribution costs.

(3) Licensing is the least costly (and potentially the least risky) form of international expansion because the licenser does not have to make capital investments in the host countries.

(4) Licensing is a way to expand returns based on previous innovations, even if product life cycles are short.

Counterfeiting is one risk to licensing strategies. Sony and Philips codesigned the audio CD. In the past, they licensed the rights to companies to make CDs and Sony and Philips collected 5 cents for every CD sold. However, the returns to Sony and Philips from CD sales were threatened by cheap counterfeit disks. Sales of counterfeit disks in China alone are estimated to exceed \$1 billion annually.

The costs or potential disadvantages of licensing include the following:

(1) The licensing firm has little control over manufacture and distribution of its products in foreign markets.

(2) Licensing offers the least revenue potential as profits must be shared between licensor and licensee.

(3) The licensee can learn the firm's technology and, upon license expiration, may create a competing product.

8.4.3 Strategic Alliances[③]

Strategic alliances enable firms to[④]:

① 授权经营。

② 通过授权经营,一家企业允许另一家外国企业在外国市场上生产并销售它的产品。

③ 战略联盟。

④ 结成战略联盟使企业可以:

(1) share the risks and resources required to enter international markets①.

(2) facilitate the development of new core competencies that yield strategic competitiveness②.

Most strategic alliances represent ventures between a foreign partner (which provides access to new products and new technology) and a host country partner (which has knowledge of competitive conditions, legal and social norms, and cultural idiosyncrasies that will enable the foreign partner to successfully manufacture or develop and market a competitive product or service in the host country market).

Strategic alliances also present potential problems and risks due to (1) selection of incompatible partners and (2) conflict between partners.

Several factors may cause a relationship to sour. Trust between the partners is critical and is affected by a number of fundamental issues:

(1) the initial condition of the relationship,

(2) the negotiation process to arrive at an agreement,

(3) partner interactions,

(4) external events,

(5) the country cultures involved in the alliance or joint venture.

British Telecommunications planned to create a virtual shopping mall in Spain through its joint venture with Banco Popular, a retail-focused Spanish bank. The two firms jointly developed a Website for business-to-business transactions. They were to use BT's portal in Spain to develop a client base of small and medium size businesses. BT would provide the common portal free of charge for the first year and Banco Popular would charge only a nominal commission for brokering sales.

Research suggests that alliances are more favorable when uncertainty is high and where cooperation is needed to access knowledge dispersed between partners and where strategic flexibility is important; acquisitions work best in situations with less need for flexibility and when the transaction supports economies of scale or scope.

8.4.4 Acquisitions③

Cross-border acquisitions have also been increasing significantly. In recent years, cross-border acquisitions have comprised more than 45 percent of all acquisitions

① 分担进入国际市场的风险及所需的资源。

② 促进产生战略竞争力的新核心竞争力的发展。

③ 收购。

completed worldwide.

Acquisitions can provide quick access to a new market. In fact, acquisitions may provide the fastest and often the largest initial international expansion of any of the alternatives.

Beyond the disadvantages previously discussed for domestic acquisitions, international acquisitions also can be quite expensive (because of debt financing) and require difficult and complex negotiations due to:

(1) the same disadvantages as domestic acquisitions,

(2) the great expense which often requires debt financing,

(3) the exceedingly complex international negotiations for acquisitions—e. g. , only about 20 percent of the cross-border bids made lead to a completed acquisition, compared to 40 percent for domestic acquisitions,

(4) different corporate cultures,

(5) the challenges of merging the new firm into the acquiring firm, which often are more complex than with domestic acquisitions—i. e. , different corporate culture, but also different social cultures and practices.

Emphasize that firms often use multiple entry strategies. For example, Auchan has used multiple entry strategies as it globalizes its operations, ranging from joint ventures in China and Latin America to acquisitions in Germany and the U. K.

8.4.5 New Wholly Owned Subsidiary①

Firms that choose to establish new, wholly owned subsidiaries are said to be undertaking a greenfield venture. This is the most costly and complex of all international market entry alternatives.

The advantages of establishing a new wholly-owned subsidiary include:

(1) achieving maximum control over the venture,

(2) being potentially the most profitable alternative (if successful),

(3) maintaining control over the technology, marketing, and distribution of its products.

While the profit potential is high, establishing a new wholly-owned subsidiary is risky for two reasons:

(1) This alternative carries the highest costs of all entry alternatives as a firm must build new manufacturing facilities, establish distribution networks, and learn and

① 拥有全部股份的子公司。

implement the appropriate marketing strategies.

(2) The firm also may have to acquire knowledge and expertise that is relevant to the new market, often having to hire host country nationals (in many cases from competitors) and/or costly consultants.

8.4.6 Dynamics of Mode of Entry①

The choice of a market entry strategy is determined by a number of factors. However, initial market development strategies generally are selected to establish a firm's products in the new market.

(1) Exporting does not require foreign manufacturing expertise; it only requires an investment in distribution.

(2) Licensing also can facilitate direct market entry by enabling the firm to learn the technologies required to improve its products in order to achieve success in international markets or to facilitate direct entry.

(3) Strategic alliances are also popular because the firm forms a partnership with a firm that is already established in the new target market and reduces risks by sharing costs with the partner.

Firms interested in establishing a stronger presence (in most instances, in the later stages of the firm's international diversification strategy) and in controlling technology, marketing, and distribution adopt riskier, more costly entry strategies, such as acquisitions or greenfield returns.

However, the entry strategy should be matched to the particular situation. In some cases, a firm may pursue entry strategies in sequential order—beginning with exporting and ending with greenfield ventures. The entry mode decision should be based on the following conditions:

(1) the industry's competitive conditions,

(2) the target country's situation,

(3) government policies,

(4) the firm's unique set of resources, capabilities, and core competencies.

① 进入模式的动力。

8.5 Strategic Competitive Outcomes[①]

Once its international strategy and mode of entry have been selected, the firm turns its attention to implementation issues. It is important to do this because international expansion is risky and may not result in a competitive advantage. The probability the firm will achieve success by using an international strategy increases when that strategy is effectively implemented.

8.5.1 International Diversification and Returns[②]

The discussion centered on product diversification where a firm manufactures and sells a diverse variety of products.

Based on the advantages discussed earlier, international diversification should be positively related to firm performance. Research has shown that, as international diversification increases, firms' returns decrease and then increase as firms learn to manage international expansion.

There are several reasons for the positive relationship between international diversification and performance.

(1) Potential advantages from economies of scale and experience,

(2) Location advantages,

(3) Increased market size,

(4) The potential to stabilize returns.

8.5.2 International Diversification and Innovation[③]

Developing new technology is critical to strategic competitiveness. In fact, Porter indicates that a nation's competitiveness depends on the innovativeness of its industries and that firms achieve strategic competitiveness in international markets through innovation.

As stated earlier in this chapter, one of the advantages of international expansion is having larger potential markets. Larger markets allow firms to achieve greater returns on innovation, which yields lower R&D-related risk. Thus, international diversification

---

① 战略竞争结果。

② 国际多元化及其回报。

③ 国际多元化及创新。

provides firms with incentives to innovate.

A complex relationship exits among international diversification, innovation, and performance. This leads, in fact, to the following circular relationship:

(1) Some level of performance is necessary to provide the resources required to diversify internationally.

(2) International diversification provides incentives (advantages) to firms to invest in R&D (innovation).

(3) If done properly, R&D and the resulting innovations should improve firm performance.

(4) Improved performance provides resources for continued international diversification and investments in R&D innovation.

It also is possible that international diversification may result in improved returns for product-diversified firms (referred to as unrelated diversification) by increasing the size of the potential market for each of the firm's products. But managing a firm that is both product and internationally diversified is very complex.

Cultural diversity may enable a firm to compete more effectively in international markets.

(1) Culturally diverse top management teams often have a greater knowledge of international markets.

(2) An in-depth understanding of diverse markets among top-level managers facilitates inter-firm cooperation, the use of strategically relevant, long-term criteria to evaluate managerial and business unit performance, and improved innovation and performance.

8.5.3 Complexity of Managing Multinational Firms①

Managers of internationally diversified firms face a number of complex challenges.

(1) Firms face multiple risks from being in several countries.

(2) Firms can grow only so large before they become unmanageable.

(3) The costs of managing large diversified firms may outweigh the benefits of diversification.

(4) Global markets are highly competitive.

(5) Firms must understand and effectively deal with multiple cultural environments.

---

① 管理跨国企业的复杂性。

(6) Systems and processes must exist to manage shifts in the relative values of multiple currencies.

(7) Firms must scan the environment to be prepared for potential government instability.

8.6 Risks in an International Environment①

Political and economic risks complicate the management of international diversification. One reason is that these risks result in competitive conditions that may differ significantly from what was expected.

8.6.1 Political Risks②

Political risks are those related to instability in national governments and to war, civil or international.

For a useful way of identifying the political risk associated with different countries, see the map on page 105 of Small Business Management: An Entrepreneurial Emphasis, by Longenecker, Moore, Petty, and Palich (2006, SWCP).

National government instability creates multiple potential problems for internationally diversified firms. Economic risks come up as governments react to a variety of events, reflected in uncertainty in terms of:

(1) economic risks and uncertainty created by government regulation,

(2) existence of many, possibly conflicting, legal authorities or corruption,

(3) the potential nationalization of private assets.

8.6.2 Economic Risks③

Economic risks are interdependent with political risks; however, some economic risks are specific to international diversification. For example, differences and fluctuations in the value of the different currencies are a primary concern to internationally diversified firms.

(1) For U. S. firms, the value of international assets, liabilities, and earnings

① 国际环境的风险。

② 政治风险。

③ 经济风险。

are affected by the value of the dollar relative to other currencies (e. g. , as the dollar value increases, the value of foreign assets decreases).

(2) The value of the dollar may make U. S. firms' exports uncompetitive in international markets because of price differentials (and, in turn make imports from other countries more attractive toU. S. customers).

8.6.3 Management Problems①

As mentioned before, firms generally earn positive returns by diversifying internationally.

However, there are limits to the advantages of international diversification.

(1) Greater geographic dispersion across country borders increases the costs of coordination between units and the distribution of products.

(2) Trade barriers, logistical costs, cultural diversity, and other differences by country greatly complicate the implementation of an international diversification strategy.

(3) Institutional and cultural factors can present strong barriers to the transfer of a firm's competitive advantages from one country to another.

(4) Marketing programs often have to be redesigned and new distribution networks established when firms expand into new countries.

(5) Firms may encounter different labor costs and capital charges.

(6) In general, it is difficult to effectively implement, manage, and control a firm's international operations.

本章课程思政学习专题

国际化战略与企业创新绩效②

1. 国际化行为与企业创新绩效

随着全球市场竞争的日益激烈,国际化战略日益成为中国企业总体战略的常规选项。2016 年中国企业对外投资达到 1961.5 亿美元,占全球对外投资的 12.6%,同比增长 34.7%,继续保持全球第二位,成为国际投资大国。作为创业企业的天

① 管理问题。

② 郝晨,张卫国,李梦雅. 风险投资、国际化战略与企业创新绩效:基于中国创业板上市公司的研究[J]. 科研管理,2022,43(4):185-191.

然高度契合投资者,风险投资对企业的成长发展起到了关键作用。但鲜有学者考虑到风险投资对企业国际化战略的影响效果。随着国际创新网络的不断发展,新兴经济体企业为了进一步拓展创新资源共享渠道、搭建创新信息交流平台也纷纷将国际化经营作为企业发展的关键战略。但现有关于国际化经营与企业创新绩效关系的研究主要以发达国家为研究对象且尚未得到一致的研究结果。与发达国家基于所有权优势和技术优势的国际化路径不同,获取更加先进的技术、提高创新能力往往是新兴经济体企业实施国际化战略的重要动因。现有文献在考察国际化战略与企业创新绩效的关系时并未区分国际化深度和广度对企业创新绩效的差异影响,但有学者发现不同维度的国际化行为对企业绩效和企业价值的作用效果并不一致。因此,有必要基于我国的特殊情境深入研究不同维度的国际化行为对企业创新绩效的差异影响。

2. 国际化战略能否提升企业创新绩效?

风险投资介入对企业国际化深度战略和广度战略的制定和实施均具有积极作用;企业实施国际化深度发展战略能够对企业的创新绩效产生显著的提升效应,而国际化广度发展战略却未能对企业的创新绩效产生积极影响,但风险投资介入能够有效增强国际化战略的创新增值作用,进而提高国际化战略对企业创新绩效的积极影响。进一步探究企业上市后风险投资是否退出以及不同特质的风险投资对国际化战略与企业创新绩效关系调节作用的差异性后发现,风险投资在企业上市后继续持股才能正向调节国际化战略与企业创新绩效之间的关系,当民营背景、外资背景、高声誉背景风险投资介入、风险资本投资期限较长、采取联合投资策略以及能够参与公司治理时,风险投资对国际化战略与企业创新绩效之间关系的正向调节作用更大,实施国际化战略对企业创新绩效的提升效应也更显著。

3. 思考问题

如何正确认识和评价我国企业国际化战略的实施动因和成效?

Chapter 9 Cooperative Strategy

Opening Case

Cooperative Action of Haier Group

Haier Group is a Chinese multinational consumer electronics and home appliances company headquartered in Qingdao, Shandong province, China. It designs, develops, manufactures and sells products including air conditioners, mobile phones, computers, microwave ovens, washing machines, refrigerators, and televisions.

The company opened a production facility in Indonesia in 1996, and the Philippines and Malaysia in 1997. The company tried to compete in the Thai market, but they completely lost to local electronics companies and had to stop the marketing there. In the US it focused upon two niche markets in compact refrigerators and electric wine cellars. Haier began to manufacture full-sized refrigerators for North American market. This would bring it into direct competition with established American companies GE, Whirlpool, Frigidaire, and Maytag. As part of its strategy, Haier built a production facility in the United States at Camden, South Carolina, opened in 2000. By 2002, US revenues reached USD \$200 million, still small compared to its overall revenue of \$7 billion. Also in 2002, Haier moved into a building in midtown Manhattan. Formerly the headquarters for the Greenwich Savings Bank, the 52,000-square-foot (4,800 m^2) building was built in 1924 in the neo-classical style. Production facilities were constructed in Pakistan in 2002 and Jordan in 2003. In Africa, Haier has plants in five countries: Tunisia, Nigeria, Egypt, Algeria and South Africa. The company also purchased a Meneghetti's factory in Italy and began placing its products in European retail chains, either under its own brand or under OEM agreements with foreign partners. Currently Haier has entered into a joint venture agreement with the government of Venezuela. Haier Appliances (India) P. Ltd initiated its commercial operations in January 2004. It was also listed among the top 20 most trusted brands in India by The Brand Trust Report, a study conducted by Trust Research Advisory. In June 2005, Haier made a bid to acquire Maytag Corporation, backed by private equity funds Blackstone Group and Bain Capital. The bid was for USD \$1.28 billion, or \$16 per share, topping a previous offer of

$14.26 per share made by Ripplewood Holdings. In the end however, Maytag was bought by Michigan based Whirlpool Corporation which offered $1.7 billion in cash and stock, or $21 per share, plus assumed debt. As of 2008, Haier had surpassed rival Whirlpool as the world's top refrigerator producer in terms of sales, according to Euromonitor, an independent business intelligence provider. Haier said it sold 12 million refrigerators worldwide, up 20% over the previous year. Its market share reached 6.3% globally. In 2012, Haier Group bought the New Zealand appliance manufacturing company Fisher & Paykel.

Introduction

A cooperative strategy is a strategy in which firms work together to achieve a shared objective. Cooperative strategy is the third major alternative (internal growth and mergers and acquisitions are the other two) firms use to grow, develop value-creating competitive advantages, and create differences between them and competitors. Thus, cooperating with other firms is another strategy that is used to create value for a customer that exceeds the cost of creating that value and to create a favorable position in the marketplace relative to the five forces of competition. A collusive strategy is a cooperative strategy through which two or more firms cooperate to raise prices above the fully competitive level. It is important to emphasize that strategic alliances can serve a number of purposes, but they are also difficult to manage.

(1) Two-thirds of all alliances have serious problems in their first two years, and 70 percent fail.

(2) A corporate alliance mindset (one through which both the strengths and risks of a firm's entire set of alliance relationships are recognized and understood by all involved with alliance formation and use) increases the probability of alliance success.

9.1 Strategic Alliances as a Primary Type of Cooperative Strategy

A strategic alliance is a partnership between firms whereby their resources and capabilities are combined to create a competitive advantage①.

Many firms, especially large global competitors, establish multiple strategic alliances. As described in the Opening Case, IBM has formed alliances with Sun

① 战略联盟指企业间形成合作关系,将双方的资源及能力整合起来,形成竞争优势。

Microsystems, SAP, Lenovo, and Cisco, among others. The goal with each cooperative relationship is different and very specific①.

In general, strategic alliance success requires cooperative behavior from all partners. Actively solving problems, being trustworthy, and consistently pursuing ways to combine partners' resources and capabilities to create value are examples of cooperative behavior known to contribute to alliance success②.

9.1.1 Three Types of Strategic Alliances

Three types of strategic alliances: joint ventures, equity strategic alliances, and nonequity strategic alliances.

A joint venture is an alliance where a new, independent firm is formed from two or more partners, with each partner firm contributing some of their resources and capabilities③.

Joint ventures are effective in establishing long-term relationships and in transferring tacit knowledge. Because it can't be codified, tacit knowledge is learned through experiences such as those taking place when people from partner firms work together in a joint venture.

An equity strategic alliance is an alliance where partner firms own unequal shares of equity in a venture formed by combining some of their resources and capabilities to create a competitive advantage④. For example, Citigroup Inc. has formed a strategic alliance with Shanghai Pudong Development Bank Co. through an equity investment totaling 25 percent. This equity strategic alliance served as a launch pad for Citigroup to enter the credit-card business in China.

A nonequity strategic alliance is an alliance where two or more firms contract to share some of their resources and capabilities to create a competitive advantage. In this type of strategic alliance⑤,

(1) firms do not establish a separate independent company and therefore don't

---

① 许多公司,尤其是大型全球性企业,建立了多个战略联盟。前面举的例子中,IBM 公司与太阳计算机系统有限公司、思爱普、联想、思科等公司建立了联盟。与不同公司的联盟目标各有不同,并且非常具体。

② 总的来说,战略联盟的成功要求所有成员相互合作。对联盟成功有意义的行为包括积极解决问题,值得信赖,不间断寻找整合联盟成员间能够创造价值的资源与能力。

③ 合资企业是指两个或以上企业合并成为联盟,每个联盟成员贡献部分资源与能力。

④ 产权战略联盟指企业内联盟成员贡献出部分资源与能力,形成竞争优势,但成员之间持有产权不相等。

⑤ 非股权战略联盟指两个或多个企业以协议形式,分享部分资源及能力,形成竞争优势。

take equity positions.

(2) these are less formal and demand fewer partner commitments.

(3) these are unsuitable for complex projects requiring effective transfers of tacit knowledge between partners.

Typically taking the form of a nonequity strategic alliance, outsourcing is the purchase of a value-creating primary or support activity from another firm.

Other types of nonequity strategic alliances include licensing, distribution agreements, supply contracts, and marketing agreements (such as code-sharing agreements among airlines).

9.1.2 Reasons Firms Develop Strategic Alliances

Technology companies cannot possibly acquire the technology they need fast enough, so partnering becomes essential. Some believe strategic alliances may be the most powerful trend in American business in a century.

Among other benefits, strategic alliances allow partners to create value that they couldn't develop by acting independently and to enter markets more quickly than they could without a partner.

In large firms, alliances account for more than 20 percent of revenue and are a prime vehicle for firm growth.

In some industries (e.g., airlines), firms compete more alliance against alliance than firm against firm.

Firms form strategic alliances to reduce competition, enhance their competitive capabilities, gain access to resources, take advantage of opportunities, and build strategic flexibility. To do so means that they must select the right partners and develop trust. ①

Slow-Cycle Markets

Firms in slow-cycle markets often use strategic alliances to enter restricted markets or to establish franchises in new markets (especially global markets).

Slow-cycle markets are becoming rare in the twenty-first century competitive landscape for several reasons, including the privatization of industries and economies, the rapid expansion of the Internet's capabilities in terms of the quick dissemination of

① 企业结成战略联盟是为了减少竞争、增强竞争能力、获取资源、利用机会和建立战略灵活性。这样做意味着他们必须选择正确的合作伙伴并建立信任关系。

information, and the speed with which advancing technologies make quickly imitating even complex products possible.

Firms competing in slow-cycle markets should recognize the future likelihood that they'll encounter situations in which their competitive advantages become partially sustainable (in the instance of a standard-cycle market) or unsustainable (in the case of a fast-cycle market). Cooperative strategies can be helpful to firms making the transition from relatively sheltered markets to more competitive ones.

Fast-Cycle Markets

Fast-cycle markets are entrepreneurial and dynamic, with new products or services imitated rapidly.

Cooperative strategies are used to increase the speed of product development or market entry or to improve strategic competitiveness.

Standard-Cycle Markets

In standard-cycle markets (which are often large and oriented toward economies of scale), alliances are more likely to be between partners with complementary resources and capabilities. Companies also may cooperate in standard-cycle markets to gain market power.

9.2 Business-Level Cooperative Strategy

A business-level cooperative strategy is used to help the firm improve its performance in individual product markets. There are four business-level cooperative strategies. ①

A firm forms a business-level cooperative strategy when it believes combining its resources and capabilities with one or more partners creates competitive advantages that it can't create by itself and that will lead to success in a specific product market.

Business-Level Cooperative Strategies

The four general business level cooperative strategies are:

(1) Complementary strategic alliances (vertical and horizontal).

(2) Competition response strategy.

(3) Uncertainty reducing strategy.

---

① 业务层面的合作策略用于帮助企业提高其在各个产品市场的绩效。有四种业务层面的合作策略。

(4) Competition reducing strategy.

9.2.1 Complementary Strategic Alliances

Complementary strategic alliances are partnerships that are designed to take advantage of market opportunities by combining partner firms' resources and capabilities in complementary ways so that new value is created.

Vertical Complementary Strategic Alliance①

A vertical complementary strategic alliance is formed between firms that agree to use their resources and capabilities in different stages of the value chain to create value. Oftentimes, vertical complementary alliances are formed in reaction to environmental changes—i. e., they serve as a means of adaptation to the environmental changes.

A critical issue for firms is how much technological knowledge they should share with their partner. They need the partners to have adequate knowledge to perform the task effectively and to be complimentary to their capabilities. Part of this decision depends on the trust and social capital developed between the partners.

Vertical and Horizontal Complementary Strategic Alliances②

A vertical complementary strategic alliance links suppliers, manufacturers, and/or distributors and represents linkages between different segments of each partner's value chain.

A horizontal complementary strategic alliance is an arrangement that links similar segments of competing firms' value chains, such as linking R&D or new product development activities.

Horizontal Complementary Strategic Alliance③

Horizontal complementary strategic alliances are partnerships that link similar activities of firms. Horizontal complementary alliances are used to increase each firm's competitive advantage and often focus on the long-term development of product and service technology.

Importantly, horizontal alliances may require equal investments of resources by

---

① 垂直互补型战略联盟。
② 垂直及水平互补型战略联盟。
③ 水平互补型战略联盟。

the partners but they rarely provide equal benefits to the partners. There are several potential reasons for the imbalance in benefits.

(1) Frequently, the partners have different opportunities as a result of the alliance.

(2) Partners may learn at different rates and have different capabilities to leverage the complimentary resources provided in the alliance.

(3) Some firms are more effective in managing alliances and in deriving the benefits from them.

(4) The partners may have different reputations in the market thus differentiating the types of actions firms can legitimately take in the marketplace.

9.2.2 Competition Response Strategy

Cooperative strategic alliances also may be established to enable partner firms to respond to major strategic actions initiated by competitors. Because they can be difficult to reverse and expensive to operate, strategic alliances are primarily formed to respond to strategic rather than tactical actions. ①

Nissan and Renault are automobile manufacturers and each suffered from being small and dealing with the standard shortcomings associated with lack of scale and scope. Both firms had similar cost structures and neither firm was competitive. Neither was able to generate any innovation in its product line. In 1999, both firms entered into a strategic alliance. This alliance was the first of its kind to involve a Japanese and French company, each with its own corporate culture and brand identity. Horizontal in nature, the Nissan/Renault partnership is an example of an equity strategic alliance. Renault holds a 44.4 percent stake in Nissan which in turn holds 15 percent of Renault's shares. Nissan has realized a significant profit turn-around as a result of the alliance, as has Renault with a goal of becoming the most profitable European auto manufacturer by 2010. The firms participate in a number of joint activities to achieve scale and scope economies, such as sharing production platforms (the partners intend to share 10 platforms by 2010) and power-trains (engines and transmissions). To generate scope economies, the firms combine their resources and capabilities to cooperate in several activities including sales, purchasing, and the use of common

① 合作企业还可以建立合作战略联盟，使合作企业能够对竞争对手发起的重要战略行动作出反应。由于战略联盟很难逆转，运作成本也很高，因此，战略联盟的形成主要是为了应对战略行动，而不是战术行动。

distribution channels in Europe. In a comprehensive and summarized sense, this alliance finds Nissan and Renault cooperating in terms of "global product development, financial policy, and corporate strategy".

9.2.3 Uncertainty-Reducing Strategy

Firms also may form strategic alliances to hedge against risk and uncertainty (especially in fast-cycle markets).

Alliances are often used where uncertainty exists, such as in entering new product markets or emerging economies. For example, Dutch bank ABN AMRO signed on to a venture called ShoreCap International which will invest capital in and advise local financial institutions that do small and microbusiness lending in developing countries. Through this cooperative strategy with other financial institutions, ShoreBank (the venture's leading sponsor) hopes to be able to reduce the risk of providing credit to smaller borrowers in disadvantaged regions. It also hopes to reduce poverty in the regions where it invests.

In other cases, firms form alliances to reduce the uncertainty associated with developing new product or technology standards. For example, the alliance between France Telecom and Microsoft is a competition response alliance for France Telecom but it is an uncertainty reducing alliance for Microsoft. Microsoft is using the alliance to learn more about the telecom industry and business. It wants to learn how it can develop software to satisfy needs in this industry. By partnering with a firm in this industry, it is reducing its uncertainty about the market and software needs. And, the alliance is clearly designed to develop new products so the alliance reduces the uncertainty for both firms by combining their knowledge and capabilities.

9.2.4 Competition-Reducing Strategy

Explicit collusion exists when firms get together to negotiate production output and pricing agreements with the goal of reducing competition. Explicit collusion strategies are illegal in most developed economies (except in regulated industries). ①

Some firms may adopt explicit alliances to reduce competition that is perceived as potentially destructive or excessive. Examples include the following:

(1) OPEC, which manages the price and output of oil companies in member

---

① 当企业为了减少竞争而聚在一起谈判生产产量和定价协议时,就存在明显的共谋。明确的共谋策略在大多数发达经济体是非法的(受监管行业除外)。

countries,

(2) manufacturing and distribution cartels in Japan,

(3) industry trade organizations,

(4) government-industry relationships,

(5) direct collusion or price-fixing agreements among participants in an industry or between industry participants and government agencies.

There are implicit cooperative alliances, such as tacit collusion, which exist when several firms in an industry observe others' competitive actions and respond to reduce industry output below the potential competitive level to maintain higher-than-competitive prices. Another form of tacit collusion is mutual forbearance, by which firms avoid competitive attacks against rivals they meet in multiple markets. Rivals learn a great deal about each other when engaging in multimarket competition, including how to deter the effects of their rival's competitive attacks and responses. Given what they know about each other as a competitor, firms choose not to engage in what could be destructive competitions in multiple product markets.

Tacit collusion tends to be used as a business-level competition-reducing strategy in highly concentrated industries.

At a broad level in free-market economies, governments must determine how rivals can collaborate to increase their competitiveness without violating established regulations.

9.2.5 Assessment of Business-Level Cooperative Strategies

Firms use business-level strategies to develop competitive advantages that can contribute to successful positioning and performance in individual product markets. To develop a competitive advantage using an alliance, the particular set of resources and capabilities that is combined and shared in a particular manner through the alliance must be valuable, rare, imperfectly imitable, and nonsubstitutable.

Complementary business-level strategic alliances (especially vertical ones) are the most likely to create sustainable competitive advantage. Horizontal complementary alliances are sometimes difficult to maintain because they are often formed between rival firms.

Although strategic alliances designed to respond to competition and to reduce uncertainty can also create competitive advantages, these advantages tend to be more temporary than those developed through complementary (vertical and horizontal) strategic alliances. The primary reason is that complementary alliances have a stronger focus on the creation of value compared to competition-reducing and uncertainty-reducing alliances, which are far more reactive.

Of the four business-level cooperative strategies, the competition-reducing strategy has the lowest probability of creating a sustainable competitive advantage. This suggests that companies using such competition reducing business-level strategic alliances should carefully monitor them as to the degree to which they are facilitating the firm's efforts to develop and successfully create competitive advantages.

9.3 Corporate-Level Cooperative Strategy

Corporate-level cooperative strategies are designed to facilitate product and market diversification through a means other than a merger or an acquisition. When a firm seeks to diversify into markets in which the host nation's government prevents mergers and acquisitions, alliances become an especially appropriate option. Corporate-level strategic alliances are also attractive compared to mergers and particularly acquisitions, because they require fewer resource commitments and permit greater flexibility in terms of efforts to diversify partners' operations. An alliance can be used as a way to determine if the partners might benefit from a future merger or acquisition between them①.

Corporate-Level Cooperative Strategies

The three corporate level strategies are:

(1) Diversifying strategic alliances.

(2) Synergistic strategic alliances.

(3) Franchising.

9.3.1 Diversifying Strategic Alliance

A diversifying strategic alliance is a corporate-level cooperative strategy in which firms share some of their resources and capabilities to diversify into new product or

① 公司层面的合作战略意在用收购以外的方法达到产品和市场的多元化。如果企业寻求多元化市场,而当地政府禁止收购,联盟便是很好的选择。与并购尤其是收购相比,企业层面的战略联盟也更具吸引力,因为后者需要的资源投入更少,合作者行为的多元化更为灵活。通过联盟,可以判断合作者是否能从双方并购中受益。

market areas. ①

Note that a diversification alliance enables firms that do not want to grow by merger or acquisition to achieve growth by forming strategic alliances. Exiting a strategic alliance is less difficult and less costly as compared to divesting an acquisition that did not contribute expected levels of strategic success. In addition, some governments restrict acquisitions (especially horizontal ones) when regulators conclude that horizontal acquisitions foster explicit collusion.

Firms might form a diversifying alliance to determine if a future merger would benefit both parties—e. g. , the formation of technology partnerships between GM and Toyota that may lead to broader linkups between the automakers.

Highly diverse networks of alliances can lead to poorer performance by partner firms. However, cooperative ventures are also used to reduce diversification in firms that have overdiversified. For example, Fujitsu, realizing that memory chips were becoming a financial burden, dumped its flash-memory business into a joint venture company controlled by Advanced Micro Devices. This alliance helped Fujitsu to refocus on its core businesses.

9.3.2 Synergistic Strategic Alliance

Synergistic strategic alliances allow firms to combine some of their resources and capabilities to create joint economies of scope between partner firms. These alliances:

(1) are similar to business-level horizontal complementary strategic alliances at the business level.

(2) create synergy across multiple functions or multiple businesses.

SBC Communications and EchoStar Communications were synergistically diversified by the arrangement to offer satellite TV billing services through SBC's system. Thus, a synergistic strategic alliance is different from a complementary business-level alliance in that it diversifies both firms into a new business, but in a synergistic way.

9.3.3 Franchising

Franchising is a corporate-level cooperative strategy used by a franchisor to describe and control the sharing of its resources and capabilities. In other words, a

① 多元化战略联盟是一种企业层面的合作战略,企业共享其部分资源和能力,以进入新产品或市场的多元化领域。

franchise refers to a contract between two legally independent companies that allows the franchisee to sell the franchisor's product or do business under its trademarks over a given time and location. ①

Franchising is a popular strategy. In fact, the companies using it account for one-third of annual U. S. retail sales while competing in over 75 industries. Already frequently used in developed nations, franchising is expected to account for significant portions of growth in emerging economies in the twenty-first century.

The most successful franchising strategy is one in which the partners (i. e., franchisor, franchisees) work closely together. The franchisor is to develop programs to transfer knowledge and skills to the franchisees that are needed to successfully compete at the local level, and franchisees should provide feedback to the franchisor regarding how their units could become more effective and efficient.

Franchising is a particularly attractive strategy to use in fragmented industries where no firm or small set of firms has a dominant share in the industry, making it possible for a company to gain a large market share by consolidating independent companies through contractual relationships.

9.3.4 Assessment of Corporate-Level Cooperative Strategies

Compared to those at the business-level, corporate-level cooperative strategies are usually broader in scope and more complex, making them relatively more costly.

Firms able to develop corporate-level cooperative strategies and manage them in ways that are valuable, rare, imperfectly imitable, and nonsubstitutable develop a competitive advantage that is added to advantages gained through the activities of individual cooperative strategies.

Corporate-level strategic decisions, such as pursuing cooperative strategies and diversification, may be the result of managerial motives instead of the appropriate desire to achieve strategic competitiveness and earn above-average returns for a company. Firms need corporate governance mechanisms to ensure managers do not use alliance strategies inappropriately. For example, without governance, top-level managers can use alliances to:

(1) increase the size of the business for the purpose of increasing his/her own

① 特许经营是特许人用来描述和控制其资源和能力共享的企业层面的合作战略。换句话说,特许经营权是指两个法律上独立的公司之间的合同,允许被特许人在给定的时间和地点销售特许人的产品或以其商标开展业务。

compensation,

(2) increase his/her worth or value to—or extend his/her tenure with—the firm by being the only top-level manager who understands the intricacies of a network of alliance partners.

9.4 International Cooperative Strategy

A cross-border strategic alliance is an international cooperative strategy in which firms with headquarters in different nations combine some of their resources and capabilities to create a competitive advantage①.

There are several reasons for the increasing use of cross-border strategic alliances:

(1) Multinational corporations outperform firms operating on only a domestic basis.

(2) A firm can form cross-border strategic alliances to leverage core competencies that are the foundation of its domestic success to expand into international markets.

(3) Limited domestic growth opportunities also cause firms to use cross-border alliances.

(4) Government economic policies can influence firms to form cross-border alliances.

(5) Strategic alliances with local partners can help firms overcome certain liabilities of moving into a foreign country, such as lack of knowledge of the local culture or institutional norms.

(6) Firms also use cross-border alliances to help transform themselves to better use their competitive advantages to exploit opportunities surfacing in the rapidly changing global economy.

In general, cross-border alliances are more complex and risky than domestic strategic alliances.

9.5 Network Cooperative Strategy

Rather than cooperative alliances between two or very few firms, alliances can also be expanded to include a larger number (or network) of partners as a complement

---

① 跨国战略联盟是一种国际合作战略,总部位于不同国家的企业将部分资源与能力相结合,创造出竞争优势。

to other forms of cooperative strategy. This is a network cooperative strategy.

A network cooperative strategy is particularly effective when it is formed by geographically clustered firms, as in California's Silicon Valley and Singapore's Silicon Island.

Alliance Network Types

An important advantage of a network cooperative strategy is that firms gain access to the partners of their partners.

The set of partnerships, such as strategic alliances, that result from the use of a network cooperative strategy is commonly called an alliance network.

Stable alliance networks often appear in mature industries with predictable market cycles and demand. Through a stable alliance network, firms try to extend their competitive advantages to other settings while continuing to profit from operations in their core, relatively mature industry.

An example of a U.S. firm's stable network is Nike's long-established relationships between the firm and its global network of suppliers and distributors.

Dynamic alliance networks often are used in industries with frequent technological innovation and short product life cycles. Thus, dynamic alliance networks are primarily used to stimulate rapid, value-creating product innovations and subsequent successful market entries.

9.6 Competitive Risks with Cooperative Strategies

Many cooperative strategies fail. Evidence suggests that two-thirds of cooperative strategies have serious problems in their first two years and that as many as 70 percent of them eventually fail. This failure rate suggests that even when the partnership has potential synergies, alliance success can be elusive.

The risks associated with cooperative strategies are significant because the firms that are cooperating may also be competing with each other. These risks include①:

(1) poor contract development that may result in one (or more) of the partners acting opportunistically and taking advantage of other venture partners.

(2) misrepresentation of partner firms' competencies by misstating or exaggerating

① 这些风险包括:(1) 合同开发不善,可能导致合作方投机,利用其他投资合伙人。(2) 夸大无形资源,如对当地市场状况的掌握,因此误判合作企业的能力。(3) 合作企业不能按照约定将互补资源用于投资。(4)有的企业可以就联盟利益做出投资,但有的企业做不到。

an intangible resource such as knowledge of local market conditions.

(3) failure of partner firms to make complementary resources available to the venture as agreed.

(4) the possibility that a firm may make investments that are specific to that alliance while its partner does not.

Managing Competitive Risks in Cooperative Strategies

The competitive risks of cooperative strategies are①

(1) inadequate contracts,

(2) misrepresentation of competencies,

(3) partners failing to use complimentary resources,

(4) holding alliance partners' specific investments hostage and can be managed by,

(5) detailed contracts and monitoring,

(6) developing trusting relationships.

9.7 Managing Cooperative Strategies

Cooperative strategies are an important option for firms competing in the global economy; however, they are complex and challenging to manage②.

The two basic approaches to managing cooperative strategies are:

(1) cost minimization,

(2) opportunity maximization.

In the cost-minimization approach, the firm develops formal contracts with its partners. These contracts specify how the cooperative strategy is to be monitored and how partner behavior is controlled. The goal of this approach is to minimize the cooperative strategy's cost and to prevent opportunistic behavior by partners.

The opportunity-maximization approach focuses on a partnership's value-creation opportunities. In this case, partners are prepared to take advantage of unexpected opportunities to learn from each other and to explore additional marketplace possibilities. Less formal contracts, with fewer constraints on partners' behaviors, make it possible for partners to explore how their resources and capabilities can be shared in multiple value-creating ways.

---

① 合作战略的竞争风险有:(1) 合同不充分;(2) 能力误解;(3) 合作者不能利用互补资源;(4) 扣留联盟合作伙伴的投资资金;(5) 合同细节化,合同监管;(6) 发展互信关系。

② 对参与全球经济竞争的企业而言,合作战略是一个重要选项,但是,管理起来很复杂,充满挑战。

Firms can successfully use both approaches to manage cooperative strategies. However, the costs to monitor the cooperative strategy are greater with cost minimization, in that writing detailed contracts and using extensive monitoring mechanisms is expensive, even though the approach is intended to reduce alliance costs.

As a strategic asset, trust can enable partner firms to reduce the cost of contracting and monitoring because the probability of opportunistic behavior is reduced if partners are able to trust each other. Trust also may enable the venture to take advantage of unforeseen opportunities.

Because trust enables partner firms to reduce venture-related contracting and monitoring costs and increase venture flexibility, a venture between trusted partners is more likely both to reduce costs and add/create value.

本章课程思政学习专题

企业合作创新战略①

1. 创新网络

开放式创新战略的应用和实践促使单体企业的创新行为和创新效应显得势单力薄,企业的创新边界模糊化,寻求外部异质性知识、技术及资源的需求趋于强烈。与此同时,由企业节点组成的创新合作网络应运而生,为企业的协同发展提供了机遇和条件。创新网络的演变受到了学术界和实务界的重视和关注,成为企业跨组织边界实现知识共享的重要手段。创新网络是为了适应系统性创新而出现的一种基本制度安排。创新网络的关键在于激发技术创新和获得竞争优势,在这个过程中强调多方创新主体间的合作与互补,同时其自身具备复杂网络的结构特征和资源特征。随着创新网络的进一步研究,国内学者依据中国情境对创新网络的理论与实践层面进行了补充,解学梅认为创新网络是指企业与外部创新行为主体通过交互构成知识创新链,具有知识溢出、知识转移和学习特征;而黄海霞等将协同创新网络视为一个自增益的循环创新生态系统,通过组织间协同关系和系统间非线性关系实现资源共享、知识传递、技术扩散以及与外界环境的交流。研究表明,创新网络的发展为多主体间的知识合作和协同创新提供了有利的发展环境,也为完善企业间的知识流动机制和创新发展创造了新的模式和渠道。

---

① 田真真,王新华,孙江永. 创新网络结构、知识转移与企业合作创新绩效[J]. 软科学,2020,34(11):77 - 83.

2. 区域创新网络对企业合作创新绩效的影响

区域创新网络开放度能够正向影响企业合作创新绩效;在开放度的基础上,包容度与企业合作创新绩效之间呈现倒 U 型关系。企业对开放式创新战略的认可有助于打开企业眼界和发展思路,强化企业对外部知识源的搜索、引进、融合和应用,推动企业积极寻求跨组织合作,加大创新技术向生产力的转化,提升企业合作创新绩效;另外,包容度的提升有助于强化企业对多元化的知识网络的过滤、精准匹配和引进,实现新旧知识及跨组织融合应用。但包容对知识具有一定的限度,过度包容容易弱化网络边界的过滤作用,造成知识的无序流动和转移,增大知识转移的风险和管理成本。该研究结果支持了以往关于开放度影响企业创新绩效的结论,验证了创新网络结构的开放度对企业创新能力和创新绩效的积极作用。

知识转移部分中介了开放度和包容度与企业合作创新绩效之间的关系。创新网络的隐形边界致使知识的流动性和应用性受到了一定的限制,但同时也为知识的跨界搜索、边界突破和协同创新抑制了风险和降低了成本。在这个过程中,知识的流动和转移成为企业创新合作的重要环节,研究指出企业间的合作形式主要通过组织间的异质性知识的转移和应用,同时知识向生产力和技术产出的转化需要通过知识的有效转移和应用才能实现。而创新网络的开放度和包容度的发展有助于为企业间的知识转移提供有利的发展环境,为知识突破双重边界限制实现跨组织共享和合作奠定了基础。

知识距离负向调节开放度与知识转移之间的关系,且负向调节包容度与企业合作创新绩效之间的倒 U 型关系。研究表明,知识距离的扩大能够弱化开放度对于知识的搜寻、引进和转移,不利于知识需求方有效寻求合作和知识资源,且不利于企业对外来知识的信任和控制,阻碍企业创新能力的提升。另外,在同一位置时,较小的知识距离对包容度与知识转移之间关系的调节作用显著高于较大的知识距离的调节作用。当包容度处于适当的位置时,知识距离的存在有助于加强网络平台对外部知识源的精准匹配和过滤,促使企业获取多元化的创新知识,形成完善的知识网络平台,为企业技术创新打造完备的知识库;但是若包容度过低或过高时,反而会抑制知识的转移,主要原因在于过度的包容容易导致创新网络缺乏对重复、无效及过载知识的过滤作用,造成知识漏斗的无序和混乱,不能充分识别有效知识和不良信息,形成企业潜在的发展风险。故而,知识距离的存在和包容度的大小均应保持在一定的范围之内,平衡发展更有助于知识漏斗发挥最优化的作用。

3. 思考问题

如何制定多元化的网络和社会环境背景下的企业合作创新战略?

Chapter 10 Corporate Governance

Opening Case

How Has Increasingly Intensive Corporate Governance Affected the Lives of CEOs?①

Daniel Zhang Yong, CEO of Alibaba Group, speaks after the November 11 Singles' Day shopping spree at the headquarters of Alibaba in Hangzhou city, East China's Zhejiang Province, Nov 12, 2014. Alibaba Group Holding is poised to overtake Walmart later this year as the world's biggest retail platform, said Daniel Zhang Yong, chief executive officer of the e-commerce behemoth, reported TMTPost. The goal includes achieving more than $1 trillion gross merchandise value (GMV) in five years, while developing more infrastructural platforms to empower businesses in the future, said the new CEO in an internal meeting on Wednesday, three days after he replaced Jonathan Lu. The change of leadership was announced earlier this month as Alibaba released its better-than-expected first-quarter results. Revenue of the Internet giant surged 45 percent in the three months through March. It's critical to achieve the sales target while retaining a thriving ecosystem, said Zhang, adding that mechanism should be improved to tackle issues such as counterfeits and bogus transactions among Taobao vendors who wished to boast sales volume to gain prominence. "Behind the $1 trillion target, the other is our new businesses apart from ecommerce, where we need more resource allocation, focus and new breakthroughs." said the 43-year-old CEO, according to the news. Cloud computing is a first, said Zhang, adding that cloud computing will serve as the engine in the new economic era, empowering all businesses to better serve consumers and improve productivity. Zhang joined Alibaba as chief financial officer of Taobao Marketplace in 2007 and acted as COO since 2013.

Although corporate governance is a necessity, it is also important to make sure it's executed properly to avoid the problems and pitfalls associated with expectations of CEO behavior and performance that have evolved as a result of greater scrutiny. In 2014, a record number of CEOs left their jobs. This exodus is due in part to increasing

① 公司治理日益精细,对首席执行官们的生活产生了何种影响?

scrutiny by boards, governance activists, and increased pressure from the market for corporate control as board members are pressured to challenge the views of the CEO if they appear to be headed in a direction that will not benefit all stakeholders.

It is found that inside CEOs have been able to provide leadership that allows firms to realize longer-term profitability and above average returns, but it takes about seven years in place to affect profitability. But the abbreviating of average CEO tenure will not accommodate this window since they are leaving their jobs before that are reaching their maximum effectiveness. Thus, corporate governance is a double-edged sword. On the one hand, it is necessary to put an end to scandals such as the Enron disaster, which led to a significant loss for all stakeholders involved, including employees. Also, CEO compensation is quite excessive relative to other managers and employees. On the other hand, governance that is overly restrictive can reduce managerial risk taking and increase governance costs excessively, as well as constrain the CEO's decision-making authority. Ironically, it inadvertently leads to increased pay for CEOs, which many governance activists rail against. Although corporate governance is a necessity, it is also important to make sure that it is executed properly to avoid the problems noted here.

Introduction

The purpose of this chapter is to present and discuss how shareholders (owners) can ensure that managers develop and implement strategic decisions in the best interests of the shareholders (owners) and not be primarily self-serving (working for the best interests of managers only, to the detriment of shareholders)①. In the absence of effective internal governance mechanisms, the market for corporate control—an external governance mechanism—may be activated. While it is a subject most frequently associated with firms in the U.S. and the U.K., the effectiveness of governance is gaining attention throughout the world. The chapter begins by describing the relationship that provides the foundation on which the modern corporation is built—i.e., the relationship between owners and managers. However, the majority of this chapter is devoted to an explanation of various mechanisms owners use to govern managers and ensure maximization of shareholder value.

Corporate governance is a relationship among stakeholders that is used to determine and control the direction and performance of organizations. At its core,

---

① 本章旨在提出并探讨下述问题:股东如何确保企业管理者制定并实施战略决策的出发点是保护股东的最大利益,而不是自私自利,只考虑自身,却损坏股东的利益。

corporate governance is concerned with identifying ways to ensure that strategic decisions are made effectively. ①

Corporate governance has been emphasized in recent years because, as the Opening Case illustrates, corporate governance mechanisms increasingly affect all stakeholders and the firm's future.

Effective corporate governance is also of interest to nations. Governments want firms operating within their countries to grow and provide employment, wealth, and satisfaction. This raises standards of living and enhances social cohesion.

Three internal governance mechanisms examined here are (1) ownership concentration, as represented by types of shareholders and their different incentives to monitor managers, (2) the board of directors, and (3) executive compensation. The external governance mechanism is the market for corporate control.

10.1 Separation of Ownership and Managerial Control

The growth of the large, modern public corporation is based primarily on the efficient separation of ownership and managerial control. ②

Shareholders make investments by purchasing stock (representing ownership), which entitles them to a share of the firm's residual income (or profits) that remain after all expenses have been paid.

(1) The right to share in residual income also means that shareholders also must accept the risk that no residual profits will remain if the firm's expenses exceed its income. ③

(2) Shareholders can manage investment risk by investing in a diversified portfolio of firms. ④

(3) In small firms, managers and owners are often one in the same—less separation of ownership and control. ⑤

(4) As family-controlled firms grow, the owners generally do not have sufficient capital or managerial skills to grow the business and seek other sources of capital and

① 企业治理指利益相关者之间的关系,用来决策或控制企业发展方向或执行。企业治理的核心在于找到有效制定战略决策的方法。

② 现代的大型公共企业的壮大,有赖于所有权与管理控制的有效分离。

③ 股东可以分享剩余所得,但这也意味着,一旦企业的支出超过收入,没有剩余所得的风险就存在。

④ 股东可以投资不同类型的企业,管理投资风险。

⑤ 小企业中,通常管理者即为所有者,所有权与管理控制不分离。

skills to support this expansion. ①

It is helpful to provide a story that would illustrate what the separation of ownership and managerial control is all about, and how it came to be. For example, it is easy for students to see that Henry Ford was involved in both the ownership and the operation of Ford Motor Company in the early days. They can see in their minds the old footage of Model T's coming off a very crude assembly line, by today's standards, and understand how much simpler operations were at the time. That has all changed with the advent of the modern, complex corporation. Today there is almost no way to bring ownership and managerial control back together again in a workable model.

10.1.1 Agency Relationships

While the efficient separation of ownership and control enables specialization both by owners and managers, it also results in some potential costs (and risks) for owners by creating an agency relationship.

An agency relationship exists when one party (the principal [s]) delegates decision making to another party (the agent [s]) in return for compensation as a decision-making specialist who performs a service. This relationship can be broader than just owners and managers—e. g., consultants and clients or insured and insurer. ②

An Agency Relationship

Note the following:

(1) Shareholders (principals) hire managers (agents) as decision makers.

(2) The hiring act creates an agency relationship wherein a risk-bearing specialist (principal) compensates a managerial decision-making specialist (agent).

The potential for conflicts of interests between owners and managers is created by the delegation of the responsibilities of decision making to managers. Therefore, managers may take actions that are not in the best interests of owners by selecting strategic alternatives that serve managerial interests rather than shareholder or owner interests.

---

① 家族企业逐渐发展壮大,所有者通常不具备足够的资金与管理技能,为了扩大企业,从别处寻找资金及管理技能。

② 一方(委托人)将决策权交于善于决策并提供服务的另一方(代理人),并支付酬金,双方之间便形成代理关系。代理关系不仅包括所有者与管理者的关系,还包括:顾问与客户的关系;被保险人与保险公司的关系。

An agency relationship enables the possibility of managerial opportunism, the seeking of self-interest with guile (i. e., with cunning or deceit), where opportunism is represented by an attitude or inclination and a set of behaviors.

Before observing the results of decisions, it is impossible to know which agents will behave opportunistically and which ones will not because a manager's reputation is an imperfect guide to future behavior. As a result, principals establish governance and control mechanisms because the opportunity for opportunistic behavior and conflicts of interest exists.

10.1.2 Product Diversification as an Example of an Agency Problem

Product diversification can be beneficial to both shareholders and managers, but it also is a potential source of agency problems.

Managers may pursue higher levels of product diversification than are desired by shareholders to capture the value of opportunities that are available to managers, but not to owners.①

(1) Increased diversification generally drives the growth of the firm and firm growth is positively related to managerial compensation. Thus, by diversifying to a greater extent than may be desired by shareholders, managers may enjoy the higher levels of compensation that accompany managing larger firms.

(2) Increased diversification also can reduce managerial employment risk (the risk of job loss, loss of compensation, or loss of managerial reputation). Increased diversification reduces managerial employment risk because the firm (and the manager) is less affected by a reduction in demand for (or failure of) a single product line when the firm produces and sells multiple products.

(3) Increased diversification also may provide managers with access to increased levels of slack resources or free cash flows, resources that are generated after investment in all internal projects that have positive net present values within the firm's current product lines. Managers may choose to invest excess funds in products or activities that are not related to the firm's existing core businesses and products if they perceive attractive (positive net present value) investment opportunities.

---

① 管理者为了追求有利的机会,通常更追求产品多样化,甚至超过股东要求的多样化程度。但这种机会只对管理者有利,对所有者无利。

Manager and Shareholder Risk and Diversification①

Curve S represents the business or investment risk profile for shareholders (owners). It spans a diversification scope from dominant business (which would be to the left of related-constrained) to a point between related-constrained and related-linked diversification. The optimum risk level is at point A, between dominant business and related-constrained diversification.

Curve M represents the managerial employment risk profile. It spans a diversification profile from related-constrained to unrelated diversification. The optimum diversification level for managers is point B, between related-linked and unrelated businesses.

As illustrated by the S-curve (owner business risk preference) and M-curve (managerial employment risk preference), there is a conflict between owners and managers regarding the desired levels of firm diversification and risk.

(1) Owners prefer that the scope be greater than a dominant business but less than related-linked diversification.

(2) Owners' optimum level of diversification is where the S-curve turns up, a point between dominant business and related-constrained diversification.

(3) However, as the curve indicates, there is a point at which managerial employment risk increases as the firm overdiversifies.

(4) The optimum level of firm diversification from a managerial risk perspective is at point B on the M-curve, somewhere between related-linked and unrelated businesses.

10.1.3 Agency Costs and Governance Mechanisms

For firm diversification to approach the shareholder optimum, managerial autonomy must be controlled by the firm's board of directors or by other governance mechanisms that encourage managers to make strategic decisions that are in the best interests of shareholders.

Agency costs are the sum of incentive, monitoring, and enforcement costs as well as any residual losses incurred by principals because it is not possible for principals to guarantee 100 percent compliance through monitoring arrangements. ②

---

① 管理者及股东风险与多样化。

② 尽管有监管安排,委托人很难保证100%的执行率,因此代理成本是激励成本、监控成本、执行成本及委托人的剩余损失之总和。

Research suggests that more intensive application of governance mechanisms may produce significant changes in strategies.① Corporate America needs more intense governance in order for continued investment in the stock market to facilitate growth. However, others argue that the indirect costs are even more telling in regard to the impact on strategy formulation and implementation. That is, because of more intense governance, firms may make decisions that are much less risky and thus decrease potential shareholder wealth significantly due to the implementation of SOX.

10.2 Ownership Concentration

Ownership concentration is defined both by the number of large-block owners and by the total percentage of the firm's shares that they own.②

Large-block shareholders are investors who typically own at least five percent (5 percent) of the firm's shares.③

Diffuse ownership (a large number of shareholders with small holdings and few/no large-block shareholders)④

(1) produces weak monitoring of managerial decisions,

(2) makes it difficult for owners to coordinate their actions effectively,

(3) may result in levels of diversification that are beyond the optimum level desired by shareholders (especially when this condition is combined with weak monitoring).

The Growing Influence of Institutional Owners

In recent years, large block ownership by individuals has declined, but they have been replaced by significant positions held by institutional owners.

Institutional owners are large block shareholder positions controlled by financial institutions, such as stock mutual funds and pension funds.

The importance of institutional owners is indicated by the fact that these shareholders now controls over 50 percent of the stock in large U. S. corporations and approximately 56 percent of the stock of the 1000 largest U. S. corporations. These ownership percentages suggest that as investors, institutional owners have both the size

① 研究表明,采用集中的治理机制可能会导致战略的重大变化。

② 股权集中由大宗股票持有者数量及其所持企业股份的百分比所决定。

③ 大宗股票持有者主要指持有企业百分之五(5%)或以上股份的投资者。

④ 股权分散(股东数量多,持股比例小,没有或少数股东持有大宗股票)。

and the incentive to discipline ineffective top-level managers and can significantly influence a firm's choice of strategies and overall strategic decisions. Initially, these shareholder activists and institutional investors concentrated on the performance and accountability of CEOs and contributed to the ouster of a number of them. They are now targeting what they believe are ineffective boards of directors.

The rising tide of shareholder pressure also is evidenced by actions taken by CalPERS.

(1) CalPERS provides retirement and health coverage to over 1.3 million current and retired public employees.

(2) CalPERS is generally thought to act aggressively to promote decisions and actions that it believes will enhance shareholder value in companies in which it invests.

(3) Institutions' activism may not have a direct effect on firm performance, but its influence may be indirect through its effects on important strategic decisions.

10.3 Board of Directors

Even though institutional ownership has increased, the majority of firms still "enjoy" the benefits or advantages of diffuse ownership (i. e., limited monitoring of managers by individual shareholders). Furthermore, large financial institution shareholders—such as banks—are effectively prevented from having direct ownership of firms and are prohibited from placing a representative on the boards of directors. These conditions highlight the importance of boards of directors to corporate governance.

Legally, the board of directors has broad powers, including:

(1) directing the affairs of the organization,

(2) punishing (disciplining) and rewarding (compensating) managers,

(3) protecting the rights and interests of shareholders (owners).

Boards are experiencing increasing pressure from shareholders, lawmakers, and regulators to become more forceful in their oversight role and thereby forestall inappropriate actions by top executives.

The board of directors is a group of elected individuals whose primary responsibility is to act in the owners' interests by formally monitoring and controlling the corporation's top-level executives. If the board of directors is appropriately structured and operates effectively, it can protect owners from managerial opportunism.

Classifications of Board of Director Members

Insiders are represented by the firm's CEO and other top-level managers.

Related outsiders are individuals who are not involved in the firm's day-to-day operations, but may have a relationship with the company. Examples might include the firm's legal counsel, a large customer or supplier, or a close relative of one of the firm's top-level managers.

Outsiders are individuals who are independent of the firm. They are neither involved in the firm's day-to-day operations, nor do they have other relationships with the firm. An example of an outsider might be the president of a university or a community volunteer.

Because the primary role of the board of directors is to monitor and ratify major managerial actions to protect the interests of owners, there is a call by advocates of board reform that outsiders should represent a significant majority of a board's membership.

Outside directors (and boards) are perceived as ineffective because:

(1) Insiders dominate the board by limiting the flow of information to outside directors.

(2) Outside directors are nominated for board membership by insiders (primarily by the CEO) and thus are indebted to insiders.

The drawbacks of outside boards:

(1) Because outside directors do not have day-to-day contact with the ongoing operations of the firm, they must obtain detailed, in-depth information about the quality of management decisions. Generally this information is obtained through frequent interactions, often developed over time, with inside directors (generally, at board meetings).

(2) In the absence of rich information, boards may be forced to emphasize financial rather than strategic controls. Potentially, this means that outsider-dominated boards—because they lack sufficient information—will evaluate managers, not on the basis of the appropriateness of their actions (which the board ratified) but based on the financial outcomes of those actions.

Enhancing the Effectiveness of the Board of Directors

Because of the board's importance, the performance of individual board members as well as that of entire boards is being evaluated more formally and intensely.

Many boards have voluntarily initiated changes, including:

(1) increasing the diversity of board members' backgrounds,

(2) strengthening internal management and accounting control systems,

(3) establishing and consistently using formal processes to evaluate the board's performance,

(4) the creation of a "lead director" role that has strong powers with regard to the board agenda and oversight of non-management board member activities,

(5) changes in the director compensation, especially reducing or eliminating stock options as part of the package.

The following comments can be used to expand the class discussion of whether a more active board is a more effective board. The findings from research regarding the effectiveness of board involvement in the strategic decision-making process are mixed, indicating the following:

(1) Board involvement in the strategic decision-making process may improve firm performance because it provides the firm's managers with access to outside opinions, and outside directors should be more objective and interested in protecting owner interests.

(2) Boards are more likely to be involved in strategic decisions when the firm is smaller and less diversified, since information regarding strategic actions is more readily available and both the scope and size of the firm are manageable.

(3) Boards are less active in large, diversified firms.

(4) The board's access to sufficiently rich information on appropriateness of strategic actions in large diversified firms is limited.

(5) Board may be limited to evaluating financial outcomes (instead of action appropriateness).

McKinsey & Co. research found that institutional shareholders were willing to pay an 11 percent premium for the shares of companies when outsiders constitute a majority of the board, own significant amounts of stock, are not personally tied to top management, and when management is subjected to formal evaluation.

Research shows that boards working collaboratively with management:

(1) make higher quality strategic decisions,

(2) make decisions faster,

(3) become more involved in the strategic decision-making process.

Because of the increased pressure from owners and the potential conflict among board members, procedures are necessary to help boards function effectively in facilitating the strategic decision-making process.

Increasingly, outside directors are being required to own significant equity stakes as a prerequisite to holding a board seat. In fact, some research suggests that firms perform better if outside directors have such a stake.

One activist concludes that boards need three foundational characteristics to be effective: director stock ownership, executive meetings to discuss important strategic issues, and a serious nominating committee that truly controls the nomination process to strongly influence the selection of new members.

10.4 Executive Compensation

As illustrated in the Opening Case and Strategic Focus, the compensation of top-level managers generates great interest and strongly held opinions. One reason for this widespread interest can be traced to a natural curiosity about extremes and excesses. But furthermore, CEO pay is an indirect but tangible way to assess governance processes in large corporations.

Executive compensation is a governance mechanism that seeks to align managers' and owners' interests through salary, bonus, and long-term incentive compensation such as stock options. ①

Sometimes the use of a long-term incentive plan prevents major stockholders (e. g. , institutional investors) from pressing for changes in the composition of the board of directors, because they assume that long-term incentives ensure that top executives will act in shareholders' best interests. Alternatively, stockholders largely assume that top-executive pay and the performance of a firm are more closely aligned when firms have boards that are dominated by outside members.

Using executive compensation as a governance mechanism is more challenging in international firms. Evidence suggests that the interests of owners of multinational corporations may be served best when the firm's foreign subsidiary compensation plans are customized to local conditions. Though unique compensation plans require additional monitoring and increase the firm's agency costs, it is important to adjust pay levels to match those of the region of the world (e. g. , higher in the U. S. and lower in Asia).

When Daimler-Benz acquired Chrysler, it highlighted the fact that top executives

① 高管薪酬是治理机制的一种,通过工资、分红、长期奖金如股票期权等来平衡管理者及所有者的利益。

at Chrysler made much more than the executives at Daimler-Benz—but higher-paid Chrysler executives report to lower-paid Daimler bosses. This example is one that students seem to be able to grasp.

Developing and implementing an effective incentive compensation program is quite challenging because:

(1) Strategic decisions made by top managers are complex and non-routine. Due to difficulties in judging decision quality, compensation is often linked to more measurable outcomes such as financial performance.

(2) Decisions made by top-level managers are likely to affect firm performance over an extended period of time. As a result, it is difficult to assess the effect of current decisions using current period performance.

(3) Many variables (or outside factors) intervene between management behavior and firm performance (e. g., uncontrollable shifts in the environment).

Although incentive compensation plans may increase the value of a firm in line with shareholder expectations, such plans are subject to managerial manipulation.

Although long-term performance-based incentives may reduce temptations to under-invest in the short run, they increase executive exposure to risks associated with uncontrollable events—e. g., market shifts, industry decline.

The Effectiveness of Executive Compensation

The compensation received by top-level managers, especially by CEOs, is often a subject of controversy.

Large CEO compensation packages result mostly from the inclusion of stock options and stock in the total pay packages. This is intended to entice executives to keep the stock price high, thus aligning manager and owner interests.

Research has shown that managers owning more than one percent of the firm's stock are less likely to be forced out of their jobs, even when the firm is performing poorly Furthermore, a review of the research suggests that over time, firm size has accounted for more than 50 percent of the variance in total CEO pay, while firm performance has accounted for less than 5 percent of the variance.

One way that boards have found to compensate executives is through giving them loans with favorable, or no, interest for the purpose of buying company stock. If done correctly, this can be a governance tool, since it aligns executives' priorities with those of the shareholders because the executives hold stock, not just options on the stock. They gain or lose money along with the shareholders.

It is important to consider that annual bonuses may provide incentives to pursue short-run objectives at the expense of the firm's long-term interests.

While some stock option-based compensation plans are well designed with option strike prices substantially higher than current stock prices, too many have been designed simply to give executives more wealth that will not immediately show up on the balance sheet. Research of stock option repricing where the strike price value of the option has been lowered from its original position suggests that action is taken more frequently in high-risk situations. However, it also happens when firm performance was poor to restore the incentive effect for the option. Often, organizational politics play a role in this.

Repricing stock options does not appear to be a function of management entrenchment or ineffective governance. These firms often have had sudden and negative changes to their growth and profitability. They also frequently lose their top managers.

Interestingly, institutional investors prefer compensation schemes that link pay with performance, including the use of stock options. Again, this evidence shows that no internal governance mechanism is perfect.

Option awards became a means of providing large compensation packages, and the options awarded did not relate to the firm's performance, particularly when boards showed a propensity to reprice options at a lower strike price when stock prices fell precipitously. Option awards are becoming increasingly controversial.

10.5 Market for Corporate Control

The market for corporate control generally comes into use as an external governance mechanism only after internal governance mechanisms have failed.

The market for corporate control is composed of individuals and firms who buy ownership positions in (or take over) potentially undervalued firms. They do this in order to form a new division in an established diversified firm, merge two previously separate firms, and usually replace the target firm's management team to revamp the strategy that caused low firm performance. ①

The market for corporate control governance mechanism should be triggered by a

① 公司控制权市场是指个人或企业买入或接管估值偏低的企业,目的是在已有多样化企业中建立新的部门,将两个原本独立的企业合并,同时替换目标企业的管理团队,改造公司绩效低下的战略。

firm's poor performance relative to industry competitors. A firm's poor performance, often demonstrated by the firm's earning below-average returns, is an indicator that internal governance mechanisms have failed; that is, their use did not result in managerial decisions that maximized shareholder value.

Managerial Defense Tactics

Because of the threat of dismissal, managers have devised a number of defensive tactics designed to both ward off takeovers and buffer or protect managers from external governance mechanisms. These tactics include:

(1) managerial pay interventions, such as golden parachutes,

(2) asset restructuring, such as divesting a business unit or division,

(3) financial restructuring—e. g. , stock repurchases, paying out a firm's free cash flows as a dividend,

(4) changing the state of incorporation,

(5) making targeted shareholder repurchases.

Hostile Takeover Defense Strategies

Most institutional investors oppose the use of defense tactics. The market for corporate control also can be plagued by inefficiency. As a result,

(1) acquisition prices were excessive.

(2) expensive defensive strategies were often implemented to protect the firm.

Despite its inefficiency, the threat of acquisition by corporate raiders can serve as an effective constraint on the managerial growth motive and result in strategies that are in the best interests of the firm's owners.

Internal and external governance mechanisms, while they may restrain managerial actions, are imperfect means of controlling managerial opportunism. This means that some combination of both internal and external mechanisms is necessary.

10.6 International Corporate Governance

Our discussion of internal and external governance mechanisms—and their effectiveness in controlling managerial behavior—has been centered on the U. S. and the U. K. But this does not necessarily apply to the systems of corporate governance used elsewhere in the world—e. g. , German and Japanese firms.

While the stability that has been associated with the German and Japanese systems has been perceived as a strength, it is possible, given the dynamic and uncertain nature of the new competitive landscape, that stability may be a potential source of weakness. ①

10.6.1 Corporate Governance in Germany

The owner-manager relationship in Germany differs from that described for the U. S. For example:

(1) In many private German firms, the owner and manager are the same person.

(2) In publicly traded firms there often is a dominant shareholder.

Banks historically have occupied a central position in German governance structure.

(1) Banks became major shareholders when companies that they financed either sought new capital in the stock market or defaulted on loans.

(2) Banks generally hold less than 10 percent of a firm's stock.

(3) Bank ownership of a single firm's stock is limited to 15 percent of the bank's capital.

(4) Three large banks—Deutsche, Dresdner, and Commerzbank—hold majority positions in large German firms through their own holdings and proxy votes for shareholders who retain shares with the banks.

(5) German firms with more than 2000 employees must have a two-tiered board structure, with supervision of management being separated from other board duties and all of the functions of direction and management being placed in the hands of the Vorstand or management board.

(6) Appointment to the management board is the responsibility of the Aufsichtsrat or supervisory board.

Despite the ability of major owners and banks to monitor and control the managers of large German firms, maximizing shareholder value has not been an historical focus. However, this is changing.

A shift is taking place in German firms' historic lack of focus on maximizing shareholder value. For example, SGL Carbon AG lost more than $71 million in the early 1990s and was later restructured to turn the corporation around. In particular the firm's governance structure was changed, transparent accounting practices were adopted, and the firm set a goal of enhancing shareholder value. The firm's

---

① 虽然与德国和日本体系相关的稳定性被视为一种优势,但考虑到新竞争格局的动态性和不确定性,这种稳定性可能是弱点的潜在来源。

performance has since improved, and many attribute this to the new governance structure.

10.6.2 Corporate Governance in Japan

Corporate governance in Japan is affected by the concepts of obligation, family, and consensus.

In Japan, obligation goes beyond principles but is more a product of specific causes, events, and relationships. It can mean returning a service for one that has been rendered.

The concept of family goes beyond the American concept to include the firm—individuals see themselves as members of a company family. And the family concept is extended to include members of the firm's keiretsu, a group of firms that are tied together by cross-shareholdings, interrelationships, and interdependencies.

Consensus represents one of the most important influences on governance structure in Japan. This requires that managers—among others—expend significant amounts of energy to win the hearts and minds of people rather than proceed by the edicts of top-level managers.

As in Germany, banks also play an important role in financing and monitoring large public firms in Japan.

(1) The bank owning the largest share of stocks and the largest amount of debt—the main bank—has the closest relationship with the company's top executives.

(2) Banks occupy an important position in the governance system, both financing and monitoring firms.

(3) The main bank—the bank holding the largest share of a firm's debt—provides financial advice and assumes primary responsibility for monitoring the firm's management.

(4) Japanese banks can hold up to five percent of a firm's stock.

(5) Groups of banks can hold up to 40 percent of a firm's stock.

(6) In many cases, bank relations are an integral part of the Japanese firm's keiretsu (an industrial group of firms that interact with the same bank).

As in Germany, Japan's corporate governance structure is changing. For example, the role of banks in the monitoring and control of managerial behavior and firm outcomes has become less significant. Japan has traditionally applied relationship-capitalism, which is based on the premise that firms help each other when they are weak and facilitate and encourage each other as they become strong. This system has been a very effective method of protection in order to keep Japanese firms Japanese. This relationship-capitalism created a system for protection against "outside" owners by having a close-knit group of insiders who manage the firm as well as a larger set of interlocking shareholders who are mutually bonded by owning each other's stock. In the 1980s, these cross-shareholdings accounted for 50 percent of the equity in Japanese firms. Recently, relationship-capitalism accounts for only 20 percent of total equity.

Foreign ownership of Japanese firms has increased from approximately 4.7 percent in 1990 to 28 percent in 2007. A parallel trend is the increase in activist foreign shareholders making proposals in governing the firms differently. Japanese managers are facing an increasing level of activism, especially by foreign shareholders. Interestingly, in Japan, shareholders can vote directly on dividends and executive pay. Thus, on the surface it would appear that Japanese stock market policies are more shareholder-friendly than those in the United States or the United Kingdom. Furthermore, shareholders can vote to dismiss the entire board without cause. However, Japanese investors do not take up this power readily and most often defer to executive proposals. Since 28 percent of Japanese shares are now held by foreign institutional investors, these practices have begun to change. Shareholder activity is becoming more common. In June 2007, firms holding their shareholders' meetings faced 30 shareholder resolutions which were twice as many as there were one year earlier. Japanese managers who are determined to maintain a tightly-knit business culture feel threatened. Some of the issues raised by shareholders included the accumulation of heavy cash reserves that could be used to pay dividends that are inline with those paid by U. S. and U. K. firms and reorganizations that would result in employee layoffs.

Japanese managers have fought back through use of the Japanese media to paint non-Japanese shareholders as short-sighted financial criminals. In fact, the long-term health of Japanese firms might be improved given that Japanese firms hold cash and securities equivalent to 16 percent of GDP, whereas American firms' long-term average of cash and securities is about 5 percent. Although these slack resources in Japan may facilitate a longer-term view, from the eyes of the Japanese firms have recently begun experiencing activist shareholders who seek to increase returns through improved dividend policy.

Were not the symptoms of change anticipated in this case? This is a clash of cultures. Japanese business culture has valued relationships and consensus which calls for the expenditure of significant amounts of energy to win the hearts and minds of people whenever possible, as opposed to top executives issuing edicts. Consensus is highly valued, even when it results in a slow and cumbersome decision-making process. Do students feel that "compromise" is a realistic strategy in addressing this apparent conundrum?

10.6.3 Global Corporate Governance

As discussed in this section, the changes in governance that are taking place in Germany and Japan are representative of the twenty-first century competitive landscape, where customer demands are becoming more similar and shareholder value is becoming a more significant focus of managerial agents. This will result in more uniform governance structures.

Examples of differences and changes in international governance follow:

(1) In France, anger has been growing over the lack of information on top executive compensation. A recent report recommended that the positions of CEO and chairman of the board be held by two different individuals. It also recommended reducing the tenure of board members and to disclose their pay.

(2) In South Korea, principles of corporate governance are being adopted to provide proper board and management incentives to pursue the interests of both the company and the shareholders and to facilitate effective monitoring.

(3) Changes in corporate governance are occurring even in transitional economies, such as China and Russia, though implemented more gradually. The use of stock-based compensation plans has influenced foreign companies to invest.

10.7 Governance Mechanisms and Ethical Behavior

Governance mechanisms discussed in this chapter are focused on ensuring that managers work effectively toward meeting their obligation to maximize shareholder wealth. However, shareholders are only one group of the firm's stakeholders.

Over the long-term, the demands of other key stakeholders—such as employees, customers, suppliers, and the community—also must be satisfied in order to maximize shareholder wealth.

For that reason, and others, governance mechanisms must be carefully designed and implemented so that managers' attention is not focused on maximizing short-term returns and to ensure that they consider the interests of all stakeholders.

本章课程思政学习专题

公司内部治理与多元化战略①

1. 公司多元化经营动因

有关上市公司多元化经营的动因和经济后果研究一直是战略管理和财务学领域的重要问题。财务多元化战略是排除了组织寻求价值最大化动机之后股东与管理者之间代理冲突的直接体现,因为它并不能通过降低企业的系统化风险而增加股东的价值。传统的理论认为,可以通过公司内部治理(股东和董事会的控制及利益一致设计)来解决由管理者的机会主义行为引发的代理问题,但却忽略了公司内部治理作为一种制度设计本身会影响管理者自身的风险感知及实施财务多元化战略成功的可能性,进而影响管理者的战略选择行为。根据弗鲁姆的期望理论,实施财务多元化的激励力度大小取决于该行动达成目标带来的效价乘以达成该目标的期望概率。

2. 内部治理是否一定能够阻止公司价值减少的战略决策呢?

公司内部治理并非"必然"能够降低财务多元化水平,公司内部治理作为一种制度设计本身就是财务多元化战略的"诱因",即控制机制和利益一致设计能够影响高管实施财务多元化战略的"可能性"和实施财务多元化战略规避风险的"效价"满足。财务多元化有损股东价值,相比于第一大股东持股,全样本控制机制中的董事会独立性和 CEO 两职性能够显著降低财务多元化水平。进一步看,在不同的分样本检验中存在差异:在主板上市公司中,董事会独立性和 CEO 两职性能够显著降低财务多元化水平,在中小板上市公司中不显著;在非国企样本中董事会独立性能够显著降低财务多元化水平,在国企样本中 CEO 两职性能够显著降低财务多元化水平;全样本中,利益一致设计中的高管薪酬敏感度显著增加了财务多元化水平,高管持股比例显著降低财务多元化水平。这说明,一定水平之上的高管可变薪酬增加了高管可感知的风险,其实施财务多元化战略进行风险规避的"效价"满足更高,进而实施财务多元化的动机更强;当自由现金流水平高的时候,董事会的独立性在降低财务多元化水平时更为有效,高管薪酬敏感度更显著增加了财务多元化水平。

3. 思考问题

(1) 高管的态度和心理特征对公司的战略决策是否有影响?

(2) 董事会监督有效性的根本决定因素是什么?

---

① 周建,罗肖依,张双鹏. 公司内部治理能阻止财务多元化战略吗[J]. 南开管理评论,2017,20(1):4-15.

Chapter 11 Organizational Structure and Control

Opening Case

Are Strategy and Structural Changes in the Cards for GE?

For more than a century, GE has occupied a spot on the Dow Jones Industrial Index. This is the result of GE's stellar performance during its 100-plus year history. For 2006, GE reported earnings of \$20.7 billion on revenue of \$163 billion, which validates that GE is performing extremely well. One of the most effective avenues to profitable growth has been GE's emphasis on innovation. In 2006, research and development spending totaled nearly \$6 billion. But analysts and investors have pointed out that all is not well with GE. In response to these concerns, there may be some changes in corporate-level strategy and structure in the offing at GE.

When Jeffrey Immelt took over as CEO at GE following the legendary Jack Welch, he initiated changes that resulted in the reduction of operating units from eleven down to six. Those six include Commercial Finance, Healthcare, Industrial, Infrastructure, Money, and NBC Universal. In announcing his decision, Immelt said that "these changes will accelerate GE's growth in key industries" while simultaneously helping the firm become more focused on emerging technologies with significant commercial potential. Even with this reorganization, GE continued using the related-linked diversification strategy at the corporate level; the SBU form of the multidivisional structure remained the structure in place to facilitate use of the related-linked strategy.

In mid-2007, a prominent analyst called for GE to sell one or more of its six businesses. Specifically, his argument called for GE to sell noncore businesses such as NBC Universal and Money (formerly called Consumer Finance) to "raise billions (and) make this colossus a heck of a lot easier for one man to manage". The thought is that these two businesses have relatively little in common with the other four, and having them in GE's portfolio of businesses is a diversion from developing additional synergies (primarily in the form of economies of scope) across the four with greater similarities. Immelt and Welch both reacted less than positively to this suggestion, with Welch saying that following this advice "would be a tragedy of enormous proportions". If these two businesses were sold, GE's corporate-level strategy would change from related linked to related constrained. If this change in strategy were to occur, the firm's structure would also need to be changed from the SBU form of the multidivisional structure to the cooperative form of the multidivisional structure. From the perspective of strategic management, the important outcome is that a change to organizational structure accompany a decision to change a firm's strategy. The reason for making such a change is that a mismatch between strategy and structure negatively affects performance.

GE's management has a deeply entrenched, highly respected profitability record. While analysts' arguments regarding diversion and dilution of management's attention away from core operations might have some validity, GE has done a yeoman's job historically of managing what could be referred to as a full-plate. With annual R and D expenditures of $5.7 billion, it seems very apparent that innovation is not taking a backseat at the feeding trough. Is this a case of analysts taking themselves too seriously? Both Immelt and Welch have successfully managed the GE stable. They've been there; done that.

Introduction

The discussion in the previous chapter described how governance mechanisms are used to align the interests of a firm's top-level managers with those of the firm's owners. It also described how those mechanisms influence the firm's ability to execute strategies that have been implemented successfully as the firm strives to achieve a competitive advantage in the new competitive landscape. The same could be said of organizational structure, the focus of the current chapter.

The match or degree of fit between strategy and structure influences the firm's attempts to earn above-average returns. Thus, the ability to select an appropriate strategy and match it with the appropriate structure is an important characteristic of effective strategic leadership. The focus of this chapter is on the structure- and control-related issues of strategy implementation, including:

(1) the pattern of growth and changes in organizational structure experienced by strategically competitive firms,

(2) the organizational structures and controls that are used to implement separate business-level, corporate-level, international, and cooperative strategies,

(3) a series of figures to highlight the structures firms match with different strategies.

11.1 Organizational Structure and Controls

When the firm's strategy isn't matched with the most appropriate structure and controls, performance declines.

Selecting the organizational structure and controls that result in effective implementation of chosen strategies is a fundamental challenge for managers, especially top-level managers. The reasons for this are:

(1) Firms must be flexible, innovative, and creative in the global economy if they are to exploit their core competencies in the pursuit of marketplace opportunities.

(2) Firms must also maintain a certain degree of stability in their structures so that day-to-day tasks can be completed efficiently.

11.1.1 Organizational Structure

Organizational structure specifies the firm's formal reporting relationships, procedures, controls, and authority and decision-making processes. ①

Developing an organizational structure that effectively supports the firm's strategy is difficult, especially because of the uncertainty (or unpredictable variation) in cause-effect relationships in the global economy's rapidly changing, dynamic competitive environments. ② Structure facilitates effective implementation of a firm's strategies when elements of that structure (e.g., reporting relationships, procedures, and so forth) are properly aligned with one another. Thus, organizational structure is a critical component of effective strategy implementation processes.

Structure specifies the work to be done and how to do it (given the firm's strategy or strategies) by specifying the processes that are to be used to complete organizational tasks.

Effective structures provide the stability the firm needs to rely on its current competitive advantages to successfully implement today's strategies while providing the flexibility required to develop competitive advantages that will be needed to use future strategies; thus, an effective organizational structure allows the firm to exploit current competitive advantages while developing new ones.

---

① 组织架构决定了企业中正式汇报的对象、程序、控制以及权威以及决策过程。

② 开发出能有效支持企业策略的组织架构并不容易,原因之一是全球经济环境变幻莫测,充满竞争,因果之间充满不确定性,变化不可预测。

Modifications to the firm's current strategy or selection of a new strategy call for changes to organizational structure. This is not uncommon since organizational inertia often inhibits structural changes, even if performance declines. Because of inertial tendencies, structural change is often induced by the actions of stakeholders who are no longer willing to tolerate the firm's inadequate performance.

11.1.2 Organizational Controls

Organizational controls guide the use of strategy, indicate how to compare actual results with expected results, and suggest corrective actions to take when the difference between actual and expected results is unacceptable.①

Properly designed organizational controls—strategic and financial—provide insights into behaviors that enhance firm performance.

Strategic controls are largely subjective criteria intended to verify that the firm is using strategies that are appropriate given the conditions in the external environment and the company's competitive advantages.② Thus, strategic controls are concerned with examining the fit between what the firm might do (external environment) and what it can do (its competitive advantages).

Effective strategic controls help the firm understand what it takes to be successful. Strategic controls demand rich communication between managers using them and those implementing the firm's strategy. These frequent exchanges are both formal and informal in nature.

Strategic controls help evaluate how well a firm is focusing on what it takes to implement its strategies.

(1) For a business-level strategy, the concern is to study primary and support activities to verify that those that are critical to successful execution of the chosen strategy are being properly emphasized and executed.

(2) With related corporate-level strategies, strategic controls are used to verify that intended levels of sharing of relevant strategic factors—such as knowledge, markets, technologies, and so forth—are taking place. When evaluating related diversification strategies, executives must have a deep understanding of each unit's

---

① 组织控制指导如何运行策略,指导如何对比预期成果和实际成果,如两者偏差过大,组织控制提供纠正措施。

② 战略控制为主观标准,考虑到企业所处的外部环境及其竞争优势,战略控制主要核查企业采用的战略是否合适。

business-level strategy. Extensive diversification often requires that financial controls be emphasized.

The use of strategic controls, which are behavioral in nature, requires high levels of cognitive diversity among the firm's top-level managers. Cognitive diversity is a term that captures differences among top-level executives regarding their beliefs about cause-and-effect relationships and outcome-related preferences.

Financial controls are largely objective criteria used to measure the firm's performance against previously established quantitative standards, and these include accounting-based (e. g., return on investment, return on assets) and market-based (e. g., Economic Value Added) measures.①

Both strategic and financial controls are important aspects of each organizational structure; thus, any structure's effectiveness is determined by using a combination of strategic and financial controls.

11.2 Relationships between Strategy and Structure

Strategy and structure have a reciprocal relationship, highlighting the interconnectedness between strategy formulation and strategy implementation.

In general, structure follows the selection of the firm's strategy. However, once in place, structure has the potential to influence current strategic actions as well as choices about future strategies.

Regardless of the strength of the relationships between strategy and structure, those choosing the firm's strategy and structure should be committed to matching each strategy with a structure that provides the stability needed to use current competitive advantages as well as the flexibility required to develop future advantages.

Using the four criteria of sustainability, the firm's strategy/structure match is an advantage when that match is valuable, rare, imperfectly imitable, and nonsubstitutable.

① 财务控制为主观标准,主要衡量企业对量化标准的完成情况,包括两个层面的衡量:会计层面,如投资回报,资产回报;市场层面,如经济附加值。

11.3 Evolutionary Patterns of Strategy and Organizational Structure

Strategy and Structure Growth Pattern

Firm structure evolves from simple to functional to multidivisional.

This evolution is caused by sales growth and/or coordination and control problems that prevent the firm from efficiently implementing its formulated strategy.

Thus, as implementation efforts falter due to growth or other problems, the firm may need to change its organizational structure to achieve an appropriate fit between strategy and structure.

11.3.1 Simple Structure

A simple structure is an organizational form in which the owner-manager makes all major decisions directly and monitors all activities, and the firm's staff is merely an extension of the manager's supervision authority.

The simple structure is characterized by:

(1) little specialization of tasks,

(2) few rules,

(3) little formalization,

(4) unsophisticated information systems,

(5) direct involvement of owner-manager in all phases of day-to-day operations,

(6) frequent and informal communications between the owner-manager and employees.

In the U. K. , some analysts believe that the simple organizational structure may result in competitive advantages for some small firms relative to their larger counterparts. These competitive advantages include a broad openness to innovation, greater structural flexibility, and an ability to respond more rapidly to environmental changes.

If they are successful, small firms grow larger; and as a result, the firm outgrows the simple structure.

(1) There is a significant increase in the amount of competitively relevant information that requires analysis.

(2) More extensive and complicated information-processing requirements place significant pressures on owner-managers (often due to a lack of organizational skills or

experience). At this evolutionary point, firms tend to move from the simple structure to a functional organizational structure.

11.3.2 Functional Structure

The functional structure consists of a chief executive officer and limited corporate staff with functional line managers in dominant functions—e.g., production, accounting, marketing, R&D, engineering, human resources.

This structure allows for functional specialization, facilitating active knowledge sharing within each functional area. Knowledge sharing usually supports career paths and professional development of functional specialists.

However, compared to the simple structure, there also are some potential problems. For example, differences in functional specialization and orientation may impede communication and coordination.

Functional specialists often may develop a myopic or narrow perspective, losing sight of the firm's strategic vision and mission. When this happens, the problem can be overcome by implementing the multidivisional structure.

The functional structure supports implementation of business-level strategies and corporate-level strategies with low levels of diversification (e.g., dominant business).

11.3.3 Multidivisional Structure

Because of limits to an individual chief executive officer's ability to process complex strategic information, problems related to isolation of functional area managers, and increasing diversification, the structure of the firm must change again. In these instances, the multidivisional or M-form structure is most appropriate.[①]

The multidivisional (M-form) structure is composed of operating divisions where each division represents a separate business to which the top corporate officer delegates responsibility for day-to-day operations and business unit strategy to division managers.

As initially designed, the M-form was thought to have three major benefits.

(1) It allows corporate officers to accurately monitor business unit performance, simplifying control problems.

(2) It facilitated comparisons between divisions, which improved the resource allocation process.

---

① 由于单个首席执行官处理复杂战略信息的能力有限，与职能部门经理隔离相关的问题，以及日益多样化，公司的结构必须再次改变。在这些情况下，多分区或 M 形结构最合适。

(3) It stimulated managers of poorly performing divisions to look for ways of improving performance.

An expanded discussion of M-form may be helpful at this point. Some facts related to use of the multidivisional structure at DuPont and GM follow.

(1) The multidivisional or M-form structure was developed in the 1920s, in response to coordination and control problems in large firms such as DuPont and GM.

(2) Functional departments often had difficulty dealing with distinct product lines and markets, especially in coordinating conflicting priorities among the products.

(3) Costs were not allocated to individual products, so it was not possible to assess an individual product's profit contribution.

(4) Loss of control meant optimal allocation of firm resources between products was difficult.

(5) Top managers got over-involved in short-run matters (e. g., coordination, communications, conflict resolution) and neglected long-term strategic issues.

The new, innovative structure adopted at General Motors called for

(1) creating separate divisions, each representing a distinct business,

(2) each division would house its functional hierarchy,

(3) division managers were given responsibility for managing day-to-day operations,

(4) a small corporate office would determine the long-term strategic direction of the firm and exercise overall financial control over the semi-autonomous divisions.

This would enable the firm to

(1) accurately monitor performance of each business, simplifying control problems,

(2) facilitate comparisons between divisions, improving the allocation of resources,

(3) stimulate managers of poorly performing divisions to seek ways to improve.

11.3.4 Matches between Business-Level Strategies and the Functional Structure

Different forms of the functional organizational structure are used to support implementation of the cost leadership, differentiation, and integrated cost leadership/differentiation strategies. The differences in these forms are accounted for primarily by different uses of three important structural characteristics or dimensions—specialization (the type and number of jobs required to complete work), centralization (the degree to which decision-making authority is retained at higher managerial levels), and formalization (the degree to which formal rules and procedures govern work).[①]

Using the Functional Structure to Implement the Cost Leadership Strategy

Firms using the cost leadership strategy want to sell large quantities of standardized products to an industry's or a segment's typical customer. The cost leadership form of the functional structure usually features:

(1) simple reporting relationships,

(2) few layers in the decision-making and authority structure,

(3) a centralized corporate staff,

(4) a strong focus on process improvements through the manufacturing function rather than the development of new products through an emphasis on product R&D.

Because of firm restructuring during the late 1980s and early 1990s—and the reduction in the number of management layers—firms now have flatter structures. "Higher" in the organizational structure has thus become a relative term.

Cost leadership strategies emphasize:

(1) centralization of decision-making to maintain cost reduction,

(2) jobs that are specialized to increase efficiency,

(3) formalization of rules and procedures to converge on the most efficient approaches.

Functional Structure for Implementation of a Cost Leadership Strategy

Key points include the following:

(1) Dotted lines from the centralized staff to each function represent tight controls and centralized coordination.

(2) The focus is on the operations (production) function.

(3) Emphasis is placed on process engineering not on new product research and development.

(4) Relatively large central staff coordinates functions.

(5) Job roles are highly structured.

(6) The overall structure is mechanical.

(7) The structure may be either relatively tall or flat (depending the on the

---

① 不同形式的职能组织结构用于支持成本领先、差异化和综合成本领先/差异化战略的实施。这些形式的差异主要是由于对三个重要结构特征或维度的不同使用:专业化(完成工作所需的工作类型和数量)、集中化(在更高管理层保留决策权的程度)和正式化(正式规则和程序管理工作的程度)。

extent of firm restructuring).

Using the Functional Structure to Implement the Differentiation Strategy

Firms offering products that are considered unique by customers usually are following a differentiation strategy.

A differentiation strategy requires:

(1) the firm to sell nonstandardized products to customers with unique needs,

(2) relatively complex and flexible reporting relationships,

(3) frequent use of cross-functional product development teams,

(4) a strong focus on marketing and product R&D rather than manufacturing and process R&D,

(5) continuous product innovation, requiring people be able to interpret and take action based on ambiguous, incomplete, and uncertain information,

(6) a strong focus on the external environment to identify new opportunities,

(7) rapid responses to collected information suggesting a need for decentralization,

(8) creativity and the continuous pursuit of new sources of differentiation and new products requiring a lack of specialization (i.e., workers have a relatively large number of tasks in their job descriptions),

(9) low formalization, decentralization, and low specialization of work tasks allowing people to interact frequently to further differentiate products while developing ideas for new products.

Functional Structure for Implementing a Differentiation Strategy

(1) The centralized corporate staff (between the president and the individual functions) has been replaced by the central staffs of R&D and marketing, which work closely together.

(2) Dotted lines between the centralized staff and individual functions have been removed, indicating a decentralization of decision making.

(3) Formalization is limited to enable emergence of new product ideas and enhanced ability to change.

(4) Job roles are less structured.

(5) The structure is organic.

Using the Functional Structure to Implement the Integrated Cost Leadership/Differentiation Strategy

Some firms may attempt to implement simultaneously both the cost leadership and differentiation strategies by providing value through:

(1) low cost relative to a differentiated firm's products,

(2) differentiated features relative to features offered by cost leadership firms' products.

The integrated cost leadership/differentiation strategy is used frequently in the global economy, though it is difficult to implement. This difficulty is due largely to the fact that different primary and support activities must be emphasized.

(1) Low-cost strategies emphasize production and manufacturing process engineering and few product changes.

(2) Differentiation strategies require an emphasis on marketing and new product R&D.

Toyota Motor Corporation has become a world leader in the auto industry primarily through its ability to implement cost leadership and differentiation at the same time. The key to Toyota's success has been the differentiated design and manufacturing process that the company has implemented through its integrated product design process.

11.3.5 Matches between Corporate-Level Strategies and the Multidivisional Structure

The firm's level of diversification is a function of decisions about the number and type of businesses in which it will compete, as well as how it will manage the businesses. Geared to managing individual organizational functions, increasing diversification eventually creates information processing, coordination, and control problems that the functional structure can't handle. This requires a shift from a functional structure to a complex multidivisional structure. ①

The demands created by different levels of diversification require that each strategy be implemented through a unique organizational structure.

From 1950 to the late 1980s, among Fortune 500 firms, diversification and

① 公司的多元化水平取决于其将参与竞争的业务的数量和类型，以及如何管理这些业务。为了管理单个组织职能，日益多样化最终会产生职能结构无法处理的信息处理、协调和控制问题。这需要从职能结构转变为复杂得多部门结构。

implementation of the multidivisional structure increased dramatically.

(1) The percentage of diversified firms increased from 30% to approximately 75%.

(2) The multidivisional structure increased from less than 20% to approximately 90%.

Three Variations of the Multidivisional Structure

The three variations of the multidivisional structure that will be discussed from the perspective of how each is best suited to specific diversification strategies are the:

(1) Cooperative form.

(2) Strategic Business Unit (SBU) form.

(3) Competitive form.

Using the Cooperative Form of the Multidivisional Structure to Implement the Related Constrained Strategy

The cooperative form structure uses horizontal integration to bring about interdivisional cooperation. The divisions in the firm using the related-constrained diversification strategy commonly are formed around products, markets, or both.

Cooperative Form of the Multidivisional Structure for Implementing a Related-Constrained Strategy

The first variant of the M-form structure—the Cooperative M-form—is characterized by an increased emphasis on integration devices and horizontal human resource practices.

All divisions are controlled by the central office and integrated by one of the integrating mechanisms (such as division managers meeting face-to-face, integrating teams, or task forces).

Integrating mechanisms are indicated by the dotted line connecting the divisions which create:

(1) tight linkages between divisions,

(2) corporate office emphasizing centralized planning, human resources, and marketing to facilitate cooperation,

(3) centralized R&D to coordinate new product introductions and/or process engineering improvements,

(4) a subjective reward system emphasizing corporate and division performance,

(5) a cooperative, sharing culture.

All of the related-constrained firm's divisions share one or more corporate strengths. Production competencies, marketing competencies, or channel dominance are examples of strengths that the firm's divisions might share.[①]

(1) Production expertise is one of the strengths of Sony's divisions, but they have had difficulties in coordinating across divisions to create joint products in online music.

(2) Outback Steakhouse, Inc. has sought to diversify across eight different chains using a cooperative M-form structure, to centralize a number of critical functions across the businesses for activities sharing, and to share its expertise in running franchise operations across contracting, advertising, training and more.

The sharing of divisional competencies facilitates the corporation's efforts to develop economies of scope (which are cost savings resulting from the sharing of competencies developed in one division with another division) that are linked with successful use of the related-constrained strategy. Interdivisional sharing of competencies depends on cooperation, suggesting the use of the cooperative form of the multidivisional structure. Increasingly, it is important that the links resulting from effective use of integration mechanisms support the cooperative sharing of both intangible resources (e. g. , knowledge) as well as tangible resources (e. g. , facilities and equipment).

The following are different characteristics of structure that are used as integrating mechanisms by the cooperative structure to facilitate interdivisional cooperation:

(1) Centralization—control at the corporate level allows the linking of activities among divisions.

(2) Frequent, direct contact between division managers—encourages and supports cooperation and the sharing of competencies or resources that can be used to create new advantages. These mechanisms include liaison roles, temporary teams/task forces, formal integration departments, and a matrix organization configuration.

(3) Coordination among divisions sometimes results in an unequal flow of positive outcomes to divisional managers. In other words, when managerial rewards are based at least in part on the performance of individual divisions, the manager of the division that is able to benefit the most by the sharing of corporate competencies might be viewed as receiving relative gains at others' expense. Strategic controls are important in these instances, as divisional managers' performance can be evaluated at least partly on the basis of how well they have facilitated interdivisional cooperative efforts.

---

① 所有受相关性约束的公司部门都有一个或多个优势(能力或资源)。生产能力、营销能力或渠道优势是公司各部门可能共享的优势。

Furthermore, using reward systems that emphasize overall company performance, besides outcomes achieved by individual divisions, helps overcome problems associated with the cooperative form.

Using the Strategic Business Unit Form of the Multidivisional Structure to Implement the Related Linked Strategy

The strategic business unit (SBU) structure is most appropriate for the related-linked (mixed related and unrelated) strategy.

A strategic business unit (SBU) structure consists of at least three levels, with a corporate headquarters at the top, SBU groups at the second level, and divisions grouped by relatedness within each SBU at the third level.

This means that,

(1) within each SBU, divisions are related to each other.

(2) SBU groups are unrelated to each other.

(3) within each SBU, divisions producing similar products and/or using similar technologies can be organized to achieve synergy.

(4) individual SBUs are treated as profit centers and controlled by corporate headquarters.

(5) corporate headquarters can concentrate on strategic planning rather than operational control.

Many of GE's SBUs attempt to form competencies in services and technology as a source of competitive advantage. Recently technology was identified as an advantage for the GE Medical Systems SBU as that unit's divisions share technological competencies to produce an array of sophisticated equipment, including computed tomography (CT) scanners, magnetic resonance imaging (MRI) systems, nuclear medicine cameras, and ultrasound systems. Once a competence is developed in one Medical Systems division, it is quickly transferred to the other divisions in that SBU so the competence can help to increase the unit's overall performance.

SBU Form of the Multidivisional Structure for Implementing a Related Linked Strategy

While the SBU M-form appears similar to the Cooperative M-form, there are several differences.

The SBU M-form includes an addition layer—the strategic business unit or SBU—between the corporate headquarters and product divisions.

(1) There may be integration and coordination between divisions in a specific

SBU.

(2) There is independence among and between SBUs.

(3) Headquarters manages approval of strategic planning of SBUs for the president.

(4) Individual SBUs may have budgets and staffs for within-SBU integrating mechanisms.

(5) Corporate headquarters staff serve as consultants to SBUs and divisions on product strategy (rather than having direct input).

Using the Competitive Form of the Multidivisional Structure to Implement the Unrelated Diversification Strategy

Firms following an unrelated diversification strategy can create value by:

(1) efficient internal capital allocations,

(2) restructuring, buying, and selling businesses.

Unrelated diversified firms should adopt the third variant of the multidivisional structure, the competitive form of the multidivisional structure, where controls emphasize competition between separate (usually unrelated) divisions for corporate capital allocations.

Competitive Form of the Multidivisional Structure for Implementation of an Unrelated Strategy

The Competitive M-form differs from both the Cooperative and SBU M-forms by:

(1) establishing a smaller headquarters office, generally containing three functions:

① legal affairs, which increases in importance when a firm acquires or divests units,

② auditing, which monitors divisional performance to ensure performance data are accurately reported,

③ finance, which manages the firm's cash flow and allocates capital.

(2) allowing independent divisions so financial performance can be monitored separately for each.

(3) setting up divisions that retain strategic control, but give up cash flow control.

(4) allowing competition between divisions for capital allocations.

The efficient internal capital market that is the foundation for use of the unrelated diversification strategy requires organizational arrangements that emphasize divisional competition rather than cooperation, and three benefits are expected from this internal competition:

(1) Internal competition creates flexibility, allowing resources to be allocated to the division that is working with the most promising technology to fuel the entire firm's success.

(2) Internal competition challenges the status quo and inertia, because division heads know that future resource allocations are a product of excellent current performance as well as superior positioning of their division in terms of future performance.

(3) Internal competition motivates effort.

Newell Rubbermaid Company (a supplier of hardware items to discount retailers) has used the competitive M-form to implement an unrelated diversification strategy. Features of the firm that match this structural selection include the following:

(1) The basic strategy of the firm was to market a multi-product offering of brand-name consumer products to mass retailers.

(2) The firm emphasized excellent customer service.

(3) Newell Rubbermaid was committed to growth by acquisition.

(4) Product lines added over time to the firm's divisions share no common characteristics.

(5) Newell Rubbermaid sold an array of products, including household products, hardware, and home and office furnishings.

(6) The firm's competitive advantage was created at the corporate level.

(7) Using a small corporate headquarters staff, the firm developed a sophisticated electronic, logistical system that was given to each division.

(8) Although not related to each other, each of Newell Rubbermaid's divisions created value from the lower cost and improved customer relations provided by the system.

Characteristics of the Structures Necessary to Implement the Related Constrained, Related Linked, and Unrelated Strategies

A handy reference that can be used to compare the structural attributes of the Cooperative, SBU, and Competitive M-form structures based on the:

(1) degree that operations are centralized or decentralized,

(2) extent to which each form uses integrating mechanisms,

(3) emphasis on subjective or objective criteria for appraising divisional performance,

(4) linkages to corporate, SBU, and/or divisional performance as bases for divisional incentive compensation.

11.3.6 Matches between International Strategies and Worldwide Structures

Forming proper matches between international strategies and organizational structures intended to support their use facilitates the firm's efforts to effectively coordinate and control its global operations. ①

Importantly, recent research findings confirm the validity of the strategy/structure matches discussed.

Using the Worldwide Geographic Area Structure to Implement the Multidomestic Strategy

Although centralization of decision-making authority has been recognized as a means of achieving coordination (and control) in organizations, some strategies require that local business units (or divisions) have the flexibility that will enable them to adapt to local market preferences. This may mean that a decentralized structure will be needed to provide this flexibility.

The multidomestic strategy is a strategy in which strategic and operating decisions are decentralized to business units in each country to facilitate tailoring of products to each country.

The structure used to implement the multidomestic strategy is the worldwide geographic area structure, an organizational form in which national interests dominate and that facilitates managers' efforts to satisfy local or cultural differences.

Worldwide Geographic Area Structure for Implementing a Multidomestic Strategy

The worldwide geographic area structure is characterized by:

(1) an emphasis on differentiation or adaptation to local market preferences or cultural requirements,

(2) individual national market operations as decentralized and independent,

(3) corporate headquarters coordinating movement of financial resources,

(4) organization representing a decentralized federation.

---

① 在国际战略和旨在支持其使用的组织结构之间形成适当的匹配有助于公司有效协调和控制其全球运营。

The multidomestic strategy requires a decentralized structure.

(1) National or country-specific preferences require local adaptation for success.

(2) Little coordination is required because of local market differences.

(3) There is no need for integrating mechanisms among divisions.

(4) The level of formalization is low.

(5) Coordination mechanisms are informal in nature.

However, firms adoptingmultidomestic strategies and the worldwide geographic area structure must give up the ability to achieve global efficiency.

Using the Worldwide Product Divisional Structure to Implement the Global Strategy

In contrast with the multidomestic strategy, a global strategy is characterized by

(1) a corporate home office that dictates competitive strategy,

(2) a firm that offers standardized products across country markets,

(3) the development and exploitation of economies of scope and scale on a global level,

(4) decisions to outsource some primary or support activities.

The appropriate structure for implementation of a global strategy is the worldwide product divisional structure, which is characterized by centralized decision-making authority at the worldwide division headquarters and the establishment of effective coordination and joint problem-solving among disparate divisional subunits.

Worldwide Product Divisional Structure for Implementing a Global Strategy

The worldwide product divisional structure is characterized by:

(1) an emphasis on inter-division coordination devices to facilitate global economies of scale and scope,

(2) information flows that are coordinated by the shaded global headquarters office,

(3) corporate headquarters allocates financial resources in a cooperative way,

(4) organization represents a centralized federation.

Multiple integrating mechanisms—which result in effective coordination through mutual adjustment via personal interaction—include:

(1) encouraging direct, face-to-face contact between managers,

(2) assigning liaison roles between departments,

(3) forming temporary task forces or teams.

Using the Combination Structure to Implement the Transnational Strategy

The last international strategy (the transnational strategy) combinesmultidomestic and global strategies by:

(1) seeking national or country-specific advantages by emphasizing adaptation to local differences,

(2) attempting simultaneously to achieve global economies of scale and scope.

The combination structure is an organizational form with characteristics and structural mechanisms that result in an emphasis on both geographic and product structures.

The transnational strategy is often implemented through two possible combination structures: a global matrix structure or a hybrid global design.

(1) The global matrix design brings together both local market and product expertise into teams who develop and respond to the global marketplace worldwide.

(2) In the hybrid structure some divisions are oriented towards products while others are oriented toward market areas.

Using the Hybrid Form of the Combination Structure for Implementing a Transnational Strategy

In this design, some divisions are oriented toward products while others are oriented toward market areas. Thus, in some products, where the geographic area is more important, the division managers are area-oriented. In other divisions, where worldwide product coordination and efficiencies are more important, the division manager is more product-oriented.

As alluded to previously, specific attributes of the transnational structure are difficult to identify because of the conflicting requirements that firms organize to provide the firm simultaneously with the

(1) flexibility required for adapting to local market preferences,

(2) coordination and control necessary to pursue global economies of scale and scope.

Firms implementing transnational strategies must encourage employees to understand the effects of cultural diversity on the firm's operations and adopt a combination structure that is simultaneously

(1) centralized and decentralized,

(2) integrated and nonintegrated,

(3) formalized and nonformalized.

A Strategic Network

The strategic center firm sits in the middle of the strategic network so that it can coordinate the activities of network members firms.

As coordinator or manager of activities carried out by partners in the strategic network, the strategic center firm—and other network partners—should note four critical aspects of the strategic center firm's functions:

(1) Strategic Outsourcing.

(2) Development of Competencies.

(3) Technology Management.

(4) Race to Learn (or Managing Learning Processes).

Strategic Outsourcing is one of the strategic center firm's key functions. In addition to outsourcing more than other members of the strategic network, the center firm also encourages member firms to go beyond contracting to solve problems and to initiate competitive actions that the network can pursue.

The Competence-related role of the center firm is to build or develop the core competencies of other network member firms and encourage them to share these with other network partners.

Technology aspects of the center firm's role include managing the development and sharing of technology-based ideas among network partners.

Emphasizing the Race to Learn implies that the strategic center firm must encourage positive rivalry among partner firms that will strengthen each partner's (as well as the network's) value chain. The effectiveness of the center firm is related to how well it learns to manage learning processes among network partners.

11.4 Implementing Business-Level Cooperative Strategies

Complementary assets at the business level can be vertical or horizontal. Vertical complementary strategic alliances are more common than are horizontal alliances and generally are focused on buyer-supplier relationships.

With Toyota's strategic network of vertical alliances in Japan, Toyota, as the strategic center firm:

(1) encourages subcontractors to modernize their facilities,

(2) supplies them with any necessary technical and financial assistance,

(3) reduces transactions costs by entering into long-term contracts which allow supplying partners to increase long-term productivity (as opposed to entering into a

series of short-term contracts based on unit pricing),

(4) provides engineers in upstream companies (suppliers) with better communication with contractees,

(5) allows suppliers and center firms to become more interdependent and less independent,

(6) is able to achieve a competitive advantage because of the imperfect imitability of the structure and the proprietary actions that it uses to manage its strategic network.

Horizontal complementary strategic alliances are much more difficult to manage than are vertical complementary strategic alliances because, in a horizontal alliance, it is difficult to select a strategic center firm when several network members have been aggressive competitors. An example is the instability of alliances between large airlines.

11.5 Implementing Corporate-Level Cooperative Strategies

It is less difficult to select a strategic center firm in corporate-level cooperative strategic alliances structured as centralized franchise networks than in those that are decentralized sets of diversified strategic alliances.

McDonald's has established a centralized strategic network in which its corporate office acts as the strategic center for its network of franchisees.

(1) The headquarters office uses strategic controls and financial controls to verify that the franchisees' operations create the greatest value for the entire network.

(2) A strategic control issue is the location of franchisee units—McDonald's believes that its greatest expansion opportunities are outside the United States.

(3) Financial controls are framed around requirements an interested party must satisfy to become a McDonald's franchisee, as well as performance standards that are to be met when operating a unit.

11.6 Implementing International Cooperative Strategies

Competing across national borders increases the complexity of the task of managing strategic networks that have been formed through international cooperative strategies and stifles the selection of a strategic center firm because great differences may exist among the regulatory environments of partners' home countries.

In response to this complexity:

(1) distributed strategic networks are formed,

(2) multiple regional strategic centers are established.

A Distributed Strategic Network

While the distributed strategic network has a primary or main strategic center firm, it also is characterized by multiple strategic center firms that are distributed throughout the world.

For example, firms such as Ericsson and Electrolux establish multiple strategic centers, which enables them to better manage multiple cooperative relationships with partnering firms that may cross national or regional boundaries or to manage specific global product markets more effectively.

The distributed strategic network form of organization enables the international cooperative network to ensure that region-, country-or product-specific market requirements are managed by the appropriate distributed strategic center firm.

本章课程思政学习专题

组织结构变革①

1. 企业组织结构变革

企业组织结构的变革,总是随着信息技术的进步而发展,从传统的塔式智能型组织结构、到矩阵型事业部结构、向扁平化联盟型组织结构演化,信息技术越发达,企业决策层掌控的幅度就能越大,模块化、扁平化和全球化的联盟趋势就更明显。供应链就属于一种常见的联盟结构,传统的供应链由上下游企业构成主体,企业主体通过原材料的供应、产品的生产、商品的销售这样的物流发生交互关系,并相互串联形成纵向的链式结构。信息技术的不断发展,会促使这种链式组织的某一级结点对供应链各级结点的掌控幅度都普遍增强,同一级就会有多家同类型可选结点出现,链式组织结构就向网络组织结构演化了。

信息技术发展的不足,导致联盟组织始终存在外部边际有界性和内部模块异质性的问题,限制了联盟组织在规模上的扩张;外部有界性和内部异质性又反过来造成了联盟成员设置更复杂的沟通机制、更冗余的交互关系,来保障彼此的信息交流和商业合作。这从根本上带来联盟组织结构的冗杂和割裂、沟通成本居高

① 胡斌,王莉丽.物联网环境下的企业组织结构变革[J].管理世界,2020,36(8):202-210+232.

不下、数据信息难以整合、组织关系协调不畅等问题。

当今物联网技术及其引起的整体环境的变化,会对消费者行为以及企业的生产经营方式,带来全新的冲击,从而导致企业组织结构根本性的改变。作为一种新兴的以"物""网络"和"信息"为三大导向的信息通信技术,传感技术、网络通信技术、追溯技术、平台技术等均是物联网技术群体的典型代表。这些新兴的信息技术,以有机的形式相互组合、协同运作、交互影响,从而形成一体化的物联网智能系统。它们在企业组织中被逐步采用并不断升级,其精准实时地对人和"物"的追溯特性和万"物"互联的平台特性,弥补了现有企业组织尤其是大规模联盟组织的结构缺陷,对联盟组织的结构特征及其运作模式产生了全面而深刻的影响。

2. 物联网环境下的企业组织结构变革

在物联网诸多技术中,实时追溯技术和平台管理技术,直接促使了企业的组织结构的变革。随着追溯技术和平台技术能力的不断进步,企业组织结构从点—线延伸结构向点—网辐射结构演变,供应链组织和联盟组织,成为物联网环境下企业组织表现形式的发展趋势。在组织结构的演变中,追溯技术和平台技术所发生的作用,离不开物联网系统计算服务能力的支持,计算服务能力的大小决定了企业组织的网络化规模的大小。物联网的典型应用领域是现代制造业和物流业。在现代制造业中,制造商先依靠物联网技术实现生产和物流执行层的技术改造,以此驱动职能层、决策层的组织结构变革,形成智能制造企业,然后依靠追溯技术和平台技术,沿着物流供应链,将上下游企业集成起来,形成从早期点—线延伸组织结构向后期点—网辐射组织结构的演变。在现代物流业中,产品经历了从制造商出厂到最终顾客这一供应链沿线的各个环节,随着物联网计算服务能力的提高,供应链沿线企业逐渐向网络化的企业集群转化,物流组织实现了从点—线延伸结构向后期点—网辐射结构演变。物联网零星技术和成套技术、甚至整体物联网环境在制造业和物流业中的实际应用比其他行业更为常见,这就限制了本文案例分析的行业范围。随着今后物联网系统及其技术的进一步普及,我们将进一步结合现实案例深入揭示物联网环境下企业组织结构的变革机理。

3. 思考问题

企业如何利用信息技术来促进组织结构演进?

Chapter 12 Strategic Leadership

Opening Case

Top-Level Strategic Leader

Jack Ma (Ma Yun) is a Chinese business magnate and philanthropist. He is the founder and Executive Chairman of Alibaba Group, a family of highly successful Internet-based businesses. He is the first Chinese mainland entrepreneur to appear on the cover of Forbes. As of November 2014, he is the richest man in China and 18th richest man in the world with an estimated net worth of $29.7 billion, according to Bloomberg Billionaires Index.

Introduction

This chapter deals with the importance of strategic leadership, its effects on organizational outcomes, and the great challenges faced by strategic leaders. This indicates that effective strategic leaders must be able to use the strategic management process effectively by

(1) guiding the firm in ways that result in the formation of its vision and mission,

(2) facilitating the development of appropriate strategic actions,

(3) providing guidance that results in strategic competitiveness and above-average returns.

Strategic Leadership and the Strategic Management Process

Effective strategic leadership shapes the formation of the firm's vision and mission which influences the①

(1) development of successful strategic actions,

(2) formulation of strategies,

(3) implementation of strategies.

which lead to②

---

① 有效的战略领导影响公司前景与任务的形成过程,这一过程会影响:(1) 策略的成功开发;(2) 战略的形成;(3) 战略的实施。

② 这一过程会导致:(1) 战略竞争力;(2) 超过平均水平的收益。

(1) strategic competitiveness,

(2) above-average returns.

Xerox presents an interesting story in strategic leadership. It is true that Xerox has committed a number of strategic blunders over the years, and yet it has enjoyed significant success in digital copy technologies. However, because of significant weakness in its many businesses, the company almost foundered after years of weak sales, high costs, and low employee morale. When Anne Mulcahy was promoted to President of the company in 2000, she took steps to try to turn the situation around—e. g., by divesting businesses, such as financial services, selling copiers and printers, and trying to strengthen the firm's services and solutions business.

12.1 Strategic Leadership and Style

Strategic leadership entails the ability to anticipate, envision, maintain flexibility, and empower others to create strategic change as necessary. In other words, strategic leadership represents a complex form of leadership in organizations.① A manager with strategic leadership skills exhibits the ability to guide the firm through the competitive landscape by②

(1) managing an entire enterprise,

(2) influencing the behavior, thoughts, and feelings of co-workers,

(3) managing through others,

(4) successfully processing or making sense of complex, ambiguous information by successfully dealing with change and uncertainty.

The strategic leader has several responsibilities, including the following:③

(1) establishing a context for efficiency,

(2) managing human capital (perhaps the most critical of the strategic leader's skills),

(3) effectively managing the firm's operations,

---

① 战略领导涉及预测、展望、保持灵活性的能力,同时有能力让他人必要时做出战略改变。换言之,战略领导是组织中领导力的一种复杂形式。

② 擅长战略领导的管理者展现出在竞争格局中引导企业的能力,能够做到:(1) 管理整个企业。(2) 影响同事的行为、想法以及感受。(3) 通过他人管理。(4) 通过处理变化和不确定性,理解和消化复杂的模糊信息。

③ 战略领导人担负着以下责任:(1) 创造高效的环境。(2) 管理人力资源(可能是战略领导力最重要的技能)。(3) 有效管理企业的运转。(4) 保持长期的高绩效。(5) 公正勇敢地做出实用的决策。(6) 征求同事、上级、员工关于决策及愿景难度的反馈。(7) 在企业内外寻求伙伴,推动愿景的实现。

(4) sustaining high performance over time,

(5) being willing to make candid, courageous, yet pragmatic, decisions,

(6) soliciting feedback from peers, superiors, and employees about their difficult decisions and vision,

(7) developing strong partners internally and externally to facilitate execution of their vision.

Strategic leaders are those at the top of the organization (in particular, the CEO), but other commonly recognized strategic leaders include members of the board of directors, the top management team, and division general managers.

The style used to provide leadership often affects the productivity of those being led. The most effective leadership style used by strategic leaders is a transformational leadership style, which encourages followers to exceed expectations, and place the organization above self interests. The strategic leadership skills of an organization's managers represent resources that can affect the firm's performance. These resources must be developed for the firm's future benefit.

12.2 The Role of Top-Level Managers

Top-level managers represent an important resource for organizations as they attempt to formulate and implement strategies effectively because of top-level mangers' roles in designing the organization and the performance outcomes that result from using that design. Thus, it is important for organizations to have a top management team with superior managerial skills.

Three factors can be viewed as determining a strategic leader's decision discretion:

(1) External environmental sources.

(2) Organizational characteristics.

(3) Managerial characteristics.

Factors Affecting Managerial Discretion

Managerial discretion is a function of three factors: external environment, organizational characteristics, and an individual manager's characteristics.

External Environment:

(1) industry structure,

(2) rate of market growth,

(3) number and type of competitors,

(4) nature and degree of political/legal constraints,

(5) degree to which products are differentiated.

Organizational Characteristics:

(1) size,

(2) age,

(3) organizational culture,

(4) availability of resources,

(5) patterns of interaction among employees.

Managers' (Individual) Characteristics:

(1) manager's tolerance for ambiguity,

(2) commitment to the firm and its desired strategic outcomes,

(3) interpersonal skills,

(4) level of aspiration,

(5) degree of self-confidence.

Other critical roles played by top-level managers include:

(1) implementing an appropriate organizational structure,

(2) implementing the organization's reward systems,

(3) shaping the organization's culture,

(4) influencing organizational activities and performance.

Remind students that, for top-level managers to make a difference—or enhance a firm's ability to achieve a competitive advantage—they generally must possess superior knowledge and skills. While all organizations have strategic leaders, the top management team's portfolio of skills must be rare, valuable, difficult for other top management teams to imitate, and not be readily substitutable if they are to result in a competitive advantage for the firm.

Top Management Teams

The complexity of the challenges faced by the firm and the need for substantial amounts of information and knowledge require teams of executives to provide the strategic leadership of most firms. Use of a team to make strategic decisions also helps to avoid managerial hubris.

A firm's top management team is composed of key managers that are primarily responsible for formulating and implementing the firm's strategy. In the case of large organizations, members of the top management team usually can be identified as those individuals with the title of vice president or above and/or individuals who serve on its board of directors. ①

Strategic actions taken by a firm's top management team will have an impact—positive or negative—on firm performance. Research indicates that there seems to be a link between the configuration or mix of expertise and skills of members of a firm's top management team and firm performance.

Top Management Team, Firm Performance, and Strategic Change

The job of top-level executives is complex and requires a broad knowledge of the firm's operations, as well as the three key parts of the firm's external environment—the general, industry, and competitor environments. Thus, firms try to form a top management team that has the appropriate knowledge and expertise to operate the internal organization, yet also can deal with all the firm's stakeholders as well as its competitors.

Research into the relationship or link between top management team composition and firm performance generally indicates that team heterogeneity is important. A heterogeneous top management team is composed of individuals with different functional backgrounds, experiences, and education.

The more heterogeneous a top management team is, with varied expertise and knowledge, the more capacity it has to provide effective strategic leadership in formulating strategy. Members of a heterogeneous top management team benefit from discussing the different perspectives advanced by team members, and these discussions can increase the quality of the top management team's decisions.

The net benefit of the actions of heterogeneous teams tends to be positive in terms of market share and above-average returns. It is also important that the top management team members function cohesively. In general, more heterogeneous and larger top management teams find it more difficult to implement strategies effectively.

Research indicates a positive relationship between higher levels of a top management team's heterogeneity, firm innovation, and strategic change. Thus, a team with diverse backgrounds and expertise is more likely to:

(1) change strategies when it is necessary to do so,

(2) identify internal and external environmental changes that require the firm to change strategic direction,

---

① 企业的最高管理团队由关键管理人组成,主要负责制定并实施企业的战略。在大型组织中,最高管理团队通常被称为副总裁,或者是董事会中的人。

(3) "think outside of the box" and thus be more creative in making decisions.

The CEO and Top Management Team Power

While the composition of a firm's top management team is important, a team that is too powerful may negatively affect firm performance. As noted in Chapter 10, the involvement of outsiders as members of a firm's board of directors also has an impact on firm performance.① In fact, involvement of outside directors in shaping the firm's strategic direction normally results in higher firm performance (than when they are not involved).

Inside directors (part of management) can affect CEO power because they

(1) report to the CEO,

(2) have a greater understanding of firm operations (information they control),

(3) can control the flow of information to outside directors.

However, in some cases, a firm's CEO and members of the top management team may "overpower" the firm's board of directors. This can happen when

(1) the CEO appoints members of the board (insiders or sympathetic outsiders),

(2) the CEO also holds the title of Chairman of the Board (sometimes called "CEO duality").

It varies across industries, but duality occurs most commonly in the largest of firms. Increased shareholder activism, however, has brought CEO duality under scrutiny and attack in both U. S. and European firms. Historically, an independent board leadership structure—in which the same person did not hold the positions of CEO and chair—was believed to enhance a board's ability to monitor top-level managers' decisions and actions, particularly in terms of the firm's financial performance.

It should be noted that a recent investigation of the relationship between CEO duality and firm performance found that the stock market was indifferent to changes in duality status. Such changes have a negligible effect of financial performance, and there is weak evidence that duality has an effect on long-term performance.

Top management team members with longer team and organization tenure have an increased ability to influence the board of directors. However, long tenure restricts an executive's knowledge base, which then limits the number of alternatives evaluated when strategic decisions are being made. The net impact is that these individuals may

① 企业的高层管理团队构成很重要,但如果团队权力过大,会对公司业绩产生负面影响。如第十章中所说,外部人员参与到企业的董事会中,对公司业绩也会产生影响。

be able to forestall or avoid board involvement in strategic decisions.

Because an unhealthy relationship between the board of directors and the top management team can potentially have a negative effect on an organization's strategic competitiveness:

(1) boards are challenged to develop an effective relationship with the firm's top management team,

(2) relative degrees of power between the board and the top management team should be examined with respect to the individual firm's situation (including firm resources and environmental volatility).

One solution to this dysfunction is to get members of the firm's management team to have a significant ownership interest in the firm. While this may provide the team with additional power, a significant level of ownership also should encourage team members to act more in the interests of shareholders, because they also are shareholders.

12.3 Managerial Succession

Because of the impact that members of a firm's top management team—especially the CEO—can have on the organization's performance, the selection of new top managers requires effective screening systems. ①

Organizations can select their strategic leaders from one of two labor markets.

(1) Internal managerial labor markets represent future promotion or transfer opportunities for managerial positions within the firm.

(2) External managerial labor markets represent the collection of managerial career opportunities outside of a manager's current firm.

Because of insiders' experience within the firm and the industry in which it completes, the benefits of using the internal managerial labor market include:

(1) familiarity with the organization's products, markets, technologies, and standard operating procedures,

(2) less turnover among existing personnel with valuable firm-specific knowledge,

① 由于企业的高层管理团成员,尤其是首席执行官,对组织业绩有一定影响,选择新一任的高层管理人员需要引入有效的筛选系统。

(3) a desire for continuity and commitment to the firm's vision, mission, and strategic actions.

Because of the perceived value of selecting an insider to succeed a CEO (or other top management team member), selection of an outsider is unusual. But there are instances which call for selecting an outsider.

(1) Executives with overly long tenure with the firm may become stale, which reduces the number of innovative approaches developed to help the firm cope with changing conditions that the firm faces.

(2) Insiders may have less of an ability to innovate or create innovation-stimulating conditions, which can be a detriment to the firm's long-term success in the twenty-first century competitive landscape.

(3) Outsiders generally have broader, less limited perspectives, which may mean that innovation and strategic change are encouraged.

Effects of CEO Succession and Top Management Team Composition on Strategy

Relationships between the source of the successor, top management team heterogeneity/homogeneity (or team makeup), and firm strategy.

(1) Internal CEO Succession: A homogeneous top management team generally results in a stable strategy. A heterogeneous top management team generally results in a stable strategy with continued innovation.

(2) External CEO Succession: A homogeneous top management team often results in changes in both top management team membership and strategy. If the top management team is heterogeneous, strategic change is likely.

To have an adequate number of top managers, firms must take advantage of a highly qualified labor pool, including one source of managers that has often been overlooked: women. Firms are beginning to utilize women's potential managerial talents with substantial success. A few firms have gained value by using the significant talents of women leaders. But many more have not done so, which represents an opportunity cost to them.

12.4 Key Strategic Leadership Actions

Exercise of Effective Strategic Leadership①

(1) Determining strategic direction.

(2) Establishing balanced controls.

(3) Exploiting and maintaining the firm's resource portfolio.

(4) Sustaining an effective corporate culture.

(5) Emphasizing ethical practices.

12.4.1 Determining Strategic Direction

Determining the strategic direction of the firm refers to developing a long-term vision. This means that a firm's managers must think beyond the current period to develop a "future" direction for the firm (normally 5 to 10 years forward). ②

The ideal long-term vision has two parts—core ideology and envisioned future. Core ideology motivates employees through the company's heritage, but the envisioned future encourages employees to go beyond their expectations and requires significant change and progress. The envisioned future serves as a guide to the firm's strategy implementation, including motivation, leadership, employee empowerment, and organizational design.

A charismatic CEO may foster stakeholder commitment to a new vision and strategic direction.

It is important that strategic leaders also recognize that, while gaining employee commitment to a new vision and strategic direction is important, factors such as the following must not be overlooked:

(1) The firm's strengths must be considered when making strategic changes for a new strategic direction.

(2) The firm's short-term needs must be balanced with long-term growth and survival.

(3) The firm can maintain long-term survivability by effectively managing its portfolio of resources.

---

① 有效战略领导的实施:(1) 决定战略方向;(2) 建立平衡控制;(3) 开发并保持企业的资源库;(4) 维持有效的企业文化;(5)强调道德实践。

② 确定公司的战略方向是指制定长期愿景。这意味着一家公司的管理者必须超越当前时期,为公司制定一个"未来"方向(通常为5到10年)。

12.4.2 Effectively Managing the Firm's Resource Portfolio

Probably the most important task for strategic leaders is effectively managing the firm's portfolio of resources.

Firms may have multiple resources that can be categorized into the following categories:

(1) financial capital,
(2) human capital,
(3) social capital,
(4) organizational capital.

Strategic leaders manage the firm's portfolio of resources by

(1) organizing them into capabilities,
(2) structuring the firm to use the capabilities,
(3) developing and implementing a strategy to leverage those resources to achieve a competitive advantage.

Exploiting and Maintaining Core Competencies

As a reminder, core competencies are those capabilities of the firm around which a competitive advantage may be built (as defined and discussed in Chapters 1 and 3).

Core competencies relate to an organization's functional skills, such as manufacturing, finance, marketing, and research and development. The key is that core competencies must enable the firm to produce and deliver products and services to customers in ways that create value for them. Before core competencies can serve as building blocks for a firm's competitive advantage, they must be distinctive. ①

The following conditions must be satisfied for core competencies to be classified as distinctive:

(1) unique to the firm,
(2) valuable,
(3) difficult for competitors to imitate,
(4) nonsubstitutable.

This means that core competencies must be emphasized as the firm implements strategy. To ensure that core competencies that are identified as distinctive (and

① 核心能力与组织的职能技能有关,如制造、财务、营销和研发。关键是核心竞争力必须使公司能够以为客户创造价值的方式生产和提供产品和服务。在核心竞争力能够成为企业竞争优势的基石之前,它们必须与众不同。

potential sources of competitive advantage) remain distinctive for longer periods of time, firms must recognize the importance of developing their human capital.

Developing Human Capital and Social Capital

Human capital refers to the knowledge and skills of the firm's workforce. This means that employees must be viewed as capital resources and as deserving of investment.

An important point to bring out in this section is that people and people-related competencies—the workforce and its capabilities (a firm's human capital)—historically have contributed more to firm (and economic) success than investment in capital equipment.

One significant problem firms face is inadequate human capital to run an organization effectively. As a remedy, many firms hire temporary employees, while others are trying to improve their recruiting and selection techniques. However, solving the problem requires more than "temp hiring" since this limits management's ability to build effective commitment to organizational goals. Hiring star players is also insufficient. It requires building effective commitment to organizational goals as well.

Effective training and development programs are important because these efforts

(1) recognize that knowledge has become more integral to gaining and sustaining a competitive advantage,

(2) help build knowledge and skills,

(3) inculcate core values,

(4) establish a systematic view of the organization,

(5) promote the firm's vision,

(6) develop organizational cohesion,

(7) contribute to the development of core competencies,

(8) improve strategic managers' capabilities in the skills that are critical to effective strategic leadership (e.g., determining the firm's strategic direction, exploiting and maintaining core competencies, and developing an organizational culture that supports ethical practices).

When human capital investments are successful, a workforce is capable of learning continuously. Learning continuously and leveraging the firm's expanding knowledge base is linked with strategic success. It is also important to promoting innovation, which is the foundation of competitive advantage.①

Layoffs can result in a significant loss of the knowledge possessed by a firm's human capital. Research has shown that moderate-sized layoffs may improve firm performance, but large layoffs produce stronger performance downturns in firms because of the loss of human capital.

Although it is also common for restructuring firms to reduce their spending on training and development programs, restructuring may actually be an important time to increase investments in these programs. Restructuring firms have less slack and cannot absorb as many errors; moreover, the employees who remain after layoffs may find themselves in positions without all of the skill or knowledge they need to perform the required tasks effectively.

Viewing employees as a resource to be maximized rather than a cost to be minimized facilitates the successful implementation of a firm's strategies. The implementation of such strategies also is more effective when strategic leaders approach layoffs in a manner that employees believe is fair and equitable.

Social capital involves relationships inside and outside the firm that help the firm accomplish tasks and create value for customers and shareholders. Social capital is a critical asset for a firm. Inside the firm, employees and units must cooperate to get the work done. In multinational organizations, units often must cooperate across country boundaries on activities such as R&D to produce outcomes needed by the firm (e. g., new products).

12.4.3 Sustaining an Effective Organizational Culture

Organizational culture represents a set of complex ideologies, symbols, and core values that is shared throughout an organization and that influences the way that it conducts business.②

Because it influences how the firm conducts its business and helps regulate and control employee behavior, organizational culture can be a source of competitive advantage.

---

① 当人力资本投资成功时,员工能够持续学习。持续学习和利用公司不断扩大的知识基础与战略成功息息相关。促进创新是企业竞争优势的基础,创新是企业竞争优势的基础。

② 组织文化代表了一组复杂的意识形态、符号和核心价值观,它们在整个组织中都是共享的,并影响着组织开展业务的方式。

Entrepreneurial Mind Set

An organization's culture will either encourage or discourage (and, in some cases, even penalize) employee efforts to tap into entrepreneurial opportunities.

IBM produced a handbook designed to infuse an entrepreneurial spirit into its culture. The handbook, Changing the World, is filled with tips designed to break mental barriers and to help employees be more creative in their jobs. Gerald Haman took a different approach. He developed a process, called the Thinkubator, to help firms build a stronger entrepreneurial orientation and boost creativity in their employees. According to Haman, the Thinkubator helps people rediscover their gifts for creativity.

One way that the pursuit of entrepreneurial opportunities might be promoted is to invest in opportunities as real options. That is, invest in an opportunity to provide the potential of exercising the option of taking advantage of the opportunity at some point in the future. Firms might enter strategic alliances for this reason. For example, they might do so to have the option of acquiring the partner later or of building a stronger relationship (e.g., developing a joint new venture).

Corporate culture characteristics and managerial actions that encourage an entrepreneurial mindset include:

(1) Autonomy—enabling employees to be self-directed in the pursuit of entrepreneurial opportunities.

(2) Innovation—encouraging the pursuit of new ideas, experimentation, and creative processes that will find new ways to add value.

(3) Risk-taking—promoting the willingness of both employees and the organization to accept risk in the pursuit of new market opportunities.

(4) Proactiveness—being a market leader rather than a market follower by anticipating the market's future needs and being the first to satisfy them.

(5) Competitive aggressiveness—taking actions that enable the firm to consistently and significantly outperform the competition.

Changing the Organizational Culture and Restructuring

As noted in the text, incremental changes to the organization's culture typically are used to improve the effectiveness of strategy implementation.

A dramatic shift in strategy from the firm's historical pattern of strategy often means that major changes in the organization's culture are required, and perhaps even the selection of a new CEO or top management team.

No matter why an organization's culture must change, the shaping and reinforcing of the new culture requires:

(1) effective communication and problem solving,

(2) selecting people with the values that managers wish to be infused throughout the organization,

(3) developing an effective performance appraisal process which establishes goals and measures individual performance toward achieving goals that fit with the new core values,

(4) implementing reward systems that encourage behaviors that reflect the new core values.

Effective strategic leadership will be reinforced by an appropriate corporate culture. This can be done using video interviews of a CEO that also profile the firm (e. g. , any of the many reports on Herb Kelleher and Southwest Airlines, when he was CEO there, will work well for this assignment). As they watch the video, have the students write down in separate columns on a piece of paper the clues they find of two things: leadership approaches taken and corporate culture employed. Upon debriefing, they will quickly see that these are mutually reinforcing in successful companies.

For cultural changes to be effective, they must be supported fully and actively by the CEO and other members of the top management team. And if large-scale change is needed, support and involvement of mid-level managers is required as they generally are adept at energizing people and aligning their interests and actions. ①

If the required cultural change is major or critical, new top management team members may need to be brought in from outside of the firm to act as a catalyst for the change.

Transforming the organization and its culture is challenging. For example, top executives at Sara Lee decided in 1997 to change the firm from a capital-intensive manufacturer to a less asset-intensive brand manager, requiring it to sell its manufacturing facilities, find excellent suppliers to replace product manufacturing, and change the firm's culture to focus on management of its brand. However, by 2000 it had become an unwieldy conglomerate, unable to capture synergies across product lines. Local managers were suspicious of managers in other product units/profit centers and thus would not cooperate with them to gain economies. The decentralized culture

---

① 为了使文化变革有效,这些变革必须得到首席执行官和其他高层管理团队成员的充分和积极支持。如果需要大规模变革,则需要中层管理者的支持和参与,因为他们通常擅长激励员工,协调他们的利益和行动。

that evolved prevents centralization, and the firm has not developed brand management as a core competence.

Another example comes from the airline industry. Continental Airlines has successfully changed its culture, building a system of teamwork that has yielded increased returns. CEO Gordon Bethune described the firm's teamwork culture not as composed of cross-functional teams, but rather as the interdependent parts of a clock. Multiple functions have value when they all work together cooperatively, and employees are rewarded for cooperating as a team. A company's reputation is linked to its culture and its strategy.

12.4.4 Emphasizing Ethical Practices

The effectiveness of strategy implementation processes increases when they are based on ethical practices. Ethical companies encourage and enable people at all organizational levels to exercise ethical judgment, but unethical practices become like a contagious disease if they evolve in an organization.

To properly influence employee judgment and behavior, ethical practices must shape the firm's decision-making process and be an integral part of an organization's culture. Research has found that a value-based culture is the most effective means of ensuring that employees comply with the firm's ethical standards.

In the absence of ethical requirements, managerial opportunism allows managers to make decisions that are in their own best interests, but not in the best interests of the firm or its stakeholders.

Recent research reports that a number of top-level executives and business students appear to be willing to commit either illegal or unethical actions. For example:

(1) 47 percent of upper-level executives, 41 percent of controllers, and 76 percent of graduate-level business students were willing to misrepresent their firms' financial statements.

(2) 87 percent of managers made one or more fraudulent decisions out of seven total decision situations.

(3) The probability of a fraudulent decision was greater when the individual valued a comfortable life and/or pleasure and placed less value on self-respect.

(4) When cheating was observed, there was a reluctance to report it.

Recent ethical lapses at high-profile corporations suggest firms need to employ ethical strategic leaders—ones who include ethical practices as part of their long-term vision for the firm, who desire to do the right thing, and for whom honesty, trust, and integrity are important. Strategic leaders who display these qualities inspire employees to develop/support an organizational culture in which ethical practices are the expected norm.

Firms must employ ethical strategic leaders who will infuse ethical values into the organization's culture by

(1) establishing/communicating the firm's ethical code of conduct to describe the firm's ethical standards,

(2) continuously revising and updating the code of conduct based on stakeholder input,

(3) disseminating the code of conduct to stakeholders, informing them of the firm's ethical standards/practices,

(4) developing/implementing methods and procedures that can be used to achieve the firm's ethical standards,

(5) creating and implementing explicit reward systems that recognize individuals that use the appropriate channels to report wrongdoing,

(6) creating a work environment that treats all people with dignity.

The effectiveness of these actions increases when they are taken simultaneously, which makes them mutually supportive. When managers/employees do not engage in these actions, perhaps because an ethical culture is lacking, problems are likely to occur. Formal organizational controls may be needed to prevent more problems. ①

12.4.5 Establishing Balanced Organizational Controls

Organizational controls are necessary to help ensure that firms meet desired outcomes: strategic competitiveness and above-average returns. ②

Controls are the formal, information-based routines and procedures used by managers to maintain or alter patterns in organizational activities to help strategic leaders. ③ These can be used to do the following: ④

---

① 当同时采取这些行动时,它们的有效性会提高,这使它们相互支持。当经理/员工不参与这些行动时,可能是因为缺乏道德文化,问题很可能发生。可能需要正式的组织控制来防止更多的问题。

② 为了确保企业达成既定的目标——战略竞争力及超出平均的收益,组织控制十分必要。

③ 控制是管理者为了协助战略领导者保持或改变模式,在组织活动中以信息为基础的管理日常及程序。

④ 上述做法的目的是:(1) 建立可信度;(2) 向利益相关者展示企业战略的价值;(3) 促进并支持组织变化;(4) 需要就战略实施做出调整,并采取纠正措施时,提供参数。

(1) build credibility,

(2) demonstrate the value of the firm's strategies to stakeholders,

(3) promote and support organizational change,

(4) provide the parameters within which strategies are implemented and corrective actions taken when implementation-related adjustments are needed.

Strategic controls represent those control systems that focus on the content of actions rather than on outcomes. This is in contrast to financial controls that focus on short-term financial outcomes (or results) rather than on the appropriateness of strategic actions that have been taken.

Strategic controls are important because they can encourage managers to make decisions that include moderate and acceptable levels of risk with a focus on the long-term impact of their decisions.

The use of financial controls alone often results in managers making risk-averse decisions, taking only the short-term financial impact into account.

The Balanced Scorecard

The underlying premise of the balanced scorecard is that firms disadvantage their future performance possibilities when financial controls are emphasized at the expense of strategic controls. Financial controls provide feedback about outcomes achieved from past actions, but do not communicate the drivers of the firm's future performance, which can promote organizational behavior that has a net effect of sacrificing the firm's long-term value creating potential for short-term performance gains.

An appropriate balance of strategic controls and financial controls, rather than an overemphasis on one or the other, allows firms to effectively monitor their performance.

The following four perspectives are integrated to form the balanced scorecard framework:

(1) Financial-concerned with growth, profitability, and risk from shareholders' perspective.

(2) Customer-concerned with the value customers perceive to be created by the firm's products.

(3) Internal business processes-concerned with the priorities for various business processes that create customer and shareholder satisfaction.

(4) Learning and growth-concerned with creating a climate that supports change, innovation, and growth.

12.4.6 Strategic Leadership in the Future

The expectations for a firm's key strategic leaders are that strategic leaders must design a process their firm will use as the foundation for earning above-average returns and consistently outperforming rivals. The simplicity of this statement belies its complexity, whether discussing strategic management today or strategic management for tomorrow.

Even though predictions of the future of strategic leadership are risky, several realities and expectations seem likely. First, it is likely that tomorrow's strategic leaders will feel even more stress than do their counterparts today. One reason is that those for whom a firm's key strategic leaders work have significant expectations of strategic leaders. Strategic leadership's demands create stress that leaders must acknowledge, and with which they must learn how to cope if they are to successfully discharge their responsibilities. Another reasonably safe prediction is that all stakeholders will continue to expect the firm's board of directors to better represent their interests. Even today, board members are on the "hot seat" to improve their performance as agents for each stakeholder group. In turn, the expectation of better board performance will find board members holding strategic leaders more accountable for achieving positive outcomes in the areas of strategy formulation and execution, effective handling of crises, particularly financial ones, ability to meaningfully link top-level managerial pay to performance, and in representing the company's best interests at all times. Tomorrow's board members and a firm's strategic leaders will undoubtedly be held accountable for their actions and the outcomes they achieve or fail to achieve.

So how do upstart high-potential wannabes enhance their ability to be an effective strategic leader in tomorrow's organizations? First, strategic leaders should be continuously curious so that they will have the foundation for seeking to learn everything they can from every person with whom they have contact. Future strategic leaders should rely on their curiosity to spot patterns that suggest future conditions. Additionally, tomorrow's strategic leaders should place even greater emphasis on the "simple rules" of effective strategic leadership than is the case today. These simple, yet vital rules are the following: Leaders make work about others, not about themselves. Once a person becomes a strategic leader, everything that person does is about "them" (the stakeholders, but especially employees) while nothing is about the leader. Leaders learn everything possible about their company from both strategic and tactical perspectives. Leaders hold individuals accountable for their outcomes. However, leaders must make themselves the most accountable for overall performance. Leaders shoulder all responsibility for all parts of their job; they always take the blame for mistakes and distribute the credit for successes to others.

This is when students need to be reminded that "leadership" is something that can be difficult to define but can be recognized when they see it. Strong corporate leaders surround themselves with people who are smarter than themselves. In addition, support people are encouraged to do their "thing" in a work "with" me; not work "for" me environment. The CEO position is not one to which everyone should aspire.

Generally speaking, strategic controls tend to be emphasized when the firm assesses its performance relative to the learning and growth perspective, while financial controls are emphasized when assessing performance in terms of the financial perspective. Study of the customer and internal business processes perspectives often is completed through relatively equal emphasis on strategic and financial controls.

Firms use different criteria to measure their standing relative to the scorecard's four perspectives. The important point is for the firm to select the number of criteria that will allow it to have both a strategic understanding and a financial understanding of its performance without becoming immersed in too many details.

Strategic Controls and Financial Controls in a Balanced Scorecard Framework

In diversified firms, successful strategic leaders also balance strategic controls and financial controls to make appropriate investments for future viability (through strategic controls), while maintaining an appropriate level of financial stability in the present (through financial control). In fact, most corporate restructuring is designed to refocus the firm on its core businesses, thereby allowing top executives to reestablish strategic control of their separate business units. Thus, both types of controls are important.

The effective use of strategic controls by top executives is often integrated with appropriate autonomy for the various subunits so they can gain a competitive advantage in their respective markets. Strategic control can be used to promote sharing of both tangible and intangible resources among the firm's interdependent businesses. The autonomy provided allows the flexibility needed to take advantage of specific marketplace opportunities. As a result, strategic leadership promotes the simultaneous use of strategic controls and autonomy. ①

本章课程思政学习专题

战略领导、人力资源柔性与组织绩效②

1．民营企业的战略领导

近些年，中国进入了深刻而全面的转型和改革时期，民营企业在吸纳就业和国民经济贡献方面所发挥的作用越来越显著。然而，在民营企业快速发展的背后，员工的思想观念、行为方式和价值追求等在不断发生变化，所表现出的自主化、个性化和差异化等特点日益突出。这直接导致转型经济下民营企业的战略领导及其他各项管理活动与过去相比，发生了很大的演变。战略领导是组织高层领导者为了组织的生存和发展，充分感知内外环境，预判未来、设定愿景、保持柔性和进行激励与沟通的行为能力。实施何种类型的战略领导来促使员工更加有效地为组织创造绩效是民营企业最为关注和迫切需要解决的现实问题。

针对转型经济面临的此种新情境和新趋势，关系导向型战略领导成为备受民营企业领导者和学者推崇的一种战略领导方式。关系导向型战略领导以塑造良好的人际关系为导向，采取对组织员工具有战略性影响的关键行为，来有效激励员工和实现组织目标，民营企业可以通过加强领导者与员工的沟通、领导者从工作和生活方面关爱员工、领导者以身作则等方式来保证经营管理的稳步推进。自此概念提出之后，学者们围绕其对组织绩效的影响机制进行了积极讨论，但研究结论存在较大分歧。例如，一部分学者认为组织绩效的提升不应归功于各类战略领导的作用，制度环境或组织文化等因素的影响作用更大，另一部分学者则通过实证研究指出关系导向型战略领导可以对组织绩效产生积极影响。该领域的研究结论之所以存在分歧，是因为现有文献在探讨关系导向型战略领导对组织绩效的影响机制时没有对中间环节进行深层次分析。我们只有打开关系导向型战略领导与组织绩效之间的“黑箱”，解析它通过何种传导机制产生影响等关键问题，才能真正认识到关系导向型战略领导的价值。可见，聚焦于关系导向型战略领导对组织绩效的影响机制，是紧扣当前民营企业的现实问题和关系导向型战略领导领域理论研究的关键问题的。

---

① 高层管理人员对战略控制的有效使用通常与各子部门的适当自主权相结合，以便他们能够在各自的市场中获得竞争优势。战略控制可用于促进公司相互依存的业务之间有形和无形资源的共享。自主权允许灵活利用特定市场机会。因此，战略领导可同时促进战略控制和自主权。

② 李召敏，赵曙明. 关系导向型战略领导、人力资源柔性与组织绩效：基于转型经济下民营企业的实证研究[J]. 外国经济与管理，2016，38(4)：73－89.

2. 战略领导对组织绩效的影响机制

转型经济下民营企业的经营管理会面临环境不确定性,企业领导可通过协调沟通、关爱下属和展示权威等方式提升人力资源柔性,借助人力资源的力量促进组织绩效的提升。而欧美发达国家的企业处在非转型期,面临的外部环境也具有不确定性。民营企业是研究对象,研究结论更具针对性。一般情况下,民营企业的经营与发展具有自身的特点,如经营理念先进、用人机制灵活、发展风险大等。需指出的是,国有企业或外资企业不具有或难以同时具有民营企业的经营与发展特点。

首先,民营企业高层领导者应全面、理性地认识关系导向型战略领导在组织绩效提升过程中所扮演的重要角色和发挥的积极作用。民营企业可通过关系导向行为的有效落实来促进组织绩效的提升,例如通过协调沟通行为妥善处理好与员工的关系,通过关爱下属行为提升员工的工作态度等。其次,民营企业可以根据外部环境的不确定程度,适当调整关系导向型战略领导的实施情况,从而更好地控制人力资源柔性。这就要求民营企业在经营管理过程中,实时关注和预测外部环境的变化程度,尽可能准确地掌握所需要的相应人力资源柔性水平,并培养与之相匹配的员工技能柔性、员工行为柔性和人力资源实践柔性,从而稳步提升组织绩效。最后,民营企业应重视和增强人力资源柔性。根据研究结果,虽然环境不确定性在人力资源柔性对组织绩效的影响过程中不起调节作用,但人力资源柔性对组织绩效确实有积极的影响作用。因此,在中国转型经济背景下,民营企业应大力提升人力资源柔性,例如切实加强员工业务技能培训、大力推行员工岗位轮换制、鼓励员工积极参与经营管理、适时调整人力资源管理策略和实践,从而为企业的各项管理活动和突发事件提供丰富的人力资源支持。

3. 思考问题

国有企业中战略领导对组织绩效的影响机制与民营企业有何不同?

参考文献(References)

[1] H.伊戈尔·安索夫.战略管理[M].邵冲,译.北京:机械工业出版社,2010.

[2] 查尔斯·W.L.希尔,加雷思·R.琼斯.战略管理:概念与案例[M].原书第10版.薛有志,李国栋,等译.北京:机械工业出版社,2012.

[3] 弗兰克·罗特尔梅尔.战略管理:英文版[M].北京:中国人民大学出版社,2015.

[4] 弗雷德·R.戴维.战略管理:概念与案例[M].13版.北京:清华大学出版社,2013.

[5] 格里·约翰逊,理查德·惠廷顿,凯万·斯科尔斯.战略管理:课文和案例[M].英文版·第9版.北京:商务印书馆,2014.

[6] 格里·约翰逊,理查德·惠廷顿,凯万·斯科尔斯.战略管理基础[M].2版.北京:清华大学出版社,2012.

[7] 杰弗里·S.哈里森,卡伦·H.圣约翰.战略管理精要[M].陈继祥,主译.大连:东北财经大学出版社,2006.

[8] 罗伯特·E.霍斯克森,迈克尔·A.希特,R.杜安·爱尔兰,等.战略管理赢得竞争优势[M].2版.北京:机械工业出版社,2009.

[9] 迈克尔·A.希特,R.杜安·爱尔兰,罗伯特·E.霍斯基森.战略管理:概念与案例[M].英文版·第10版.刘刚,吕文静,雷云,等译.北京:中国人民大学出版社,2012.

[10] 迈克尔·波特.竞争战略[M].陈小悦,译.北京:华夏出版社,2005.

[11] 王圣元,王小波,沈毅,等.市场营销学[M].南京:东南大学出版社,2014.

[12] 威廉·G.齐克芒德,巴里·J.巴宾,乔恩·C.卡尔,等.商业研究方法[M].3版.刘启,王引,李宇华,等译.北京:清华大学出版社,2012.

[13] 韦斯特三世,班福德.战略管理:英文版[M].北京:中国人民大学出版社,2011.

[14] 魏江.企业战略管理:理念、方法与案例[M].杭州:浙江大学出版社,2003.

[15] 小阿瑟·A.汤普森,玛格丽特·A.彼得拉夫,约翰·E.甘布尔,等.战略管理:概念与案例[M].英文版·原书第18版.黄嫚丽,蓝海林,等译注.北京:机械工业出版社,2012.

[16] 杨锡怀,王江.企业战略管理:理论与案例[M].3版.北京:高等教育出版社,2010.

后　记

战略管理是指对一个企业或组织在一定时期的全局的、长远的发展方向、目标、任务和政策以及资源调配做出的决策和管理艺术。战略管理是企业确定其使命,根据组织外部环境和内部条件设定企业的战略目标,为保证目标的正确落实和实现进度谋划,并依靠企业能力将这种谋划和决策付诸实施,以及在实施过程中进行控制的一个动态管理过程。战略管理是经济与管理类专业的必修课程。国外的战略管理教材很少使用中国企业的战略管理案例,由于文化背景差异较大,其案例不适合国内教学活动。国内专家学者编写的战略管理英文教材较少。在全球化背景下,战略管理教学中需要一部有中国特色的战略管理英文教材。

本书在撰写过程中大量使用中国企业的战略管理案例,设置课程思政环节,注重实践教学,调动学生的积极性。教材符合人才培养目标,符合教学规律和认知规律,注重素质教育,具有启发性,能够激发学生学习兴趣。教材的撰写有较强的适应性,既可以在纯英文教学环境中使用,也可以在双语教学中使用。

本书由赵彤、王圣元、徐萌、吴小兰共同撰写完成。王圣元负责全书的总体结构设计,吴小兰负责英文校对,赵彤负责全书的统稿。本书受到江苏高等学校重点教材建设项目资助,在撰写过程中得到了学校领导与同事的大力支持。特别感谢责任编辑孙松茜老师的辛勤付出。由于水平有限,不足之处敬请各位读者指正。

作　者

2021 年 10 月